KEALAKEKUA BAY, IN THE DAYS OF CAPTAIN COOK.

# LIFE IN THE SANDWICH ISLANDS:

OR,

# THE HEART OF THE PACIFIC,

## AS IT WAS AND IS.

BY REV. HENRY T. CHEEVER,

AUTHOR OF "THE ISLAND WORLD OF THE PACIFIC," "THE WHALE AND HIS CAPTORS," ETC.

WITH ENGRAVINGS.

Histories make men wise; poetry, witty; the mathematics, subtle; natural philosophy, grave; logic and rhetoric, able to contend; voyages and travels, to entertain and illustrate.

LORD BACON.

NEW YORK:
PUBLISHED BY A. S. BARNES & CO.,
NO. 51 JOHN-STREET.
CINCINNATI:—H. W. DERBY & CO.
1856.

Stereotyped by
RICHARD C. VALENTINE,
New York.

# PREFACE.

WE call this book "The Heart of the Pacific," for two reasons: first, because the Sandwich or Hawaiian Islands, which form its subject-matter, hold about the same relation to other parts of the Pacific as the heart does to the rest of the human body. Second, because these Islands bid fair to become the religious Protestant Heart of the great Ocean, whose pulsations at different times we have herein marked and interpreted.

Although independent and whole of itself, it has a connection which will be seen with "The Island-World of the Pacific." The writer believes it may fulfil a useful part, in directing the general interest now felt in the young Island-Kingdom of Hawaii. The perpetuity of the pure Hawaiian race there is daily becoming more and more doubtful. But, as it has been remarked of New Zealand, the natives, though melting away, are not lost. They are emerging into another and a better class. In this process there lacketh not sin on man's part; but Providence will overrule it for good, and bring forth an order of things which shall be far better for the world, for the Church of Christ, and for the new race.

Perhaps it is in the providential plan of the world's great Ruler, that the Sandwich Islands should yet be adopted into the great American Confederacy. Won as they have been from the lowest barbarism by American missionaries,—having had expended upon them in the process, nearly a million and a half of dollars from America, and the services of fifty families now possessing there valuable homesteads,—harboring a permanent American population, foremost in energy and influence, now little short of one thousand, besides a floating American population that touch and recruit annually to the number of fifteen thousand, in whale-ships and merchantmen,—and consuming yearly a million of dollars' worth of American merchandise;—on all these grounds there would seem to be a propriety in their enjoying an American Protectorate, if not an admission under the flag of the American Republic.

"American enterprise," says a writer* who has been for many years familiar with the history and progress of the Hawaiian Islands, "both commercial and philanthropic, has invested the group with its present political importance—bestowing upon the inhabitants laws, religion, civilization—and will soon add to these gifts

* J J. Jarves.

language; for the English tongue is rapidly superseding the Hawaiian. The Islanders have thus a moral claim upon the American nation for protection. In no way can this be more efficiently bestowed than by receiving them into the family of this great Republic. The native population are as well prepared to be American citizens, as the multitude of European emigrants. Unlike the generality of *them*, they can read and write, and have already acquired democratic ideas under the operation of their own liberal constitution of government, which will readily enable them to incorporate themselves under our institutions. They are destined to be supplanted in numbers and power by a foreign race. They desire us to be their successors and protectors. The present revenues of the Islands are more than adequate to the expenses of its government—time, opportunity, the interests of the inhabitants and ourselves point to this result."

Events will soon determine whether they are to retain their independency, or to be merged in the nation that has civilized them. In either event they are to constitute no mean a portion of the kingdom of Christ; and if this book shall be found to have helped at all to the production of that better order of things, when HE WHOSE RIGHT IT IS SHALL REIGN, the labor bestowed on it at a time when the decay of health, and circumstances not to be controlled, precluded the exercise of the Ministry, will be amply rewarded. It is one man's mission in this world to do; it is another's to record and perpetuate the memory of worthy deeds. And, in John Newton's judgment, it would make little difference to an angel who should visit our earth, upon which of the two he were sent by the angels' Lord.

Next, at least in our view, to the honor of being one's self a laborious and successful foreign missionary, is that of being permitted to describe and preserve the achievements of other missionaries, and to portray the benign results to society at large, which have been realized by good men and true, on the noble field of Protestant Missionary benevolence in the Pacific. Having steadily aimed to present to his readers none other than the real, which is the hopeful aspect of the missionary life and enterprise at the Sandwich Islands, the author believes that this volume will gain a grateful echo from the great Heart of Christian Philanthropy, as it is a true report from that portion of our common humanity whence it purports to issue.

But in this and three previous volumes, though pleased to minister both pleasure and profit to all our readers, we have written mainly for Seamen; and while aiming to entertain and instruct them, have desired also to cultivate and quicken their perceptions of the true, the good, the sublime, and the beautiful in man, nature, art, and religion. We have, therefore, felt justified in making free use of the rich treasures of English poetry,

> To point a moral, and adorn a tale.

We have desired, in so doing, to enhance the value of this book to the class of readers for whom it has been made, without lessening its interest for any—

> Lectorem delectando simul atque monendo.

With these remarks, while the work is honestly commended to the patronage of all classes, the author would be happy if it might find such favor with the liberal merchant and ship-owner, that they should secure it a place in The Cabin Boy's Locker. The design of furnishing a suitable Literature for the sea, in a convenient, accessible, and cheap form, is one which we have for some time entertained, since observing the lamentable destitution of it on the Ocean. By leave of a gracious Providence, and with aid from others, we mean to do something to supply this deficiency, and to put it out of the power of shipmasters to plead, that they do not know where to procure a suitable Library for the Sea.

To them and to their Seamen this volume is accordingly dedicated, as being an humble attempt to furnish something better than the medley of Flash Literature usually found in the Cabin-Locker and the Sailor's Chest.

The Appendix is meant to supply to business men and travellers, as well as to Seamen, those reliable statistics respecting the government, resources, commerce, growth, and prosperity of the Hawaiian Islands, which all visitors, or any persons who are seeking accurate information respecting a country, desire to have at hand. In lieu of something more perfect, it is hoped that this may answer as a guide-book and vade-mecum to tourists in the Pacific.

In connection with the tinted engravings, the author and publishers regret certain typographical errors, which were not observed till the edition was in part printed. The candid reader is therefore requested to read on the vignette title-page, Kaahumanu, for Kaahamann, and Hawaiian, for Hawanan.

New York, *August 20th*, 1851.

# CONTENTS.

## CHAPTER I.

LOCAL TRADITIONS OF CAPTAIN COOK, AND GLIMPSES OF OLD PAGANISM IN THE HEART OF THE PACIFIC.



## CHAPTER II.

KEALAKEKUA BAY NOW AND THIRTY YEARS AGO.

## CHAPTER III.

### LAHAINA AND ITS ENVIRONS ON THE ISLAND OF MAUI.



## CHAPTER IV.

### THE FOOTSTEPS OF BEAUTY TRACED BY A TRAVELLER IN NATURE, LANGUAGE, AND RELIGION.

## CHAPTER IX.

### REMINISCENCES OF LAHAINALUNA, AND SKETCHES OF THE FIRST HAWAIIAN COLLEGE.



## CHAPTER X.

### HAWAIIAN LITERATURE AND LETTER-WRITERS.

## CHAPTER XI.

### RIDE AROUND THE ISLAND OF OAHU, AND NOTES BY THE WAY.



## CHAPTER XII.

### SIDE VIEWS OF HAWAIIAN CHARACTER AND DESTINY.

## APPENDIX.



---

## LIST OF ENGRAVINGS.

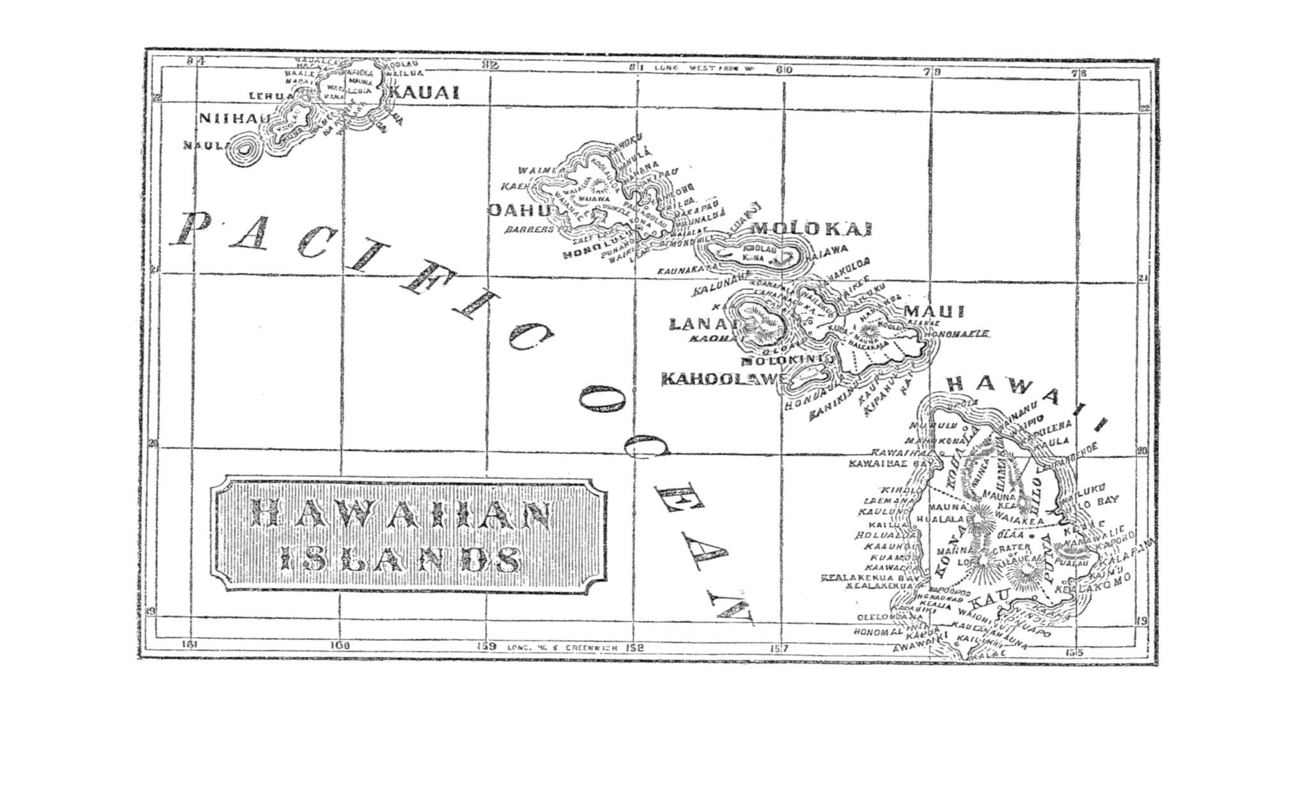

HAWAIIAN ISLANDS
PACIFIC OCEAN
NIIHAU
KAUAI
OAHU
HONOLULU
MOLOKAI
LANAI
MAUI
KAHOOLAWE
MOLOKINI
HAWAII
KOHALA
HILO
KONA
PUNA
KAU
HAMAKUA
KAWAIHAE BAY
KEALAKEKUA BAY
LONG. WEST FROM W.
LONG. W. F. GREENWICH

# LIFE IN THE SANDWICH ISLANDS.

## CHAPTER I.

### LOCAL TRADITIONS OF CAPTAIN COOK, AND GLIMPSES OF OLD PAGANISM IN THE HEART OF THE PACIFIC.

GLIDING through Magellan's Straits,
Where two oceans ope their gates,
Now th' immense Pacific smiles
Round ten thousand sunny Isles.

A notable wonder—Curious fancies of the Natives respecting the first Ship—They venture nigh in Canoes—They recognize their god Lono—They pay divine worship to Captain Cook—They grow familiar with the Haöles—They smart under indignitics and exactions—The bent bow snaps—They are undeceived—The denouement—He groans—He is not a god—The fight—The fall—The retreat—The burning of the navigator's body—The exploits of Phillips—The narrative of Ledyard—The revenge—The providence—We stand where Cook fell—We visit the spot where his body was burned—Monumental inscription—Natural reflection upon his end—Forms of the old idolatry—Pagan notions respecting the soul—The realms of Wakea and Milu—Providence and Grace in the Heart of the Pacific.

THREESCORE and thirteen years ago there appeared in the serene waters of a far island in the Pacific a notable wonder, which has been succeeded by a greater wonder still. Two ships, significantly called the Resolution and Discovery, cast anchor in an unknown bay, called by its aborigines Kaawaroa, or Kealakekua. They were commanded by an intrepid navigator, of the most intrepid and daring race that has ever ploughed the seas. Their prows had ventured into strange oceans, and had broken the primeval stillness of bays and roadsteads which are now whitened with the wings of Commerce, and struck by the propellers of mighty Steamers, then an idea all unknown but to the Creative Mind who has since given the steamboat, through Fulton, as a benignant boon to our race.

These adventurous ships had anchored in the night, as upon the coast of an undiscovered country, with thoughts, perhaps, like those which a navigator in a balloon would now have, whose anchor should catch at midnight on some floating island of the great ocean of air. In the morning, when the natives on shore first behold the strange sight, they were wild with amazement and conjecture. Unable to tell whence the wonder came, or what it was, or how to express their astonishment at the sight, they cried out, "Moku! moku!" the Hawaiian word for island, as if it were a moving island; and that is their name for a ship to the present day.

Then, as they gazed from a distance at the ship's towering masts and branching spars, they exclaimed, "It is a forest that has moved into the sea!" Soon the chiefs commanded some of their men to go in canoes and find out what this wonderful thing, this new moku, might be. They approached so near as to survey, with curious dread, the different parts of the ship and the men on board; and then they returned, all wild with excitement, and with the vain effort of their undisciplined minds, to describe what they had seen.

They had beheld the strangers as they looked over the ship's sides eating something red, (being watermelon from Monterey,) and to their imagination it was the raw flesh of men: they had seen fire and smoke about their mouths from cigars, and they reported them, therefore, to be Fire-gods—gods of the Volcano. They told in an exaggerated manner of the whiteness of their skin, the brightness of their eyes, their garments rough and strange, their heads horned like the moon, and their speech all unintelligible gibberish—"A hikapalale, hikapalale—hioluai, oalakai."

The fire, they said, burns at their mouths like Pele—the Volcano. They have doors in their sides for property; openings going far down into their bodies, where they thrust their hands, and draw knives, and iron, and beads, and cloth, and nails, and every thing else, for their bodies are full of treasure. Then a warrior by the name of Kapupuu, hearing of the great quantity of iron about the ships, (which they had learned the value of by what had occasionally drifted ashore in strange pieces of wood,) at once said, "I will go and seize the iron, for plunder is my business." He boldly went, according to his boast, but while in the act of purloining was shot. Then the cluster of canoes with him fled, and reported that Kapupuu was slain by a fire-ball, a *pu* from the volcano—the *pu* being the only instrument like a gun which they were acquainted with.

The succeeding night there was a discharge of cannon from on board the ships, and a display of fire-works that filled up the measure of wonder and dread in the minds of those rude barbarians. Unable to believe any thing else than that the new-comers were supernatural beings, they called the Captain Lono, that being the name of a fabled god of theirs who had gone into a foreign land, and now they supposed had come back.

It was a tabu-week with them, when canoes were ordinarily forbidden from being on the sea, and it was death to be seen in one at such a time. But when they saw Lono's moku there—the moving island of their god—they were not afraid to use their canoes, because their god had come to them, and his ship must be a *heiau*, a temple. When they observed the seamen calking the sides of the vessels, they called them Mokualii's company, Mokualii being the god of canoemakers. Those who had fire at their mouths they denominated Lono-pele-poe, or Lono's volcano-company.

But every wonder has its day and its end, and familiarity with the *haöle*, as they called the strangers, at length began to breed dislike, if not contempt, on the part of the eager natives. They found the foreigners to be like themselves in lusts and covetousness, if superior in power. At length the unwarranted act of the great Lono in breaking down the wooden fence of their sacred morai, or *heiau*, and loading his boats with it, in order to supply his ships with wood, provoked their indignation beyond the power of their superstitious dread of the gods to restrain.

Thefts, reprisals, insults, and bloodshed followed quick upon one another, until a deep, uncontrollable resentment was kindled among the natives. But Captain Cook—for he was the Lono, even according to the narrative of Ledyard, one of his men, who landed with him on the morning of his death, and was near him during the fatal contest—blinded by some fatal cause, could not perceive it, or, too self-confident, would not regard it.

There is an historical work of much value written in the Hawaiian tongue, a few years ago, by some of the early adult pupils of the Seminary at Lahaina-luna, and called Ka Moolelo Hawaii. Its materials were derived from old men then living, and the accounts they gave were afterwards compared and corrected by their teacher, Rev. Sheldon Dibble, until a valuable authentic volume grew therefrom. The authors of this say, that owing to their conviction that Lono (Captain Cook) was a god, the people generally paid him divine honors. They offered him hogs, food, *kapa*, (native cloth,) and other articles, as they were accustomed to bestow them on their deities, not expecting any thing in exchange. The priests approached him with prostrations, and cast their red kapa over his shoulders; then receding a little, they presented hogs, and a variety of other offerings, with long addresses rapidly enunciated, which were a repetition of their prayers and religious homage.

"If on any occasion he went inland, the mass of the people fled through fear, while all who remained fell down and worshipped him. He was led into the houses and temples of the gods, and worshipped there also; and all this adoration was received without remonstrance, as in the case of Herod. Wherefore, some, perhaps, may think for this cause, and for another already mentioned, he was smitten of God, and died."

These were the circumstances of that melancholy event, as gathered from the Moolelo Hawaii, and the Life of Ledyard: In a contest that ensued after the demolition of the morai by Captain Cook, the stealing of one of the ship's boats, and the killing of a chief in a canoe, by a shot from one of the ships, the Captain imprudently struck a high chief with his sword. Upon this the chief, Kalaimano-Kahoowaha, seized him instinctively with his powerful grasp in order to hold him, but with no idea of taking his life, Lono being, in his view, a god that could not die. But when he struggled to free himself, and groaned as he was about to fall, the chief cried, "He groans, he is not a god," and instantly slew him.

The fight then became general, in which many of the natives were killed and some of the Captain's guard. In the end the savages were routed and fled inland, taking with them the bodies of the fallen Navigator, and four of his companions. The king there presented the body of the captain in sacrifice to the gods, and after that ceremony was performed, they proceeded to remove the flesh from the bones in order to preserve them. The flesh was consumed by fire; the heart was eaten by some children who had mistaken it for the heart of a dog. Their names were Kupa, Mohoole, and Kaiwikokoole, one of whom was living only a few years ago. Some of the bones of the dead were afterwards returned to the ship, and the rest preserved by the priests, and worshipped.

Ledyard's account of the same transactions is this:

"Cook, perceiving the people determined to oppose his designs, and that he should not succeed without further bloodshed, ordered the lieutenant of marines, Mr. Phillips, to withdraw his men and get them into the boats, which were then lying ready to receive them. This was effected by the sergeant; but the instant they began to retreat Cook was hit with a stone, and perceiving the man who threw it, he shot him dead. This occasioned the guard to face about and fire, and then the attack became general. Cook and Mr. Phillips were together, a few paces in the rear of the guard, and perceiving a general fire without orders, quitted Teraiobu, and ran to the shore to put a stop to it; but not being able to make themselves heard, and being close pressed upon by the chiefs, they joined the guard, who fired as they retreated.

"Cook having at length reached the margin of the water, between the fire of the boats, waved with his hat for them to cease firing and come in; and while he was doing this, a chief from behind stabbed him with one of our iron daggers, just under the shoulder-blade, and it passed quite through his body. Cook fell with his face in the water, and immediately expired. Mr. Phillips not being able any longer to use his fusee, drew his sword, and engaging the chief whom he saw kill Cook, soon dispatched him.

"His guard, in the mean time, were all killed but two, and they had plunged into the water and were swimming to the boats. He stood thus for some time the butt of all their force, and being as complete in the use of his sword as he was accomplished, his noble achievements struck the barbarians with awe. But being wounded, and growing faint from loss of blood and excessive action, he plunged into the sea with his sword in hand and swam to the boats; where, however, he was scarcely taken on board, before somebody saw one of the marines that swam from the shore, lying flat upon the bottom. Phillips, hearing this, threw himself in after him, and brought him up with him to the surface of the water, and both were taken in.

"The boats had hitherto kept up a very hot fire, and lying off without the reach of any weapon but stones, had received no damage; and, being fully at leisure to keep up an unremitted and uniform action, made great havoc among the Indians, particularly among the chiefs, who stood foremost in the crowd and were most exposed. But, whether it was from their bravery, or ignorance of the real cause that deprived so many of them of life, that they made such a stand, may be questioned, since it is certain that they in general, if not universally, understood heretofore, that it was the fire only of our arms that destroyed them.

"This opinion seems to be strengthened by the circumstance of the large, thick mats they were observed to wear, which were also constantly kept wet; and, furthermore, the Indian that Cook fired at with a blank discovered no fear, when he found his mat unburnt, saying, in their language, when he showed it to the bystanders, that no fire had touched it. This may be supposed at least to have had some influence. It is, however, certain, whether from one or both these causes, that the numbers that fell made no apparent impression on those who survived; they were immediately taken off, and had their places supplied in a constant succession.

"Lieutenant Gore, who commanded as first lieutenant under Cook in the Resolution, which lay opposite the place where this attack was made, perceiving, with his glass, that the guard on shore was cut off, and that Cook had fallen, immediately passed a spring upon one of the cables, and, bringing the ship's starboard guns to bear, fired two round-shots over the boats into the middle of the crowd; and both the thunder of the cannon and the effects of the shot operated so powerfully, that it produced a most precipitate retreat from the shore to the town."

It will be seen thus that the two records, Hawaiian and English, of the melancholy transactions which give such unwonted interest to this spot, substantially agree. Hereafter pilgrim tourists in the Pacific visiting this place, will find it replete with historical associations mellowed by time; and glowing perhaps with enthusiasm, they will quote the oft-reiterated words of Johnson:—Far from me be such frigid philosophy as would conduct us indifferent or unmoved, over any ground dignified by wisdom, bravery, or virtue.—But, although I have trodden the lava rock where the justly incensed barbarians slew the great navigator, calling aloud, "He groans,—he is not a god;" and have swum in the Bay's blue waters at that very point; and have read the copperplate inscriptions upon the stump of the memorable cocoanut-tree put there by British men-of-war; and have been to the place further inland, where a rude monument tells us that his flesh was burned;—yet at neither locality could I start productively the meditative or heroic mood.

Perhaps it is because the imaginative notions of my boyhood, respecting the Great Captain and Discoverer in the Island World of the Pacific, have been reluctantly corrected by the more accurate information obtained here on the spot in Hawaii-nei. The footprints Cook has left on the sands of time, great as he was in many respects, will never wear out; but the place and the manner of his death we should contemplate less painfully, had the illustrious navigator, whose blood threescore and ten years ago crimsoned these peaceful waters, done more to direct the untaught natives to the Great Jehovah, *instead of receiving divine homage himself.*

God will not have his glory given to another, nor will he with impunity let selfish gain be made out of the principle of reverence for higher powers, which himself has implanted in the human constitution. Captain Cook wrongly attempted this, although, as we would fain believe, not aware to what extent the offerings paid him were meant as homage to a God. Hence, in the order of retributive Providence, his ignominious death at the hands of the very incensed barbarians whom he had allowed to worship him.

A glimpse of the besotted idolatry which the aborigines of this Island Kingdom of Hawaii were then addicted to, and of the moral state of Hawaii AS IT WAS, may be gathered from the engravings we give of some of their idol gods.

It is a matter of curious interest to the philosopher, in tracing the origin of the religious and mythological notions of different savage tribes, to observe how they are always modified by the physical objects, usages, and scenery with which they are chiefly conversant. The most terrific and impressive of all visible things to Hawaiians being the Volcano, or Lua Pele, and its cause unknown, they attributed all its phenomena to gods there living, and those gods their imaginations made like unto themselves.

Thus, the conical craters in the bed of the volcano they regarded as the houses of their gods, where they amused themselves by playing at *konane*, the favorite Hawaiian game of drafts. The roaring of the volcano's furnaces, and the crackling of its sulphurous flames, were deemed by them the *kani* to the *hula* of their gods, that is, the music of their dances, which were naturally attributed to them, from their own addictedness to the same. The red flaming surge in the caldron of the volcano they called the surf, where their gods played like themselves with surf-boards on the great Pacific rollers.

In like manner, the Greenlanders and Esquimaux of the Arctic regions, when first visited by Moravians, believed every thing in heaven to be after the pattern of things on their earth; and they found it difficult to be satisfied with the Bible promise of the Christian heaven, because it did not contain seals. The arch of heaven, in their view, turns round on the pivot of a high, sharp peak, far to the north. The Great Bear they compare to a sort of bench, on which they fasten their ropes and harpoons for the capture of seal. The belt of Orion consists of Greenlanders, who were placed there because they could not find the way to their own country. The Pleiades are howling dogs, which surround a white bear. The red stars take their color from eating seals' livers, the white from eating seals' brains. The Northern Lights are caused by the souls of the dead playing at ball. In the sky there is an immense lake, confined by a dam; when the water overflows this dam, it rains; and if the dam should break, heaven would fall, and crush the earth.

The deities worshipped by Hawaiians were called by the general name Akua, and the number of them was unlimited, expressed by their word *kini*. Mr. Dibble says the Hawaiians had six deities to whom they gave names, but oftener addressed only four, Ku, Lono, Kane, and Kanaloa. After naming these four, and sometimes six, they then added the expression, the forty thousand, and the four hundred thousand gods, meaning an indefinite number.

These deities they regarded as spirits who had their residence above, or in the clouds. They attributed to them all the proud, fierce, cruel, and impure passions of men; and supposed them of course to delight in the

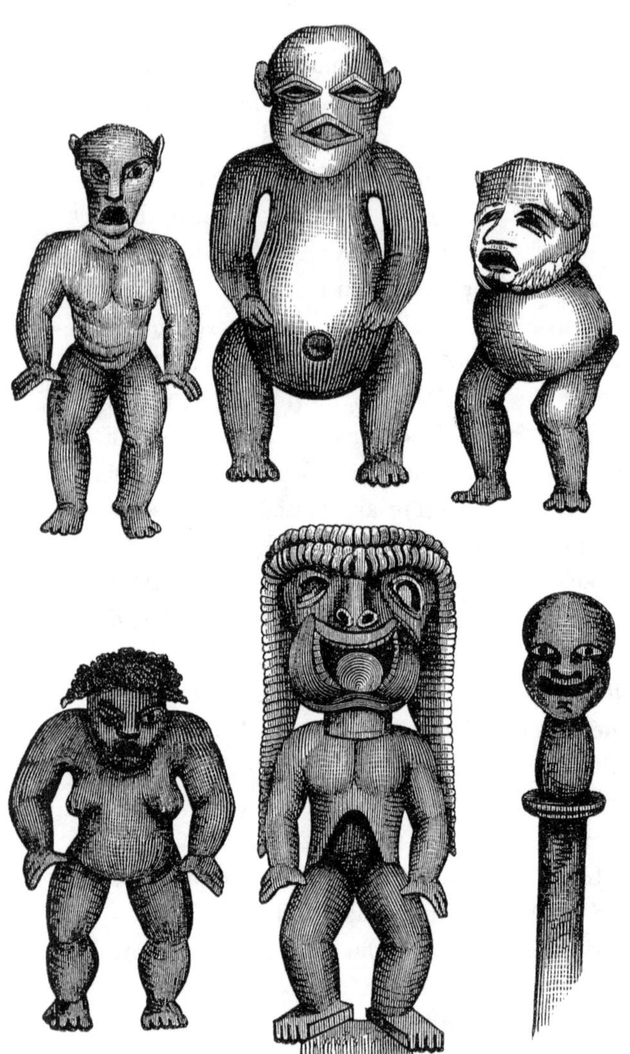

OLD HAWAIIAN IDOLS.

sufferings, and in the immolation even of human victims. The people worshipped them usually by means of idols, supposing that after the performance of certain ceremonies on the images, they became repositories, or at least suitable remembrancers of the spirits above. The people deny that they actually worshipped the wood and the stone, and to explain their use of images, they refer at once to the practice of the Romanists with pictures and symbols.

"In regard to the soul, they had very inadequate and confused notions. They supposed that after death the soul, or rather the ghost, lingered for some time about the deceased body, haunted in dark places, and made its attempts occasionally in the night to strangle its enemies. If any one was afflicted in the night with the incubus, or night-mare, he regarded it as the attack of some ghost upon his throat. On the evening of a dark night I heard a horrid shriek in the street; it was that of a strong, athletic man running with all speed, with both hands at his throat, endeavoring to tear something away. He soon reached the door of a house, burst his way in, and fell on the floor, terrified even to faintness and insensibility. He imagined that the ghost of a chief, who had deceased the day before, had a firm gripe upon his throat, and was about to strangle him."*

The old Hawaiian notion of a future state was, that after death the ghost went first to the region above belonging to Wakea, the name of their first progenitor.

* History of the Sandwich Islands, by Sheldon Dibble, p. 99.

If in this life the man had observed religious rites and ceremonies, the ghost was allowed to remain there in comfort and pleasure with Wakea. But if the dead had failed to be religious here, the soul found no one there in the region of Wakea to entertain it, and was forced to take a desperate plunge into a place of misery below ruled by one they called Milu.

There are several precipices from the verge of which unhappy souls were formerly supposed to take the leap into the world of woe. Three in particular are pointed out to the traveller: one at the northern extremity of the island of Hawaii, one at the western termination of Maui, and a third at the southern point of Oahu.

We can hardly believe that the confused and indistinct notions of the Hawaiians respecting a future state, or their absurd system of mythology,* at all prepared

* Idols were of every variety imaginable, from hideous and deformed sculptures of wood, to the utmost perfection of their art. The features of their religion were embodied in these images; the most desired object in their manufacture being to inspire fear and horror, sentiments which in a more refined people would, from such exhibitions, have been converted into disgust. Pele was the chief goddess. Her principal followers were Ka-ma-hu-alii, the King of Steam and Vapor; Ka-poha-i-kahi-ola, the Explosion in the palace of life; Ke-ua-ke-po, the Rain of night; Kane-kekili, Thundering god; Ke-o-ahi-kama-kaua, Fire-thrusting child of war. These were brothers, and, like Vulcan, two of them were deformed. Ma-kole-wawahi-waa, Fiery-eyed canoe-breaker; Hiaka-wawahi-lani, Heaven-dwelling cloud-breaker; and several others of longer names and similar definitions; these latter were sisters.

The whole family were regarded with the greatest awe. The volcano was their principal residence, though occasionally they renovated their constitutions amid the snows of the mountains. On such occasions their journeys were accompanied by earthquakes, eruptions, heavy thunder and lightning. All were malignant spirits, delighting in acts of vengeance and them to receive the revelations of Christianity. But as it was the work of Divine Providence to make a way for the entrance of Divine truth externally, so was it the work of the Divine Spirit internally to procure its reception to a degree, so unprecedented and remarkable, by the mind and heart of the Hawaiian nation. Some of the steps in that process, and the triumphant issue of the same in the Heart of the Pacific, we will endeavor to trace in succeeding chapters that shall present the Island Kingdom of Hawaii AS IT IS.

---

destruction. Many tributes were assessed to avoid or appease their anger; the greater part of which went to support the numerous and wealthy priesthood and their followers, who regulated the worship of Pele. These were held in the highest reverence, as holding in their power the devouring fires of the all-powerful goddess. To insult them, break their taboos, or neglect to send offerings, was to call down certain destruction. At their call, Pele would spout out her lava and destroy the offenders. Vast numbers of hogs, both cooked and alive, were thrown into the crater when any fear of an eruption was entertained, or to stay the progress of one commenced. Offerings were annually made to keep her in good humor, and no traveller dared venture near her precincts without seeking her good-will.—*History of the Hawaiian Islands*, by James Jackson Jarves, pp. 28, 29. Honolulu, 1847.

## CHAPTER II.

### KEALAKEKUA BAY NOW AND THIRTY YEARS AGO.

Till missionaries' feet made glad
The solitudes by sin made sad;
Till songs to Christ took place of cries,
Shrieked o'er the monarch's sacrifice,—
No good was there,—no Godhead's beam,
No light did o'er the future gleam.

TAPPAN.

The trail from Kailua—Observed wealth of nature—Insight of the spiritual through the veil of the natural—Analogy drawn and lessons derived—We view the ocean from on high—Coffee plantation of a man from Maine—A relic from the times of Kamehameha the Great—The premises of a missionary heave in sight—Primitive hospitality—City of refuge at Honaunau—The Iona of Hawaii—Ellis's account of it quarter of a century ago—The hideous corpse of paganism—The deeds of despots—Legendary exploit of an Hawaiian Gracchus—Sole feature of humanity in the system of paganism—Human sacrifices—Numbers once immolated—Last at Kealakekua—Comparison of Christianity with paganism—Incredible change—The theme of song—The transforming agent—Investment of a Massachusetts wheelwright—How to make eighteen hundred per cent. by a donation to missions—Death and life springing from the same Bay of Kealakekua—Sketches of Obookiah—Providential voyage to America, and adoption at Cornwall—Other links in the chain of Providence—Adventures of Thomas Hopu—Hopes from the Cornwall school—Natural disappointment—The Heart of the Pacific in 1820 and 1850—Blessedness of the change.

In order that we may survey in this Chapter more minutely an interesting portion of the Hawaiian Heart of the Pacific, I will take the reader upon my trail from Kailua, Hawaii, to Kealakekua, on the same great Island. The path runs, for six miles along the sea, through villages of cocoanut-palm groves, from which the bronzed inhabitants, with little else than the habiliments of nature, peeped and stared upon a stranger, as I came that way, with curious eyes. I passed two snug little bays that used to be favorite resorts of Kamehameha the Great, in one of which was his bathing-place, tabu to every one else, and the *heiau* and house of his favorite war-god *Kaili*.

At Kiauhou, the path turned inland two miles, up a rugged hill of lava, in ascending which, the beast I rode made as much ado as if he had been brought up on a Brussels carpet or an English lawn, instead of the hoof-hardening pastures of Kailua. The path was slightly worn by the bare feet of the natives, much as the stone toe of St. Peter at Rome is kissed smooth by the worshippers of baptized Jupiter Capitolinus. On both sides were heaps and depressions of rough scoria and slag, great boulders of lava, black broken masses, crumbling cylinders, and spheroidal volcanic stones, the surface of which had been fused, and in some places had peeled off like a crust or shell, while the centre of some of them was of a dark-blue color and compact texture, and did not appear to have been at all affected by the fire which had reduced the surface.

Jammed into clefts of lava, where there seems not a particle of sand or earth, you may see there the splendid pink-white caper, (capparis,) with its hundred stamens, and delicious odor, and light-green leaves, lavishing alone its fragrance and beauty upon rough, unsightly rocks. Even so, perhaps Jeremy Taylor would say, have I seen beauty adorning the face of deformity, virtue flourishing amid vice, and the wealth of warm affections and generous natures spent unpaid upon selfish, sterile hearts. So, I would rather say, it is the way of benignant nature to show the affluence of her resources, to reveal the might and glory of a creative, wonder-working God.

> "She has a world of ready wealth,
> Our minds and hearts to bless;
> Spontaneous wisdom breathed by health,
> Truth breathed by cheerfulness."

No one who has been through the barren parts of Hawaii, or East Maui, can fail to have noticed this beautiful shrub; how, as by elective affinity, it chooses those unwatered, desolate tracts of lava, where there is not a green thing else to sympathize with it, or be its rival. There have I often observed it cheerfully exhaling its odors and hues, not unheeded by God and his angels, though unnoticed of men. Even like a retiring, virtuous woman—

> "Wisely she shuns the *broad way and the green*,
> And with those few is eminently seen,
> That labor up the hill of heavenly truth.
> Her care is fixed, and zealously attends
> To fill her odorous lamp with deeds of light,
> And hope that reaps not shame."

A half hour of such travel, as slow as it could be and yet be called motion, brought me in sight of silvery *kukuis* and the oak-green bread-fruit tree, with its eight-lobed leaves and golden fruit. At half past ten I reached a beautiful table-land, where, by the lapse of time and the action of frequent rains, the lava has become disintegrated, and covered over with a prolific soil. The sight of the plain of ocean, noiseless in the distance, whitened here and there by the sail of a fishing-canoe, and extending off in its azure glory, till it seemed to rise up into an eminence high as that I was riding upon, was very beautiful.

I stopped a while to rest at the place of a man from Maine, who was discharged here from a ship in 1811, and entered into the service of Kamehameha, who gave him his lands. In the evening of his days he has become a member of the church. When under discipline, a few years ago, for intoxication, he was addressed by a Romish priest at Kailua: "The missionaries have turned you out of the church for drinking, have they?" "Yes," he replied. "I deserved it; for I could not go to the table of the Lord defiled with sin."

The Jesuit rejoined, "You have committed no crime. God is willing we should enjoy ourselves, and what is the harm of drinking a little brandy? God will forgive you. These missionaries are keeping you in fetters and superstition. I wish to see you at liberty and enjoy yourself. If you will only join my church, I will pledge my honor that you shall never be turned out." Disgusted with such a gross attempt to flatter and seduce him, the man retorted, somewhat warmly, "Yes; and I suppose the devil would not turn me out of hell, if he got me there!" He is now restored, and is living in good standing with the native church.

Coffee is being extensively cultivated by this man and his son-in-law. The tree, laden with fruit and ruffled leaves, its branches proceeding from the trunk horizontally, and filled out to the end with red coffee-berries, looking very much, when ripe, like the cranberry, is a very beautiful specimen of tropical vegetation, deserving to be cultivated for its looks alone. The tree here is said to be from twenty months to three years in attaining its maturity. It will then bear, I am told, two crops a year for twenty years. It is usually cut off at the top when about five and a half or six feet high, and will then produce about a peck of berries at a time, or ten pounds of dried coffee annually, which sells here for two reals or more a pound.

After a delay at this plantation of a couple of hours, I proceeded hither by a path shaded with *ohias*, bread-fruit, and kukuis. Long before reaching it, the missionary establishment hove in sight, with its thatched roofs and whitened walls, and an air of taste and cultivation giving just promise of hospitality, intelligence, and piety. My guide and baggage-carrier had reached here before, so that I found a room and entertainment ready, with a missionary's cordial welcome to it. Would that every Christian wayfarer could find where-e'er he wanders, for health or to do God's will, hospitality as grateful and cheering!

There is a passage in "Colman's Christian Antiquities," in regard to the hospitality of primitive Christians, which I have often read with pleasure, and will quote here, because it is so happily paralleled in what

I am now experiencing among missionaries: "The followers of Christ, how widely soever they were scattered throughout the world, were then united as one great family, and agreeing, as they did, in the happiness and spirit of concord, to regard any local varieties of custom as matters of indifference, kept up a constant and friendly correspondence with all the branches of the Church universal; so that, whenever any of them went abroad, either on their own private affairs, or on missions connected with the state and progress of religion, they were received with open arms by the Christians of the place as brethren.

"Go under whatever name they might, and travel to remotest places, among people of foreign manners and an unknown tongue, the pilgrims of the faith were sure, wherever they met with a Christian, to find a friend, whose house would be thrown open for their reception, whose table would be spread for their entertainment, and who would welcome them with a warmer heart and a kindlier smile, than they were often met with by their kinsmen and acquaintances at home. They were treated by the family that received them as one of themselves, had their feet washed by the wife on their first arrival, and at their departure were anxiously and tenderly committed to the divine care, in a prayer by the master of the house."

On the other side of this Bay of Kealakekua, and off to the south, is the celebrated old Puhonua or Hawaiian city of refuge, at Honaunau, the ancient residence of kings, where Kalaimoku, he that was afterwards called the Iron Cable of Hawaii, fled for refuge after the sanguinary battle that made Kamehameha the Great sovereign of the whole island. I say celebrated, because this and one of the same kind in Waipio, Kohala, are the only sanctuaries of the kind ever known to have existed among pagans; and this has been frequently spoken of by missionaries as a unique object among the ruins of Paganism, to be contemplated with unusual interest.

When Ellis visited it in the year 1824, there was standing within it a house called the House of Keawe, which would seem to have been to Hawaii what Iona was to Scotland—a sacred depository of the bones of departed kings and princes, probably first erected for the custody of his remains whose name it bore, a king that reigned in Hawaii about eight generations back. By pushing one of the boards across the doorway a little on one side, Mr. Ellis says they could look in and see many large images, some of wood very much carved, others of red feathers, with wide-distended mouths, large rows of sharks' teeth, and glaring pearl-shell eyes. They also saw several bundles apparently of human bones, cleaned, carefully tied up with cinet made of cocoanut fibres, and placed in different parts of the house, together with some rich shawls and other valuable articles, probably worn by those to whom the bones belonged, as the wearing apparel and other personal property of the chiefs is generally buried with them.

On the outside of the inclosure there were rudely

carved male and female images of wood, some on low pedestals under the shade of an adjacent tree, others on high posts on the jutting rocks that overhung the edge of the water. "At the southeast end of the inclosed place twelve of them stood in grim array, forming a semicircle, as if perpetual guardians of the mighty dead reposing in the house adjoining. Once they had evidently been clothed, but now they appeared in the most indigent nakedness. A few tattered shreds round the neck of one that stood at the left-hand side of the door, rotted by the rain, and bleached by the sun, were all that remained of the numerous and gaudy ornaments with which their votaries had formerly arrayed them.

"A large pile of broken calabashes and cocoanut-shells lay in the centre, and fragments of kapa, the accumulated offerings of former days, formed an unsightly mound before each of the images. The horrid stare of these idols, the tattered garments upon some of them, and the heaps of rotten offerings before them, seemed no improper emblems of the system they were designed to support; distinguished alike by its cruelty, folly, and wretchedness."

The traveller at this day sees none of these hideous relics of the corpse of Paganism, that was then just slain, and lay rotting, unburied, like a carcass thrown to carrion-birds. To visit here at that time, was like looking down into one of those wide pits of living death and festering decay, into which Defoe says they used to cast the victims of the great plague in London. It was, as it were, stepping into the very rank tomb of idolatry, where the horrid monster had been lately tumbled all naked and gory, weltering in his own blood and foulness, as he had long revelled in that of his murdered victims—

> "——— besmeared with blood
> Of human sacrifice, and parents' tears."

There now remain only a low fence of posts, and the stone walls of the irregular parallelogram that constituted the Place of Refuge. These are 715 feet long, 404 feet wide, about 12 feet high, and 15 feet thick. Holes are still visible on the parapet or raised terrace, where large images formerly stood about four rods apart, through the whole extent. There are fragments of lava in these walls that must be of two or more tons weight each, six or eight feet above the ground, which it is difficult to imagine how Hawaiians could have raised (as they must) without machinery, by the mere force of the unassisted human hands. But the despots here of old knew how to use the bones and sinews of their subjects with great executive effect, in hauling heavy timber for their idols, and putting up immense *heiaus*, as well as to give their bodies a sacrifice to

> "The devils they adored for deities,"

whenever the priest* or their own caprice called for the Moloch offering.

* If a temple was to be built, the people had the stones to collect for the walls, and the timber and posts to put up; they had the thatch-

Sometimes they made their lives so bitter with hard bondage, imposed such intolerable burdens upon the abject people, and bent the bow of their servile compliance so far that it suddenly snapped, with death to the tyrant that strained it. In the mountainous parts of Kau there is a steep, round hill, up which it is a tradition among the people that a chief once required his subjects to drag a huge log, which he was going to set up there for his idol, to overlook all the land and sea. They had succeeded, at intervals of time, in drawing it two-thirds of the way up, when some Hawaiian Gracchus, heading the people, and gaining them all over to his purpose, laid this plan to get rid of their task and task-master. He feigned himself extraordinarily zealous in forwarding the work, got all the people to man the lines, and then approached the chief, who sat looking on, with this request—that he would but put his shoulders once to the log from be-

ing to do; a levy for sustaining the service was made on them of hogs, cocoanuts, bananas, kapa, red fish, bundles of baked kalo, fowls, and other articles. The priest looked at the king, saying, "Let there be men for the god." The king consented. "Let there be a house for the god." The king consented. "Let there be land for the god." The king consented. Then the priest addressed the king again, "Let a hog be hanged up for the god; let there be certain fish for the god; the first fish for the god." The king consented. Then the priest proceeded, "Let the land of the priest be sacred, free from taxes; let the house of the priest be sacred, no one wantonly entering it; in short, let all that belongs to the priest be in safety." Thus the priest says to the king. The king and the priest were much alike, and they two united were the nation's main burden.—*Ka Moolelo Hawaii*, in *Hawaiian Spectator*, vol. II., p. 440.

hind, and, at a given signal from himself, they would all strain themselves to the utmost, and at one pull run it up to its place. The purblind chief consented, and with a simultaneous joyful effort they started the log forward a few feet, and then suddenly let it go back, crushing with its whole length and weight the body of their oppressor, and thundering down the side of the mountain, as on the slide of the Alpnach, till it lodged in the level below, where they say a part of it may be seen to this day.

But to return to the *Puhonua*,* at Honaunau.

---

* The Puhonuas were the Hawaiian Cities of Refuge, and afforded a most inviolable sanctuary to the guilty fugitive, who, when flying from the avenging spear, was so favored as to enter their precincts. This had several wide entrances, some on the side next the sea, the others facing the mountains. Hither the man-slayer, the man who had broken a tabu, the thief, and even the murderer, fled from his incensed pursuers, and was secure. To whomsoever he belonged, and from whatever part he came, he was equally certain of admittance, though liable to be pursued even to the gate of the inclosure. Happily for him, those gates were perpetually open; and as soon as the fugitive had entered, he repaired to the presence of the idol, and made a short ejaculatory address expressive of his obligations to him for reaching the place in safety.

Whenever war was proclaimed, and during the period of actual hostilities, a white flag was unfurled on the top of a tall spear, at each end of the inclosure, and until the conclusion of peace, it waved the symbol of hope to those who, vanquished in fight, might fly thither for protection. It was fixed a short distance from the walls on the outside, and to the spot on which this banner was unfurled the victorious warrior might chase his routed foes; but here he must himself fall back. The priests and their adherents would immediately put to death any who should have the temerity to follow or molest those who were once within the pale of the *pahu tabu;* and, as they expressed it, under the shade or protection of the Spirit of Keawe, the tutelar deity of the place.

Whether it was first instituted by priests, as a means of increasing their power by binding to their interests all who should owe safety to its protection; or by some Hawaiian Alfred, in order to mitigate the cruelty of idolatry, and provide an offset to the sanguinary character of their wars; or whether it was derived, as some suggest, traditionally from the Israelitish cities of refuge, it is not easy to determine. However the institution may have originated, the Place of Refuge itself is an interesting spot, which no visitor on this side of Hawaii will fail of going to see.

The grim idols that received the man-slayer within their strangely-friendly pale, like a wolf turning his den into a sheep-fold, are gone. The high-priests of idolatry are all dead, and there are few surviving who can tell you any thing of the transactions that have taken place here. The Gospel of Christ precluding and extinguishing murder and war, supersedes the necessity of this singularly humane feature of cruel Paganism. It is almost too great a tax on the traveller's

---

In one part of the inclosure, houses were formerly erected for the priests, and others for the refugees, who, after a certain period, or at the expiration of war, were dismissed by the priests, and returned unmolested to their dwellings and families; no one venturing to injure those who, when they fled to the gods, had been by them protected. The Puhonua at Honaunau is very capacious, capable of containing a vast multitude of people. In time of war, the females, children, and old people of the neighboring district, were generally left within it, while the men went to battle. Here they awaited in safety the issue of the conflict, and were secure against surprise and destruction in the event of defeat.—*Ellis's Missionary Tour through Hawaii*, pp. 137, 138.

credulity to ask him to believe that a people now so remarkably peaceable and gentle, among whom the safety of human life and property is unparalleled anywhere on the face of the earth—that only one generation back they were the warlike, ferocious, infanticide race, sacrificing each other to their gods, which unquestionable facts make them to have been.

The last human sacrifices are said to have been made at this place in 1818. One man was then sacrificed for putting on the *malo* (girdle) of a chief, one for eating a forbidden article of food, one for leaving a house that was tabu and entering one that was not, and a woman was put to death for going into the eating-house of her husband when intoxicated. On the authority of natives, former kings have immolated eighty victims at once, as in the days of Umi, whose blood-thirsty god, after one of his victories, kept calling from the clouds, Give, give, until the priest and himself were all that remained of his train.

In the revolution so marvellously effected at these Islands, how remarkably is fulfilled that prediction of Holy Writ in the Prophecy of Zephaniah, *The Lord will* FAMISH *all the gods of the earth; and men shall worship him every one from his place, even all the* ISLES *of the heathen!*

When the first band of missionaries landed at Kailua, only fifteen miles from this Bay, in the spring of 1820, just thirty-one years ago, the appearance of the natives was thus described by one of that heroic company:—"A first sight of these wretched creatures was almost overwhelming. Their naked figures and wild expression of countenance, their black hair streaming in the wind as they hurried the canoe over the water, with all the eager action and muscular power of savages; their rapid and unintelligible exclamations, and whole exhibition of uncivilized character, gave to them the appearance of being half-men and half-beast, and irresistibly pressed on our minds the query: '*Can they be men? Can they be women? Do they not form a link in creation connecting man with the brutes?*' This, indeed, seemed to be the general impression. The officer heading the boat sent to the shore, on his return exclaimed, as he ascended the deck, 'Well, if I never before saw *brutes in shape of men*, I have seen them this morning;' and, addressing himself to some of our company, added, 'You can never live among *such a people as this:* we shall be obliged to take you back with us.'"

Some of their number, says Mr. Bingham, with gushing tears, turned away from the spectacle. "Others, with firmer nerve, continued their gaze, but were ready to exclaim, 'Can these be human beings! How dark and comfortless their state of mind and heart! How imminent the danger to the immortal soul, shrouded in this deep pagan gloom! Can such beings be civilized? Can they be Christianized? Can we throw ourselves upon these rude shores, and take up our abode, for life, among such a people, for the purpose of training them for heaven?' 'Yes,' (they replied,) though faith had to struggle for the victory, 'these interrogations could all be answered in the affirmative.'"

These were the hopes of the pioneers themselves, sustained by secret refreshings from on high, and their life hid with Christ in God. But tell us now, ye men of the world, judging according to sense, what can these humane but Quixotic fanatics, as they were then deemed, what can they do with these untutored abjects of humanity in the remote heart of the Pacific? What, think you, will become of them, left all defenceless with these "brutes in the shape of men?" Two husbands and wives from the realm of Christendom, unbacked by navies, unsupported by armies, planting themselves at the very heart of the most abject paganism, among a horde of naked, squalid savages, already doubly brutified and debased below the level of ordinary savageism, by contamination from those moral ulcers which had been bred by the riffraff of civilization —what shall they do there?

What means do they possess of transforming such miserable creatures into intelligent, conscientious, civilized and Christianized men and women? Will they succeed in the experiment? Or will they fail? Will the labor and money expended upon them be thrown away to no purpose? Or, going forth and weeping, bearing precious seed, will they come again with rejoicing, bringing their sheaves with them? Let the harvest of 1850 answer, just one generation from the deposit of the first germ:— TWENTY-TWO THOUSAND MEN AND WOMEN IN THE CHRISTIAN CHURCH; SEVENTEEN THOUSAND PUPILS IN CHRIS-

TIAN SCHOOLS; and their contributions in the year 1849, while decimated by a wasting epidemic, to different religious objects, over Seven thousand Dollars!

Statesmen and philosophers, and socialist reformers, have started innumerable plans and theories for the improvement of our race and the reconstruction of society. But while we behold here a triumph of the Gospel over the direst combination of evil influences, what instance is there on record, in the annals of the human family, of a nation emerging from barbarism by any other means, and ascending to a moral position so eminent, in a single generation? Is there any other agency known to man, but the "foolishness of preaching," capable of producing such results? We say with certainty, No, there is not.

Had Napoleon obtained for France to the full his three wishes—"I desire Ships, Colonies, and Commerce"—they would never have done for France, or for the countries colonized and traded with, what Christianity has done for the Island Heart of the Pacific. The transformation here accomplished is little less than miraculous.

Never, in the history of man, has so great a change been effected in so short a time. Where robbery and murder but a few years ago were practised as trades, and were events of every-day occurrence, life and property are now safer than under any long-established government that can be named. Great as is the Hawaiian love of *waiwai*, (property,) and degraded and bad as they still are in many ways, yet such is now the force of law and the effect of the Gospel, that we might almost say a man may travel afoot and by canoe, through the entire cluster of Islands, from Hawaii to Niihau, and with a net bag of shining dollars, without fear of molestation, unless it be from some desperate runaway foreigner, or a straggling Hawaiian sailor, hardened by his cruises abroad. If the same be true of any other land, we have yet to know it. To the Gospel, that has wrought the change, be all the glory.

Christianity as the Cause, Commerce and Civilization as the consequents and handmaids, have done it all. Without the missionary, carry to them all you could of modern art and culture, Hawaiians to this day would have lived and died in as besotted and gross barbarism as in the days of Cook. God would not be in all their thoughts; and where God is not honored, civilization can neither be established, nor can it hold its own. It was because the glorious Gospel of the Son of God went first to this Island Heart of the Pacific in the year 1820, that facts like the following turn up in the year 1850.

When the Sandwich Islands Mission was first started, a young wheelwright in Massachusetts was called upon to contribute for it, and was told that his quota would be a dollar. He paid it, but with the feeling then that the dollar was thrown away. Within the present year this same wheelwright has received an order from those Islands for twenty pairs of cart-wheels and bodies, at ninety dollars a pair.

Now we say with confidence, that without the Christianity there* which this wheelwright's *first dollar* helped to establish, Commerce, with all its boasted facilities, could never have returned him the *eighteen hundred.* And the fact shows that, if men wish to invest their money where it will yield a dividend of eighteen hundred per cent., they had better put it into the treasury of Missions.

The religion of the Gospel is the only lever that can pry up the nations, and put them in the way of improvement by commerce and civilization. Christianity is itself the most perfect civilizer hitherto discovered. John Williams very truly remarks, that, until the peo-

* The money-value of Christianity at the Sandwich Islands is further shown in these two facts. A plantation on the Island of Maui, which a few years ago cost less than $5000, has recently (in 1851) been sold for $30,000; and a small store-lot at Honolulu, purchased of a chief about the time of the arrival of the missionaries for a mere trifle, has lately sold for $10,000.

The gross domestic exports from the Islands in 1849 were valued at $103,743.74. In 1850, $380,323.63. Increase more than three-fold. Gross value of imports in 1849, $729,730.44. In 1850, $1,053,053.70. Increase nearly two-fold. Number of vessels that visited the Islands in 1849:—Merchant vessels, 180; whalers, 274; vessels of war, 13: total, 467. In 1850:—Merchant vessels, 469; whalers, 237; vessels of war, 14: total, 720. Value of supplies furnished these vessels in 1849, $81,340.00. In 1850, $140,000.00. Both the number of vessels and value of supplies nearly doubled in a year. The gross value of the supplies and exports for 1850 was $536,522.63. The exports of sugar increased from 653,820 lbs. in 1849, to 750,238 in 1850; of coffee, from 28,231 lbs. in 1849, to 208,428 in 1850; of Irish potatoes, from 858 bbls. in 1849, to 51,957 in 1850; of sweet potatoes, from 306 bbls. in 1849, to 9,631 in 1850.

The number of framed houses erected in Honolulu and vicinity during the year 1850 was three hundred and fifty.

ple are brought under the influence of religion, they have no desire for the arts and usages of civilized life; but that invariably creates it. While nations are under the power of their superstitions, they evince an inanity and torpor, from which no stimulus has proved powerful enough to arouse them, but the new ideas and new principles imparted by Christianity.

Was it that the savage Sandwich Islanders, in the days of Cook, did not discover God by the light of nature? Were not the invisible things of him from the creation of the world clearly seen, being understood by the things that are made, even his eternal power and Godhead?

Knew they not God?—They might have seen
His beauty in the glorious green
Of these fair Isles, and heard his voice
In Nature's song, that bade Rejoice!
And witnessed in the soil they trod,
Heaved up in coral wonder—God!
And marked HIS footsteps, bathed in wrath,
On the volcano's fiery path.
But all in vain;—though every hill
Its Maker knew; each conscious rill,
Leaping and sparkling, told of HIM;
Morn's blush, and Evening's twilight dim,
Proclaimed their God; though valleys rang,
And the blue-waved Pacific sang;
And mountain, mead, and rock replied,
"*God! God!*"—they heard not, raved, and died!—

God was not in all their thoughts until enthroned there by Christianity, brought in God's own providential time, and inaugurated in his own way in the Heart of the Pacific, so as best to answer the part to be fulfilled by these Islands in the conquest of the entire Island World of the Pacific, and of the great continents that lie upon it, for the Lord Jesus Christ.

It is remarkable to notice how, in the providence of God, death to the first discoverer of the Sandwich Islands, and spiritual life to their depraved aborigines, should both issue instrumentally from the bosom of this Bay of Kealakekua. This was the birth-place of Opukahaia, or Obookiah, and it was his embarkation at this port, accidental as it seemed, in 1809, on board an American trader, that forged the important link in the chain of events which was finally completed in 1819, just ten years after, in the embarkation of the missionary band from Boston for Hawaii in the brig Thaddeus.

On board the American trader there was a pious student of Yale College, who took much pains on the voyage to America to instruct the tawny Hawaiian sailor in the rudiments of knowledge. Along with his companion, Thomas Hopu, he was taken, on their arrival, to New Haven, where the spark of missionary zeal may be said to have been first struck out, in the successful efforts of some of the students there, to initiate these youth into the elements of learning and Christianity. "The friends of Christ in New England were led to look upon these sons of Paganism, thus providentially brought to their doors, as having a claim for sympathy, care, and instruction in the Christian doctrine; and, in attempting to meet this claim, they cherished the reasonable hope that suitable efforts to enlighten and convert them would tend to the evangelization of their idolatrous nation."*

Aiming to secure the salvation of these strangers, and to make their agency available in disseminating the Gospel through heathen countries, the American Board of Commissioners for Foreign Missions established, in the year 1816, a trial school at Cornwall, Connecticut, for whatsoever sons of unevangelized barbarians they could gather together. Hereby was fanned the nascent flame of the Island Mission, which in due time was to irradiate the Heart of the Pacific with so wide a blaze.

Let us pause and mark here the hand of God. "The time of blessed visitation," says Hollis Read, "had come for the isles of the sea. The English churches had already taken of the spoil of their idols, and were rejoicing and being enriched by their conquests. The American Zion must participate in the honor and profit of the war. Hence Henry Obookiah, an obscure boy, without father or mother, kindred or tie, to bind him to his native land, must be brought to our shores; be removed from place to place, from institution to institution, everywhere fanning into a flame the smoking flax of a missionary spirit, and giving it some definite direction; be made the occasion of rousing the slumbering energies of the Church on behalf of the heathen, and of kindling a spirit of prayer and benevolence in the hearts of God's people; and finally, and principally,

* Bingham's History of the Sandwich Islands, p. 57.

his short and interesting career, and perhaps, more than all, his widely lamented death, must originate and mature a scheme of missions to those Islands, the present aspect of which presents scenes of interest scarcely inferior to those of the apostolic age."*

The companion of Opukahaia, Thomas Hopu, I met at Kailua. He was then fifty-two years of age, and was the sixth man living of those that came from Cornwall, all but one of whom were then said to be in good standing in the church, although they had all been wayward and unstable.

He gave me a graphic account of sundry early adventures of his when a sailor, before he went to Cornwall: how he was the means of saving all on board the schooner he was in, when it was overset at sea, and the masts sprang out as she capsized. He dove under and bit off a rope that held the boat; then got it to the floating masts, and, freed of water, helped the crew into it, and rigged a sail out of the captain's shirt, through which, by a propitious Providence, they reached, just alive, one of the West Indies. Though a wicked sailor, he said he often prayed then to God in the Lord's Prayer, which he had learned while first going to America with Henry Opukahaia.

From the West Indies he shipped again to the United States; but it being the time of the last war with England, the brig was captured by a British cruiser not far from Newport, and carried into Tarpaulin Cove.

* Hand of God in History, by Hollis Read. Hartford, 1849. P. 138.

There, according to his story, he prevailed upon his shipmates to seize a Yankee sloop the British had brought in there. They succeeded in the enterprise, and returned with the sloop to the very port where it was owned.

Reclaimed from the sea, and adopted by the benevolent, Hopu now lived for three years at Cornwall, where, although he never enlisted the sympathy and interest that were attracted to Obookiah, he was fitted for an important part, at first, as interpreter to the early missionaries, and a teacher in the schools.

While at the Cornwall Mission School, it is related of him that he took a journey into the country with a friend, and spent an evening with a company who were much entertained by the questions proposed to him by an irreligious lawyer, and his amusing answers. At length Thomas said, in substance, "I am a poor heathen boy. It is not strange that my blunders in English should amuse you. But soon there will be a larger meeting than this. We shall all be there. They will ask us all one question, namely, 'Do you love the Lord Jesus Christ?' Now, sir, I think I can say, Yes. What will you say, sir?"

He ceased, and an oppressive stillness pervaded the room. At length it was broken by a proposition of the lawyer, that, as the evening was far spent, they should have a season of devotion, in which Thomas should lead. It was acceded to; and Thomas, in his accustomed meek and affectionate manner, addressed the throne of grace. Soon he prayed for the lawyer in person, alluding to his learning and talent, and besought that he might not be ignorant of the way of salvation through Christ.

As he proceeded thus, the emotion of the lawyer rose above restraint. He sobbed aloud. The whole company were affected, and sobs drowned the speaker's voice. When they separated for the night, and retired to their respective rooms, there was no rest to the lawyer, for the question of Thomas still rung in his ears, "*What will you say, sir?*" Nor did its echo cease till the Spirit of God renewed his heart, and he truly found the Saviour.

This same Thomas Hopu is now bronzed and wrinkled beyond his years, and his lamp of life must soon go out. Though his conduct as a Christian since his return is said to have been by no means always exemplary, nor his influence upon his countrymen what was to have been looked for from his advantages, we must lean to the side of charity in our judgments both of him and his fellows.

Mr. Dibble very properly says, that too much had been expected of them. They were found exceedingly ignorant, and of course, therefore, were miserable interpreters, and very poor teachers. They were often found teaching doctrines and precepts altogether opposed to the precepts of the Bible, and to the spirit of the Gospel. Those of the Cornwall youth especially, that came with the first reinforcement, were deemed a hindrance rather than a help. "To have visited a foreign land, to be better clad than their fellow-countrymen, to receive some attention from chiefs and foreigners, were distinctions which their weak brains and undisciplined minds could not endure."*

These youth having so far failed as interpreters, the missionaries were thrown upon their own skill and application for getting a mastery of the Hawaiian tongue. To this great work, therefore, of learning and reducing to writing a language barbarous and unknown, they accordingly devoted themselves with a patient, yea, heroic assiduity. The marvellous result of their labors the universal world of humanity now knows and feels. How vast the difference between the Hawaii which they found in 1820, and the Hawaii which, under God, they have made in 1850!

In the marvellous change thus effected at this long-lost Atlantis of the Pacific, we catch a glimpse of what may be realized the world over, when that prophecy of Holy Writ shall be fulfilled which says that THE EARTH SHALL BE FILLED WITH THE KNOWLEDGE OF THE GLORY OF THE LORD AS THE WATERS COVER THE SEA. THEY SHALL NOT HURT NOR DESTROY IN ALL MY HOLY MOUNTAIN.

* Dibble's History of the Sandwich Islands, p. 173. Lahainaluna Mission Press, 1843.

# CHAPTER III.

## LAHAINA AND ITS ENVIRONS ON THE ISLAND OF MAUI.

Happy, oh! happy he, who not affecting
The endless toils attending worldly cares,
With mind reposed, all discontent rejecting,
In steady pace his way to heaven prepares;
Deeming his life a scene, the world a stage,
Whereon he acts his useful pilgrimage.

Anon.

Good-bye to Hawaii—Grateful reminiscences—The continental character of missionaries—Portraiture of a good priest—Run to Maui by whale-ship—Facilities for recruiting at Lahaina—Seamen's chaplain—Gratuitous services of missionaries—Sailors always careless when not cared for—Winding up of a liberty-day at Lahaina, in the season of ships—An honorable pre-eminence—Hawaiians a surf-playing—Sea-bathing a national passion—Array of arguments for the people supporting their own ministers—Peculiar advantages at Lahaina—The Hawaiian democracy—Remarkable running out of the race of rulers—Precious dust in God's acre—Character and influence of the high chief Hoapili—A striking anecdote—Vistas of prophecy opened—Tendency of things—Cheering progress.

Turn we now, in prosecuting this survey of the moral Heart of the Pacific, to another portion of the Hawaiian group. We pay a reluctant farewell to the hospitable Island of Hawaii, in whose missionary families, churches, and schools, as portrayed in "The Island World of the Pacific," I find myself to have become more deeply interested than I could have believed. The friendships of studious years have been renewed. New ones, that will be ever cherished and fragrant, have been formed. The good fruits of the Gospel, and the benign results of faithful missionary labor, have been observed; and a debt incurred of that kind which, while it cannot be cancelled from the mint, a debtor loves to be paying, and a creditor to be receiving from the mental mine of genuine affection, good wishes, and prayers.

It is that kind of obligation which a truly hospitable and good man likes to have others under to himself, and it is the only debt which does not worry, and which he is willing to be burdened with himself, as answering the apostolic injunction, *To owe no man any thing, but to love one another*. It is a commodity which it were happy indeed if all Christians lived so much within their means, and with such true Christian simplicity and prudence, as to be able to pay all their debts in. The pressure of the times would be little felt if a plenty of that were in circulation, and if discounts were oftener made between man and man in that genuine currency. Its quality, like that of mercy, is not strained,

> Both blessing him that gives and him that takes.

It is of the kind words, attentions, hospitality, and help which love dictates between friend and friend, and from his host to the traveller, and which humanity calls for from the rich and prospered in society to the unfortunate and needy, that our American poet Dana says,

> They make not poor:
> They'll come again full-laden to your door.

Lord Bacon, too, has beautifully said, If a man be gracious to strangers, it shows that he is a citizen of the world, and that his heart is *no island* cut off from other lands, but a *continent* that joins them. The friends with whom I have been sojourning, are eminently continental in their make and their manners. With the great Continent of Humanity, and every member of it, they are closely allied, and nothing human is foreign to them. Though their range be but an island, their sympathies embrace the world; and the sweep of their prayers and their charities is as wide as that of the glorious ocean that laves their shores.

A man that lives to do good, (the only life worth living,) may think himself well off to have his lot cast among the missionary band of Hawaii. Assured of a steady living, and delivered from so much that is artificial and hollow in society, they have only to devote themselves to their families and to their proper missionary work. Theirs is not the bread of idleness. And if they labor hard, and have some discouragements and trials, not easily appreciated by men that live in America, they have the solace, too, that their toil is not unblessed, and that the sympathy and prayers of many are with them. Some of them realize to a rare degree Bishop Ken's portraiture of "A Good Priest:"

Give me the Priest these graces shall possess:—
Of an ambassador the just address;
A father's tenderness, a shepherd's care,
A leader's courage, which the cross can bear;
A ruler's awe, a watchman's wakeful eye,
A pilot's skill, the helm in storms to ply;
A fisher's patience, and a laborer's toil,
A guide's dexterity to disembroil;
A prophet's inspiration from above,
A teacher's knowledge, and a Saviour's love.

They are a united and affectionate body, that have eminently the confidence and love one of another, and they have the confidence and love of the Hawaiians to the utmost. May it be so always, and may every fresh accession to their forces be an accession of executive and moral strength! May peace be on them and mercy, and upon the Israel of God of which they have the charge! *Peace be within her walls. May they prosper that love thee. For my brethren and companions' sake I will now say, Peace be within you.*

The disability of bodily indisposition prevented my making the tour of Hilo and Puna with the pastor, Rev. Mr. Coan, and afterwards going across Mauna Kea to Waimea, the station occupied by Rev. Lorenzo Lyons. I wished, also, to be near at hand to this port in the shipping season, in order to take advantage of any good opportunity that might occur for America. Taking passage, therefore, in a whale-ship that touched at Hilo for supplies, I am here, after an easy run of two days.

The roadstead of Lahaina, as usual in spring and fall, is anchored in all over by large whale-ships, that have come in from the different cruising-grounds of the Pacific to recruit, where supplies of all kinds can be obtained on more advantageous terms, and with less detriment to the men, than at any other place in this ocean. It has been visited the last two seasons, fall and spring, by about four hundred ships, that spend on an average, at a very moderate estimate, three hundred dollars each, making the sum-total of $120,000 yearly disbursements at this port. The estimated value of the

LAHAINA AND LAHAINALUNA FROM THE ANCHORAGE.

whale-ships and cargoes entered at Lahaina and Honolulu, between 1844 and 1845, was $17,733,411; of disbursements there, $150,000.

The supplies furnished by the natives are goats, hogs, poultry, fruit, and vegetables, especially Irish potatoes, for which they get money and cloth, or other articles of exchange. Fresh beef, also, is supplied by foreigners. Other supplies, as of salt provisions, bread, cordage, and ship-chandlery in general, are furnished almost exclusively by one American house, that take bills drawn upon ship-owners in America and Europe, at a rate of twenty per cent. for exchange.

The concurrence here of such large whaling fleets makes Lahaina a most desirable place of labor for a seamen's chaplain. Estimating twenty-five seamen only to a ship, the port will be visited by ten thousand annually: not, indeed, ten thousand different seamen, but that number in two different times.

From the first year, 1823, in which this was made a missionary station, to the present time, more or less of a chaplain's work has been done for them by the resident missionaries. Until he left, in 1825, it was Mr. Stewart's special department; in whose time were perpetrated the atrocious outrages upon government and the mission by disappointed sailors and their infamous captains.

Rev. Mr. Spalding, the lamented associate of Mr. Richards, labored some years after among them with great acceptableness. On his failure, the work fell upon Mr. Baldwin, who had at the same time the pastoral care of the church in the absence of Mr. Richards, and the medical department for Maui. A building has been erected, and an upper room finished for a chapel, by the contributions of shipmasters and foreigners at Lahaina.

During one year, the Rev. Lorrin Andrews, for some years a missionary of the American Board, now in the employ of government, was engaged by the residents here to supply the desk. Two hundred and forty dollars were contributed by shipmasters and residents for his support. He labored, however, only on the Sabbath, and preached once the same day in a school-house to a little congregation of natives, in a remote part of Lahaina.

A man was needed to labor daily among the residents and seamen, who might come into personal rencontre, and employ what Dr. Beecher used to call the short-sword and dagger of personal conversation and Tract-giving. Through the providence of the American Seamen's Friend Society, such a laborer is now supplied in the person of Rev. Mr. Taylor, who has been stationed here since the year 1848 as the local seamen's chaplain. It will be in his power, through God's blessing, to preclude much sin and suffering on the part of those otherwise unfriended seamen, who, having no man to care for their souls, are likely to care little for themselves, except how they may secure the pleasures of sin for a season.

It was painful to go out among them here about sundown, when their liberty expires, and, drunk or sober, they must be off to their ships, or into the fort. Liquor and lust had by that time done their best to inflame many of them, and your ears would be shocked by ribald oaths, and the language of lewdness, caught up and repeated by native boys; and you would see some reeling to and fro at their wit's end, and hustled along by some less drunken comrade; and others without shame, caressed and hung upon by native girls, who flock here in the ship season, from other parts, to get the ready wages of sin. The populace of both sexes were out to see what was a-going, and to catch the contagion and cant of vice. It was a scene of vileness, disgust, and abomination, which no virtuous man, if possible, would see but once.

You seemed to behold busy devils scouting about one of the breathing-holes of hell, running into the drunken herd, and chuckling with Satanic glee over the human victims which they were making ten-fold more the children of hell than themselves. It was a sight to make a missionary weep, and any foreigner in whom virtue and shame have not become extinct,

> To blush,
> And hang his head to think himself a man;

a countryman, perhaps, of those who were making themselves and the recent heathen so vile.

It ought to be added to this picture now, that, just after my visit at Lahaina, the sale of ardent spirits was prevented, and a great deal of mischief and vice stopped. The only license for its sale (which government deemed itself under the humiliating obligation to grant in consideration of the forced French treaty) was bid off at auction to a temperance man, with the tacit understanding that he should not be a loser, for the sum of $1500. In a riot just before, and a fight of the seamen with the native constables, the rioters for a time held the town, and it was found absolutely necessary for the safety of life and limb, and to preclude similar or worse scenes of riot and noise, that the one great mischief-breeder should be bound and rendered impotent. This port and Hilo are now probably the only two places in all the Pacific Ocean frequented by ships, where a sailor cannot get drunk. May the honorable difference never be lost through any fault of theirs!

It is highly amusing to a stranger to go out into the south part of this town, some day when the sea is rolling in heavily over the reef, and to observe there the evolutions and rapid career of a company of surf-players. The sport is so attractive and full of wild excitement to Hawaiians, and withal so healthful, that I cannot but hope it will be many years before civilization shall look it out of countenance, or make it disreputable to indulge in this manly, though it be dangerous, exercise.

Many a man from abroad who has witnessed this exhilarating play, has no doubt inly wished that he were free and able to share in it himself. For my part, I should like nothing better, if I could do it, than to get balanced on a board just before a great rushing wave, and so be hurried in half or quarter of a mile landward with the speed of a race-horse, all the time enveloped in foam and spray, but without letting the roller break and tumble over my head.

In this consists the strength of muscle and sleight-of-hand, to keep the head and shoulders just ahead and clear of the great crested wall that is every moment impending over one, and threatening to bury the bold surf-rider in its watery ruin. The natives do this with admirable intrepidity and skill, riding in, as it were, upon the neck and mane of their furious charger; and when you look to see them, their swift race run, dashed upon the rocks or sand, behold, they have slipped under the belly of the wave they rode, and are away outside, waiting for a cruise upon another.

Both men and women, girls and boys, have their times for this diversion. Even the huge Premier (Auhea) has been known to commit her bulky person to a surf-board; and the chiefs generally, when they visit Lahaina, take a turn or two at this invigorating sport with billows and board. For a more accurate idea of it than can be conveyed by any description, the reader is referred to the engraving.

I have no doubt it would run away with dyspepsia from many a bather at Rockaway or Easthampton, if they would learn, and dare to use a surf-board on those great Atlantic rollers, as the Hawaiians do on the waves of the Pacific. But there is wanting on the Atlantic sea-board that delicious, bland temperature of the water, which within the tropics, while it makes sea-bathing equally a tonic, renders it always safe.

The missionaries at these Islands, and foreigners generally, are greatly at fault in that they do not avail themselves more of this easy and unequalled means of retaining health, or of restoring it when enfeebled. Bathing in fresh water, in a close bath-house, is not to be compared to it as an invigorating and remedial agent; and it is unwise, not to say criminal, in such a climate, to neglect so natural a way of preserving health, as washing and swimming in the sea. In those who live close to the water, and on the leeward side of the Islands, it is the more inexcusable, for it could be enjoyed without exposure in the dewless evenings; or in some places, a small house might be built on stone abutments over the water, and facilities so contrived that both sexes could enjoy this great luxury of a life within the tropics.

But we come back to Lahaina, to speak of a charming grove of young cocoanut-trees in the northwestern part of the town, planted by the excellent chief Hoapili, or Hoapiliwahine. They are not the tall, lank, ghostly-looking things which the full-grown tree is, that becomes at these Islands, from the places in which you most often see it, a synonym of desolation and sterility, but a luxuriant, youthful growth, more beautiful than

HAWAIINA SPORT OF SURF PLAYING.

any thing in the form of woods that I have seen since leaving America.

Six or seven years ago there was a fine grove of large green Kou-trees in the opposite part of the town, near where the King lives, covering an acre and a half or two acres, and so ancient and shady as to afford ample covering for all the canoes in Lahaina, and all the people too. But before any one knew it, and not until it was too late to remonstrate against such a piece of savageism, the King took a freak to have them all cut down to make into bowls, and spittoons, and pounding-boards for *kalo*. Could the outraged trees have wept like the sacred grove in the Ænead, they would have dropped tears of blood at the indignity.

So, on the island of Molokai, there was a fine forest of Kamani-trees, the only ones at the Islands. It is a tree of slow growth, and of great value for its beautiful wood. But the chiefs a few years ago had them all mercilessly cut down, without any care to propagate young ones, happening to want the timber to repair some vessels. It was a fair specimen of ordinary barbarism: how unlike the wisdom of Kamehameha the Great, who, when birds were caught for him to pluck certain feathers for his *leis* and *kahilis*, would not let them be killed, but set loose again, to give feathers, he said, to his sons. And when they cut young sticks of sandal-wood, he remonstrated with them, and said, "Is it, indeed, that you do not know my sons? To them the young sandal-wood belongs."

A sure sign of thrift and civilization, which I have

seen a very few times in Hawaiians, is the planting of trees. Ask them why they don't do it more in a land where shade is such a blessing, and they will answer, it will do them no good; they would never enjoy them; it is a *mea lapuwale* for them. But such improvidence is not at all to be wondered at, when we consider the uncertain tenure upon which they have hitherto held their lands. Any improvements made by a common man would have been only a premium to covetousness and injustice on the part of his chief, and would be likely to insure the alienation of property whose enhanced value made it a Naboth's vineyard to some Hawaiian Ahab.

The planting of trees anywhere indicates the possession of a freehold, and the beginning of a prosperous and sound state, in which the rights of property are respected, and justice is rendered between man and man. It is what Washington Irving, speaking of the English fondness for trees, calls "the heroic line of husbandry, worthy of liberal, free-born, and aspiring men. He who plants an oak looks forward to future ages, and plants for posterity. He cannot expect to sit in its shade, nor enjoy its shelter; but he exults in the idea that the acorn he has buried in the earth shall grow up into a lofty pile, and shall keep on flourishing, and increasing, and benefiting mankind, long after he shall have ceased to tread his paternal hills."

The laws framed within three or four years nominally secure the right of property to Hawaiians; but in their administration justice was far from being even, especially on the Island of Hawaii, under the management of Governor Adams, who was averse to quitting the ancient *régime*, or waiving any of the privileges of the chiefs. But liberty and law are everywhere gaining force, and a revolution is in progress which will insure good government and equal rights, if the people only survive to enjoy them. The philanthropist and Christian cannot help ardently desiring it, and deprecating as most melancholy the decay of the race, just as it might be beginning to enjoy the liberty and all the benign ameliorations of the Gospel.

But if, in the all-wise providence of God, the event be contrary to what we naturally desire, they who have been laboring sincerely to save the nation will not lose their reward. They are laying the foundations for many generations, and the good of their labors shall redound for ages. *Their reward is with them, and their work before them.* The church they have planted *shall continue so long as the sun and moon endure, throughout all generations. The Lord shall have here a seed to serve him* to the end of time.

And though the nation's blood run out, and there be left a mongrel race of self-glorifying Anglo-Americans and other foreigners, that like the Jews of Nehemiah's day, "married wives of Ashdod, of Ammon, and of Moab, and their children spake half in the speech of Ashdod," yet it shall be not less a people to serve God, to reap the benefit of, and to be moulded by, the institutions of the Gospel planted now. Meanwhile, although the Hawaiians melt away, and it be sad to see a nation dying out, we will take the consolation given by the chorus in Milton's Samson Agonistes—

> All is best, though we oft doubt,
> What the unsearchable dispose
> Of highest wisdom brings about,
> And ever best found in its close.

Lahaina is one of those places which you like much better as you approach or recede from it, than when you are actually in it. A little way off it seems sweetly embosomed in bread-fruit trees, and all fresh and lovely with sunshine and verdure, calmly inclosed seaward within a fence of foam, made by the sea breaking upon the coral reef. Ride over the rollers in a whale-boat or native canoe, get to the sun-burnt, dusty land, walk up a few rods, perhaps with white pantaloons, to the mission-houses, and make acquaintance on the way to your heart's content with Lahaina dust and caloric, and you will probably by that time be saying to yourself—

> 'Twas distance lent enchantment to the view.

However, dirt, fleas, mosquitoes, and heat to the contrary notwithstanding, Lahaina has so salubrious and dry a climate, and advantages for healthful sea-bathing all the year round, that one who is any thing of an invalid likes to be there, or, what is better, two miles above, at the seminary of Lahainaluna. It is said that the greatest observed elevation of the mercury here in Fahrenheit's thermometer, for ten years, was 86 deg.; the lowest, 54 deg. The wind is the alternating land and sea breeze. A steep mountainous ridge in the rear entirely breaks off the trades, and, receiving all their rain, carries it distilled below in a fertilizing stream that irrigates all the valley and vega of Lahaina, and is spent before it reaches the sea.

Two or three times in a year the trades whirl over the mountain, and then woe to the man's eyes that are so luckless as to be found in it. From hill and plain there are caught up great, suffocating volumes of red dust, that envelop all the town, and even roll off to ships in the roadstead, and redden the sea. Closed doors and windows are as mere lattice-work for it. It traverses stone walls and *adobes*, human lungs and ears, and I know not but livers, and permeates every thing. If a man's eyes only escape being filled and getting the ophthalmia, he is well off. But the blow over, all is well again. The sea or the translucent Lahainaluna water is there to wash in, and, merrily making your ablutions within and without, you'll sing—

Cold water for me, cold water for me!
But wine for the tremulous debauchee!

The mission-house here, being the first built, and (until his embassy abroad) occupied by Mr. Richards, and the one now occupied by Mr. Baldwin, are situated in the very busiest and dirtiest part of the town. Probably it was a retired spot, surrounded by kalo patches, when selected and given by Keopuolani, in 1824. But the concourse of business and ships have so increased both the population and noise, that the place has become a most undesirable one for residence, and especially for rearing children. Juvenal's caution can hardly be kept there:

> Nil dictu fœdum, visu que hæc limina tangat
> Intra quæ puer est—
> Maxima debetur puero reverentia.*

Somewhat more than a quarter of a mile to the southeast, within a verdant and shaded inclosure, is the large galleried Stone Church and burying-ground. It is the first stone meeting-house built at the Islands, and does credit to its architect, the Rev. Mr. Richards. When he found its steeple to have settled away a little from the main body of the house, so as to threaten a fall, he cleverly made it fast by iron clamps and chains. It will accommodate two thousand people.

The Gospel preached there has been sometimes quick and powerful, and full of edification and life to good old chiefs and common kanakas. The veteran Hoapili, when unable to sit up but a few minutes, had himself carried there only ten days before his death in 1840, to be once more blessed by the ordinances of God's house. No serious blot, say the missionaries, is known to have attached to the Christian character of this chief while living, and now that he is gone, his memory is sweet. Those who saw and conversed with him while he was waiting the summons of death, were much affected with

* Let nothing foul to eye or ear be ever seen or heard about those doors which inclose your boy. To eager and imitating childhood we owe a scrupulous reverence and care.

his deportment. He was wakeful and deeply interested in the prospect of the change that awaited him, and he longed to depart and be with Christ.

"He seemed to be emptied of self, to be lowly in his own eyes, and to cast himself with much confidence on Christ. The word of God and prayer were his delight, and from these he sought solace till he was insensible to every thing earthly. His last interview with the king was said to have been tender and affecting in the extreme. After conversing with him in a dignified manner for a time, alluding to his own dependence, and beseeching the king to abandon his sins, and become a good man, he became much affected, laid his head on the lap of the king, and burst into a flood of tears. As he lay dying, he gave a charge concerning his bones, strictly forbidding wailing on the occasion of his death, and desiring that his grave might be an humble one near the sleeping-place of Mr. McDonald, a departed missionary."

There they lie in the burying-ground, hard by together, the missionary teacher and the converted heathen chief, with a little group of baptized missionaries' children, whom Christ has taken from the care of parents to be safe with himself.

> "God their Redeemer lives,
> And ever from the skies
> Looks down and watches all their dust,
> Till he shall bid it rise."

The good old chief then will come forth in his new attire, with the vigor of immortal youth, wondering at the grace of a Saviour to a dark-minded savage; and, methinks, it will be with no common energy that he will lead a file of ransomed Hawaiians in that blest song, "Worthy is the Lamb:"

> Loud as from numbers without number,
> Sweet as from blest voices uttering joy!

How beautiful is that poem by Longfellow called God's-Acre, which I can never enter a Christian burying-ground without calling to mind!

> I LIKE that ancient Saxon phrase, which calls
> The burial-ground God's-Acre! It is just;
> It consecrates each grave within its walls,
> And breathes a benison o'er the sleeping dust.
>
> God's-Acre! Yes, that blessed name imparts
> Comfort to those who in the grave have sown
> The seed that they had garnered in their hearts,
> Their bread of life, alas! no more their own.
>
> Into its furrows shall we all be cast,
> In the sure faith that we shall rise again
> At the great harvest, when the archangel's blast
> Shall winnow, like a fan, the chaff and grain.
>
> Then shall the good stand in immortal bloom,
> In the fair gardens of that second birth;
> And each bright blossom mingle its perfume
> With that of flowers which never bloomed on earth.
>
> With thy rude ploughshare, Death, turn up the sod,
> And spread the furrow for the seed we sow:
> This is the field and Acre of our God;
> This is the place where human harvests grow!

It was of this remarkable Hawaiian chief, now peacefully sleeping in God's-Acre at Lahaina, that a story is told which well illustrates his native strength of mind.

Upon the publication by the missionaries of a little treatise on the true principles of geography and astronomy, surprise and doubt were expressed by some, and they disputed before Hoapili about the figure of the earth. "Stop," said the old chief; "do not be so quick with your objections to the foreign theory. Let us look at it. This is what I have always seen. When I have been far out at sea on fishing excursions, I at first lost sight of the beach, then of the houses and trees, then of the hills, and last of the high mountains. So when I returned, the first objects which I saw were the high mountains, then the hills, then the trees and houses, and, last of all, the beach. I think, therefore, that these foreigners are right, and that the earth is round."

The influence of Hoapili and Hoapiliwahine his wife was valuable and excellent many ways. Among other things, they taught the people at Lahaina to be liberal to their ministers, and it should be said to their praise, that they are more than usually attentive at this station in bringing poultry, fruits, vegetables, dried fish, &c., as marks of their aloha (love) both to Christ and their worthy pastor. This liberal spirit can be easily encouraged and turned to good account, so as entirely to support among them the institutions of the Gospel.

The Church at this station, by the annual report for 1849, numbers 637 members—ordinary attendance on the Sabbath at the meeting-house, twelve or thirteen hundred. Some of them are, for Hawaiians, men of considerable substance; are owners of horses and cattle, make molasses from the sugar-cane, have lands on which they raise potatoes for ships, besides kalo-patches that furnish their own food, and are officers of government.

Almost the same may be said of their pecuniary ability at Honolulu, and particulars might be given of the ways in which Hawaiians at these ports can now get money, and of the ease with which much of it can be applied to support the preachers of the Gospel. They make out a strong case why the missionaries at these places, the two central stations first taken, and from which there is constantly emanating a powerful influence throughout the entire group, should have been supported by the people for two or three years past;* and the late action of the American Board in 1849, is altogether wise and feasible, that proposes to the Sandwich Islands Mission to become independent of the home treasury, and to throw itself upon the people for support.

The readiness of the missionaries to accede to this proposition and to make the experiment of self-support, trusting under God to the generosity of the people, is worthy of all praise, as it is in keeping with the character they have won before all the world for ability, zeal, and devotion. The general success of this experiment can hardly be doubted, though it may fail at some particular stations for reasons purely local.

We do not think the objection valid, that you cannot

---

* The whole amount of contributions for all benevolent and religious purposes, in the two Native Churches of Honolulu for the year 1850, is $1733.92.

expect the people to give seven or eight times as much to their teacher as it takes to support one of their own families. Hawaiians know the wants of foreigners are more than theirs, are glad to have it so, and would be unwilling that their teachers should live like themselves. And as to any natural scruples at receiving from people so poor, and that live so miserably destitute of the comforts of civilized life, we think they had better be set over against the contributions of many at home, who give *out of the abundance of their joy and their deep poverty*, by rigid economy, and the voluntary deprivation of luxuries which are missed far more than the poor Hawaiians' *hapaha*, or *hapalua*, or dollar would be, if given to his minister.

Ships put in circulation here a good deal of money, spent by sailors, and in lieu of fresh supplies. Many of the reals, and half-dollars, and dollars so distributed, fall into the hands of common church members, who being supplied, for the most part, otherwise with food, and having as yet few artificial wants, might as well as not bestow many of them upon their teacher.

In this connection, we cannot help saying, that we think it would be far better for American missionaries everywhere to be allowed to hold property, and honorably help themselves, and to be in every respect upon the same footing as ministers at home; and that they should be enjoined to urge the people to whom they preach to contribute all in their power for their support. We think there would in this way be more economy, and more manliness and proper independence both in the missionary ministers and their families, and in the churches. The dangers of undue acquisitiveness, neglect of missionary work, and worldly-mindedness might be guarded against. Missions generally, certainly those that are so far advanced as the Sandwich Islands Mission, would thus cost the Board less, and do the people more good, by stimulating them early to maintain their own religious institutions. This always leaning upon America, David Malo says, is not good. If America should give way, we should break our backs. We had better learn early to stand alone.

It is upon the Hawaiian democracy mainly that the support of the Church at these Islands must henceforth depend; for with the decease of Hoapili and Kapiolani the race of godly chiefs seems to have become extinct. Few are surviving that can boast of chiefs' blood. Hoapili died without issue. The governor of Hawaii dies childless. The king and the premier (Auhea) have no offspring; nor is there a high-chief living that has a lineal heir. Most of the chief boys and girls in school at Honolulu are half-breeds, or adopted heirs, and the children of the former premier Kinau.

It is a remarkable fact, and would seem to argue somewhat of Providence and destiny, that so large a body of rulers by birthright should so soon give out. Their rapid extinction is even more manifest and significant than that of the people. Perhaps in the mysterious counsels of the Most High, their days are numbered, and the end of their existence as a nation is near. If it prove to be so, it will remain to be remarked how the date of their depopulation and decay, like that of all the other islanders of the Pacific, and the tribes of North and South America, synchronizes with their discovery and the offer made them of the Gospel.

Through their acceptance of the latter, although they now become extinct, the prophecy will be made good, that *in him* (*Christ*) *shall all nations of the earth be blessed. Redeemed unto God out of every kindred, and tongue, and people, and tribe, and nation*, there shall be some to sing, " Thou, Lord, art worthy." With thanks and everlasting joy the ransomed Hawaiian, the Indian, the Hottentot, the South Sea Islander, the " natives of Ormus and of Ind," shall come up to the general assembly and church of the first-born.

From every isle, from every clime they come,
To see thy beauty and to share thy joy,
O Zion! an assembly such as earth
Saw never, such as heaven stoops down to see!
Bright as a sun the sacred city shines:
All kingdoms and all princes of the earth
Flock to that light; the glory of all lands
Flows into her; unbounded is her joy,
And endless her increase. Thy rams are there,
Nebaioth, and the flocks of Kedar there:
The looms of Ormus and the mines of Ind,
And Saba's spicy groves pay tribute there.
Praise is in all her gates; upon her walls,
And in her streets, and in her spacious courts,
Is heard salvation. Eastern Java there
Kneels with the native of the farthest West;
And Ethiopia spreads abroad the hand,
And worships. Her report has travelled forth
Into all lands. Thus heavenward all things tend.

COWPER.

## CHAPTER IV.

### THE FOOTSTEPS OF BEAUTY TRACED BY A TRAVELLER IN NATURE, LANGUAGE, AND RELIGION.

There's beauty all around our paths, if but our watchful eyes
Can trace it 'midst familiar things, and through their lowly guise.
Yes! beauty dwells in all our paths—but sorrow too is there:
How oft some cloud within us dims the bright, still summer air!
But know that by the lights and clouds through which our pathway lies,
By the beauty and the grief alike we are training for the skies.

Mrs. Hemans.

A canoe takes us to Wailuku—Elements of the beautiful at home and abroad—Morning on the mountain—Effect of natural scenery upon childhood—Curious Hawaiian etymologies—A catalogue of queer appellatives—The peculiar genius and idioms of the Hawaiian tongue—Words to be domesticated into English—Conversational uses of the native—Commendable solicitude of Hawaiians for the purity of their language—Classical discussion at an assembly of teachers—Fear of barbarous innovations from abroad—A book of fables suggested—Their uses illustrated—Isaac Taylor on the employment of the Esopian vehicle of instruction—Notices of the Wailuku church and pastor—Resolutions for the independent support of the ministry—Praiseworthy instance of Hawaiian gratitude—Mr. Green's experiment at Makawao—Beneficial results—Reasonings of natives—Union of faith and works—Affecting tests of Christianity—Resolves of pastors preparatory to independency—Initiatory steps—Remarkable consummation in the jubilee year of the nineteenth century.

Six hours' sail by canoe along the coast of Maui, and a walk of eight miles, have brought us to Wailuku, the windward station of this island, where constitu tions debilitated by the long-continued heat and confinement of a leeward residence, find repair and health from the bracing trades and exercise on horseback, for which latter there are more facilities in roads and horses than at any station yet visited.

The mission-houses are situated on a gently sloping plain, about half a mile from the base of an abrupt mountainous ridge, that rises in some of its peaks to the height of six or seven thousand feet. The tract is watered by a side canal from a stream that is abundantly supplied by mountains,

> On whose rugged breast
> The laboring clouds do often rest.

The plain looks towards the east, and slopes downward to the sea on both sides, at the north and south, being traversed by a range of sand-hills that separate East and West Maui. These were once two islands, and are now divided only by the sand and a low isthmus, daily enlarging, which, together with the tracts on each side, furnish pasturage for large herds of cattle, horses, and goats.

There is beauty here, material and moral, human and divine, on the blue sea always in sight, and on the green or sun-dried land. There is beauty within the mission-houses, and beauty abroad in the daily paths of usefulness trodden assiduously, by the laborious men and women to whom Providence has here assigned a sphere of duty, in which they cheerfully revolve. There are trials, and sorrows, and crosses, too, here, as always in the lot of man, which true piety, however, is converting daily into elements of beauty. Hence it is that we have taken the motto of this Chapter from that beautiful composition of England's Poetess, "Our Daily Paths," written in

> The cheerful faith that all which we behold
> Is full of blessings.

I have said there is beauty abroad; for as you look off to the east, towering up to heaven in calm majesty, there is the beautiful long mountain of Hale-a-Ka-La, or The House of the Sun. From its top, ten thousand feet above the rest of the world, the bright eye of day opens every morning with a golden glory, and sends his level beams across to the opposite range on West Maui, and aslant down the mountain's fire-worn sides, showing the cones and chasms of old volcanoes. Sometimes a snow-drift lies on its summit in the morning. Always it is there, the same great object in its quiet beauty, which from morning to morning it does one good to behold.

To rise up a little before the sun, and look out upon the azure face of that calm mountain, beautiful in its distance and repose, and lofty and vast as the Almighty made it, can hardly fail of filling a heart with joy that is at peace with God.

By half past nine or ten, clouds have drifted on to its bosom, and there they are all day long, the blue crown of the mountain alone visible above them, until nightfall, when they generally vanish or sail away, and leave it open to the beams of the moon and stars.

The salutary moral influence of opening one's eyes every morning upon such a scene, though it may be imperceptible at the time, is very great. It is well for a family of children that they may drink it in and have joy in it, although they do not know why; and in beholding all the beautiful things of nature, which they never stop, in their innocent delight, to call beautiful, or once think what it is that is making them so happy.

Yet all the while, if their training within doors be only right, by such joyous intercourse with nature in a happy childhood, they are laying a broad foundation of permanent after peace. Even as we are instructed in the "Excursion,"

> Thus deeply drinking in the soul of things,
> We shall be wise perforce; and while inspired
> By Truth, and conscious that the will is free,
> Unswerving we shall move, as if impelled
> By strict necessity along the path
> Of order and of good. Whate'er we see,
> Whate'er we feel, by agency direct
> Or indirect, shall tend to feed and nurse
> Our faculties, shall fix in calmer seats
> Of moral strength, and raise to loftier heights
> Of love divine, our intellectual soul.

There are in this region four streams in succession from the different gorges of the mountain, significantly named, it is thought, from the events of battles which have transpired upon them. *Waikapu*—The *water* where the *conch* was blown, and the engagement began. *Waiehu*—The *water* where the combatants *smoked with dust and perspiration. Wailuku*—The *water of destruction*, where the battle began to be fierce and fatal. *Waihee*—The *water* of total *rout and defeat*, where the army melted away.

The Hawaiians were particularly fond of annexing a *wai*, (water,) if possible, in the names of places. It is like the Eastern word *wadi*, (water,) that occurs so often in the names of places in Arabia, as Wadi Mousa, Wadi Seder, &c. Undoubtedly it is the same word, with the mere ellipsis, for euphony's sake, of the consonant *d*.

And it might be remarked, in passing, that not a few of such verbal analogies go far towards proving the original identity of the languages of Polynesia and the East. Almost all valleys in Hawaii-nei, and places that have the precious boon of water, are called *wai* with some descriptive epithet, as *Waiohinu*, sparkling water; Waialua, two waters, or double water; Kawaihae, broken waters, &c.

In giving names to each other, and to their children, Hawaiians were often not a little whimsical and droll. The most trifling circumstance or accident fixed their nomenclature; and names were as likely to be taken from things and qualities disgusting and vile, as from the opposite, and to be borne without any disgrace.

You might know that a people must have been vile from the vile names they assume and wear without shame—names that one would be unwilling to translate. All evil appetites and qualities, bodily organs and deformities, mischievous acts and vices, were turned into names. Thus there are persons named Moekolohe, (adultery;) Kekuko, (lust;) Kahahu, (anger;) Haaheo, (pride;) Kalili, (jealousy;) Kaino, (bad;) Aihue, (thief;) Wahahe, (liar;) Pelapela, (filth;) Molowa, (lazy;) Pupule, (crazy;) Puhi-baka, (tobacco-smoker;) Inurama, (rum-drinker,) &c.

It is not a little amusing sometimes, though it be disgusting at others, to trace out their etymologies. When the chief woman, Kapiolani, at Kealakekua, was sick, and had submitted to a surgical operation, a child of a common man happening to be born about that time, was called Four-Inches-Long, in order to commemorate the length of the wound.

So, not to mention a great variety of natural objects from which they derived names, there are some men noways deformed, called Pupuka, (crooked;) Makaino, (ugly-face;) Kamakalepo, (dirty-face;) Kealiiopunui, (big-bellied-chief;) Blind-of-one-eye, Lame-of-one-leg, &c.

The names of the Diabolonians and Men of Man-Soul in Bunyan's Holy War, or of the soldiers of Cromwell's army, are not more whimsical and odd than are to be found often in Hawaii-nei. Messrs. Jolly, Gripe, Griggish, Rake-all, and their excellencies, Mr. Carnal-sense, Live-by-feeling, Love-lust, Hate-good, Mr. Facing-both-ways, Sergeant Bind-their-kings-in-chains, Captain Hew-Agag-in-pieces-before-the-Lord, and others, compare very well with the queer appellations by which Hawaiians often call each other and foreigners.

Missionaries were for a long time called the *Ai-oe-oe*, (long-necks,) because, when the Hawaiians first saw the missionary wives with bonnets, making them to appear as if long-necked, they cried out, *Ai-oe-oe.* Chiefs among them went by many names, all expressive of something; and a new name was frequently assumed after any exploit or event of their lives, to keep it in memory, as the Romans honored their successful generals with appellations derived from the cities or countries which they had conquered; as, Caius Marcius Coriolanus, Scipio Africanus, Cato Uticensis, &c. The names of the present King, Kaui-ke-ao-uli, and of the Premier, Ke-kau-luohe, mean Hanging-upon-the-blue-sky, and Bamboo-grove.

The Hawaiian language, that admits so readily of these compounds, is simple in its structure, and very easy and uniform both in its orthography and pronunciation. Aside from the facile genius of the tongue, this is owing to the good sense and judgment of the missionaries who first reduced it to writing. They admitted no silent letters, and adopted the uniform Spanish designation of the vowel-sounds. Hence, as in that beautiful language, a, e, i, o, and u, always have each but one, and its own sound, varied only by quantity: so that, unlike what is found in the English and French, the language is spelt and pronounced just as it is written, and vice versa. Any one that has a knowledge of the Spanish at once slides into the pronunciation of the Hawaiian vowels.

The variety of only twelve letters expresses every Hawaiian sound, by reason of which, and the constant repetition of vowel terminations, the language to foreigners sounds monotonous. Also, no word ever ends in a consonant, nor can two consonant sounds come together, but a vowel is always interposed. Thus, an Hawaiian, in writing or pronouncing Boston, London, Bedford, will say *Bosetona*, *Lonedona*, *Bedefoda*.

Some of the idioms are very peculiar and curious. There is no auxiliary verb *to be*, nor any word to express the abstract idea of being or existence. Good idiomatic Hawaiian is, therefore, in short sentences, or clauses thereof, and the same word may be a noun or a verb, according to the sense to be expressed, without change. This, and the destitution of general terms, while specific ones are numerous, constitutes a state of the language favorable to the art of poetry.

There are no variations in nouns for case, number, or person; but the mood and tenses of verbs are pretty clearly distinguished by simple prefixes and suffixes. The mode of conjugating verbs, the existence of a causative form, and the derivation of words from roots of two syllables, are thought to indicate a resemblance and cognate origin with the Hebrew and other Oriental tongues.

The use of the particle *no* in the way of affirmation or affirmative emphasis, like yes indeed, no indeed, is very peculiar, as being so the reverse of all the languages of Europe, where it is negative. Tell an Hawaiian to stop or leave off any thing he is doing, as *ua oki, ua oki pela*, and he answers, I stop indeed, *oki au no*, or *stop no!*

Ask a man a question to which he does not know or wish to give the answer—as, What did you do it for?—and the reply commonly heard will be, *He aha la!* what indeed! Ask a native about the climate of a place—as, whether it is rainy or not—and he will think he gives you a very wise answer, though it is a most amusing and unsatisfactory one to the asker: *Ina ua, ua no*, (If or when it rains, it rains;) *Ina aole, aole no*, (If not, no indeed;) *Ina ua pinepine, pinepine no*, (If it rain often, often indeed it rains;) *A i hiki i ka manawa ua, ua no*, (And when the rain-time has come, there is rain indeed!)

So, when you ask a native, sometimes, where he is going, he will answer you very respectfully, *E hele au makahi E hele ai*, I am going where I'm going, or what amounts to the English expression, without any of its impudence, I am following my nose! Ask a man whom you are employing what shall be done in any exigency, and he generally answers, *Eia no ia oe*, (That's with you, that's for you to say.)

There is one Hawaiian word which, for its singular convenience and expressiveness, I would be glad to get domesticated into English, and that is *Pilikia*. They use it to signify any strait, or difficulty, or perplexity a man is brought into, by accident, or sickness, or the mismanagement or ill conduct of others.

In the speech of the King at the forced cession of the Islands to Paulet, it occurs very aptly. "Hear ye! I make known to you that I am in perplexity (*pilikia*) by reason of difficulties into which I have been brought without cause; therefore I have given away the life of our land. Hear ye! But my will over you, my people, and your privileges, will continue, for I have hope that the life of the land will be restored when my conduct is justified."

When one becomes familiarized with this term, there is no word that can be thought of half so expressive to denote one's extremity and strait; and hence you will hear it used in conversation by missionaries in the midst of their English, as if it were legalized old Saxon. The same is true of the word *akamai*, expert, skilful, ready at any thing.

The compound word for hope is beautifully expressive: it is *manaolana*, or *the swimming thought*—faith floating and keeping its head aloft, above water, when all the waves and billows are going over one—a strikingly beautiful definition of hope, worthy to be set down along with the answer which a deaf and dumb person wrote with his pencil, in reply to the question, What was his idea of forgiveness? "It is the odor which flowers yield when trampled on."

At a convocation of teachers held at this place, to consider their disabilities, and petition government for a redress of grievances, I have been highly pleased with the solicitude which some of them have manifested to maintain the purity of their Hawaiian tongue. They were over ninety in all, a respectable, orderly body, having their President and Secretaries, and disposing of all questions in due form and order.

One of the subjects first discussed was the name by which they should call their meeting, as it was a new thing under the sun for Hawaiians. It was proposed to adopt, so far as they could, the English word Society, and call the convention The Teachers' Society, *Sokieke o na Kumu*.

To this some of them resolutely objected, just as we may imagine Cicero or Pericles would to an unauthorized innovation upon the classic Latin or Greek, that their *language was getting barbarous;* that foreigners were *corrupting and running away with it;* and that, if they did not take care, it would soon become a mongrel, and they should not know their own tongue.

At length, with the help of their minister, they hit upon a vernacular compound that met the case, and they called the assembly *Ahahui*, or The United Company.

I cannot but venture to suggest here, that a well-selected book of the best fables extant would be a great boon to the Hawaiian Nation in the present stage of its progress. It could not but interest and quicken the minds both of youth and adults; and a Reading Book might be made of them of singular utility and attractiveness, that would constitute a mine of wealth. Hawaiians are now familiar with almost all the animals that afford subjects of fable—the ass, the dog, the horse, goat, sheep, cattle, and swine; besides cats, rats, and mice, (those prolific fable-breeders,) domestic fowls, and birds.

It is remarked by Isaac Taylor, in his admirable work entitled "Home Education," that the distinctive characteristics of animals bear such an analogy to the varieties of human character, as has in all ages suggested the mythic form of instruction, and such as imparts to fable a degree of fixedness, or, one might say, authenticity, which hardly admits of its being disturbed.

The relative dispositions and habits of the bee and the wasp, the dog, the wolf, and the fox, and the moral picturesqueness of temper which we attribute to the ass, the magpie, the parrot, the viper, the owl, the jackal, the ape, are such as force themselves upon our notice as samples of humanity in caricature.

The first stirring of intellectuality in a people, as they emerge from barbarism, shows itself by catching at these same analogies; and what is true of a nation in its infancy, is true of childhood itself; for the mind no sooner opens than it seizes upon these very resemblances, and nourishes itself with them.

"The usage of employing the Esopian fable in the conveyance of language, must be considered as well adapted for securing several ends; inasmuch as, while it affords a sparkling entertainment, it brings together almost exclusively the descriptive portion of language, an early familiarity with which is in itself highly important."

Backed by such authority, I cannot but commend the preparation of a collection of fables like that here indicated, to the hard-working Professors of Lahainaluna and Wailuku, and to the literature-founders of newly civilized nations generally. It would be giving to the people a grant of ideas, resources for the imagination, and a fund of mental activity, not soon to be exhausted; and it would materially aid the hitherto necessarily slow process of intellectualizing and Christianizing barbarous tribes.

We find the church at Wailuku to include eleven hundred and thirty-four members, under the pastoral care of Rev. E. W. Clark. The riding abroad necessary in performing the duties of a pastor, and change of climate, have proved partially restorative to his health, which had been much impaired by his severe sedentary labors in the Mission Seminary at Lahainaluna. Although far from being robust and strong, he is able now to execute the round of a missionary's work, in which, like all other business, it is happily true in practice,

"That use doth breed a habit in a man,"

and render it comparatively easy.

His church, self-moved, has just taken a stand, and adopted a series of resolutions for the independent support of the Gospel ministry among them, that must be highly agreeable to the feelings of a Pastor, as indicating a manly mind and Christian spirit on the part of the people.

The movement augurs well. It is an omen of good that may justly encourage the American Board and its patron churches. It has led the way to the independent support of the Gospel ministry at the Hawaiian Islands. The following is a translated copy, furnished me by the Pastor, of resolutions adopted at a full meeting of the church called on the previous sacramental Sabbath:

Resolutions adopted by the church included in the territory from Waihee to Kahikinui:

I. That we decline the support received by Mr. Clark from the Missionary Society of America, and that this church of Wailuku unite together to supply all his wants in this thing and that thing, which he needs for his support.

II. That his support from America be sent to those places where the name of the Saviour has not been heard.

III. That certain persons be appointed to stir up the people to this work, and that the collections be made four times in a year.

IV. That collectors be appointed in different parts of the district, whose duty it shall be to take care of the property contributed by the church.

V. That the contributions at the monthly concert, and contributions for other definite objects, be kept distinct from what is contributed for the support of the pastor.

VI. That the names of all who assent to this proposition be attached to this engagement entered into by this church, and that it be the duty of the collectors to take down the names.

VII. In this manner shall each one give according to his ability—some one dollar, some fifty cents, some twenty-five cents, some twelve and a half cents, some six cents—according as each one receives, from the highest to the lowest, so shall he give.

VIII. To carry out these resolutions is the great thing; for it is an important work, and a work by which both our country and ourselves will be benefited.

IX. That this church engage, if they are out on a journey on Saturday, that they will not travel on the Sabbath, but remain and keep the Lord's day.

It is natural to mention in the same connection the recent instance of a man (not a church member) who had been early taught at Lahainaluna, and had become, through his knowledge and skill there acquired, a man of wealth and standing. He brought lately to Mr. Clark a present of four dollars, saying it was a *mea aloha*, (a thing of love;) that it was to his instructions he owed his property and place, and that he was going to make such a present to Mr. Andrews also, the first teacher in the Seminary, but now disconnected with it and the American Board.

You hear it often said that there is little or no gratitude in the Hawaiian mind, and they have even no word in their language to give thanks by. Be this as it may, there are few, I think, who would not agree, in this particular instance, that this man, at least, possessed both a sense of obligation and the feeling of gratefulness, which it would be pleasing often to see evinced as substantially by men in other lands, that have a better name for refinement than his, and where the institutions of Christianity are of older date than here.

A great stimulus to this action of the Wailuku church undoubtedly is the example of a neighboring church at Makawao, where Mr. Green retired after leaving the American Board, organized a church, and was settled as its pastor, on a promise of being supported.

He told them before he went that they must raise wheat for his breadstuff, and immediately they began in a district called Kula, and have succeeded in furnishing the best bread eaten at these Islands. He tells his *lunas*, persons appointed for this purpose, when he wants any thing, and forthwith they do all the *paipaiing* (stirring up) among the people, and it comes.

They also supply his domestics with food, haul all his wood and timber, have put up the *adobe* dwelling he now lives in, and are making ready to build a good stone or wattled house.

The pastor of Makawao received from his people on January 4th, 1851, five hundred and thirty dollars in money, as their free-will offerings to aid him in the support of himself and his family. In addition, they paid about forty dollars to a licensed native preacher of the Gospel, who has been laboring among them. They have also paid, during the year 1850, eight hundred dollars in money towards the erection of a house for public worship, and more than one hundred and fifty dollars for other than domestic objects. And they have promptly furnished their pastor with such comforts for his table as their fields afford.

The so far successful experiment he is making in a place by no means the most favorable for it, will go far to convince the native churches and the mission that missionaries can be supported on the spot, not only without impoverishing, but to the actual enriching of the people, by the efforts it demands, and the productive energy it constrains them to put forth. It is as true here as anywhere, that the *liberal soul is made fat, and he that watereth is watered also himself. There is that giveth and yet increaseth. There is that withholdeth more than is meet, and it tendeth to poverty.* Giving here, no more than in America, does not impoverish; withholding doth not enrich.

The churches at Wailuku and Makawao are beginning to find it out. The more they give, the more (say they) they have. It was not a little amusing, as well as affecting, to hear them sagely debate and express their minds, at the meeting in which this church unanimously resolved to support their teacher.

Various and interesting were the reasons given for so doing. One old man, bronzed with the tropical suns of sixty summers, said, with a native eloquence and emphasis not to be forgotten, that once his dollars and *hapahas* used to go for tobacco and his sins, and it was all *poho*, that is, sunk; and now it was a small thing to give them for the support of the Gospel, by which he had been led *to leave off his sins.*

Another said they were once thieves and murderers,

and their property and lives were insecure; and now it was but fair to give for the Gospel, by which it was that they had made their property, and were able also to keep it, and were so much better off than they used to be.

Another said, if they supported their own teacher, he would be theirs. Now they had had Mr. Green, and he had gone; Mr. Armstrong, and he had gone; and their tears had fallen, but they had murmured and wept in vain. But if they themselves should pay their teacher, he *would be theirs;* they should *hoopaa* him, that is, make him fast.

Another said that in this thing they must not promise and then not perform, but whatever they said they would give they *must* give. That he himself was *hewa* (that is, wrong) in this matter; he had sometimes promised what he had not yet performed. Then, after meeting was over, he came to Mr. Clark with three dollars, saying it was a part of five which he had promised a good while ago to the American Bible Company, for printing the Hawaiian Bible, of which he was so glad to have a copy.

Any benevolent patron of Missions, to have been there and heard them debate, and to have witnessed the evidence of their sincerity, would have thanked God from his inmost soul for having ever been able, or induced, to give to carry the Gospel where it had produced such benign results. And he would have said, Let me deny myself in order to give this blessed Gospel to all the world; for this same Gospel, if applied to all the world as at the Sandwich Islands, would, there is every reason to believe, produce the same results—results that have all been secured within less than thirty years since missionaries were first planted there among a race of indescribably depraved and debased heathen.

After this action on the part of the church at Wailuku, a committee of missionaries, on the subject of the support of pastors by their people, reported to the General Meeting convened at Oahu as follows :

1. That we regard the subject one of great importance to the prosperity of Christian institutions in these Islands; and that it is peculiarly gratifying to learn that some churches and congregations have resolved to make the attempt to support their pastors, and are actually taking measures to effect the object.

2. That, considering the increase of means, and the advancement of correct principles among the people, we believe the time has come when several of the more able congregations might be induced to support their pastors wholly, and many others might do it in part; and we believe the present is a peculiarly favorable time to present this subject to our several congregations, inasmuch as there is already, in many intelligent natives, an interest awakened to this subject.

3. That every pastor take great pains to instruct his people, and especially the church members, in the right use of money; to teach them to curtail all useless superfluities, such expenses as are incurred merely for show and ornament; and to induce them to appropriate their means to useful objects only, such as will secure to them all the advantages and comforts of complete civilization, and especially to sustain among themselves all the institutions of the Gospel, as the foundation upon which their temporal and eternal welfare must depend.

4. In order to bring this subject in the most advantageous manner before the congregations which are able to support their pastors, in whole or in part, we recommend that the pastor, together with such two members of the mission, and perhaps such influential native Christians as he may call to his aid, be a committee to present this subject before the people, and, in concert with them, to devise such practical and efficient measures as will secure the object; and we recommend further, that these efforts be made as soon as practicable after the close of the present General Meeting.

These initiatory steps, beginning, it will be noticed, with the people under the training of missionaries, have resulted, in the year 1849, in an offer and acceptance, on the part of the Sandwich Islands Mission, of a proposition of independency from the American Board.

The fiftieth year of the nineteenth century closes auspiciously with the grand experiment of a self-supporting Mission in the Heart of the Pacific successfully under way. Who of our readers does not earnestly implore for it the blessing of the Almighty Lord God, whose providences have been so marked and many towards that infant Christendom, the foundations of which have been thus gloriously laid?

## CHAPTER V.

A GLANCE AT THE PROVINCE AND RESULT OF MISSIONS IN THE HEART OF THE PACIFIC, AND A VISIT TO THE PALACE OF THE SUN.

I WATCH with throbbing heart the zeal,
Whose all-incorporating plan
Can teach a million souls to feel
For all that's man—for all that's man!
And every human title blend
In those of Brother and of Friend.

BOWRING.

A passing tribute to the true modern apostles—Character of Protestant civilization—Theory and practice at Wailuku—History and progress of the Female Seminary—Province of woman in the work of civilization—How fulfilled—Examination of schools—Hawaiian girls—Trip to the crater of Hale-a-ka-la—We reach the brim—Novel scene opened at the top—Spectacle of grandeur and glory presented by the clouds—A play-ground for the youth of heaven—Feelings belonging to such a position—Man's nothingness and the Creator's glory—Rhapsody of Rowland Hill—Luther's view of the majestic vault of God—Lesson we learned from the lofty look-out of Hale-a-ka-la—A sight from the cliffs of eternity—Montgomery's imprecation—We are let down safely—We pass to the sugar-making on East Maui—Farming lands—Horseback route through Haiku—Sand-hills and ancient Golgotha—Reflections on a skull—Evidence of former culture and dense population—Present record of deaths and births—Mortality of the year 1848 by measles—Culture of rice by Chinamen—Fine appearance of the garden and terraces of Wailuku—Entertainment at the Seminary—Sports with the children.

WITHOUT being of the craft,—an honor which providences have forbidden,—we freely confess to what may already have been discovered in these pages, namely, to an unfeigned love and respect for foreign missionaries. Well knowing whereof we affirm, we hold them worthy of all honor. They are Civilization's pioneers and explorers, as well as the tamers of mankind and preachers of the Gospel.

It is of them that Tacitus might have said most truly, Emolliunt mores, nec sinunt esse feros—They soften and improve both the manners and the morals of men, and forbid their living like beasts. They are Humanity's best teachers; Freedom's truest champions; Labor's ablest lifters; Society's real equalizers, and the clearest expounders of the rights of man. They are, indeed, the only true Apostles of Liberty, Fraternity, Equality—the world's working Socialists. They are the heralds and advance-guard of Agriculture, Science, and Art, and of all true social reformation, as well as of virtue and religion.

In their relations to barbarous tribes, and to the wide world of suffering humanity, they alone do truly blend in one the Christianizer, Civilizer, Benefactor, Brother, Friend. They act in the spirit of John Hampden's motto, Nulla vestigia retrorsum—No steps backward.

A practical demonstration of this is now seen at Wailuku; and it is pleasant to be able to testify of a station which, up to 1850, has enjoyed the labors of resident missionaries for eighteen years, that the people seem to be better clad, better housed, and to live better than at any other part of this Heart of the Pacific yet visited. Three special reasons may be assigned for it: First, The region is a fruitful one, supplying kalo and potatoes in abundance, and furnishing pasturage for herds, in which natives begin to hold property. Second, A good market is opened for their products at Lahaina, within thirty miles, at which they can obtain cloth. Third, Something has been done in the way of agriculture and internal improvements by the missionaries.

The station was first taken by the Rev. J. S. Green, with whom was afterwards associated the Rev. Richard Armstrong, both laborious and practical men. Much benefit has also been derived here from the residence and labors of the blind preacher, Bartimeus, the first convert to Christianity at these Islands. He died, beloved and lamented, in September, 1844. But his works do follow him, and shall be had in everlasting remembrance. A little memoir of this good man has been published, and a larger work on his Life and Times is said to be in preparation by the first pastor of the Wailuku church.

The influence of the Female Seminary located here has undoubtedly also been great and salutary. It was commenced by Mr. Green, in 1837, by the erection of a substantial stone building, fifty-six feet long by twenty-four wide, and two stories high. Thirty pupils were admitted that year, and an excellent female teacher associated in the instruction and care of them, who continues to occupy a post of so much usefulness. In 1840, the charge of the school was given to Mr. Bailey, which he still retains. The largest number of pupils at any one time has been seventy. The present number is fifty-two.

Besides the stone building first erected, there are

now a fine Chapel forty feet long, furnished with desks, seats, and school apparatus; two neat lecture and recitation rooms, floored, painted, and whitewashed; two ranges of adobe buildings for dormitories, one hundred and twenty feet long, in front and rear of the chapel; thirty acres of land inclosed and under cultivation by a native farmer attached to the institution, and eight native laborers.

The time of the pupils is employed as follows: one hour from early rising in the garden, then prayers and breakfast, recreations and miscellaneous work till nine; then two hours with Miss Ogden in spinning, knitting, and sewing; bathing, relaxation, and dinner, till two; then two hours of recitation and study with Mr. Bailey, followed by an hour's work in the garden; supper between five and six; evening prayers at half past seven; hours of retiring eight and nine, according to their ages.

More time was at first spent within doors and in study. But it was found detrimental to health, and that the Hawaiian constitution, used to indolence, freedom, and sunshine, could not bear much confinement without giving way. Weekly excursions are now taken with their teacher to the mountain or sea-shore, and care is used to keep them much in the open air. The health of the school is consequently better, and they form a company of hearty, happy girls, as fond of a romp and ball-playing, and as glad to be noticed, as ever boarding-school girls are in America.

Five of them are members of the church, and several others are hopefully pious. Ten or twelve having finished their course, have been married to graduates from Lahainaluna, and others are held in reserve for the same market.

The design of the female seminary, says Mr. Dibble, is to take a class of young females into a boarding-school, away, in a measure, from the contaminating influences of heathen society, to train them to habits of industry, neatness, and order, to instruct them in employments suited to their sex, to cultivate their minds, to improve their manners, and to instil the principles of religion; to fit them to be suitable companions for the scholars of the Mission Seminary, and examples of propriety among the females of the Sandwich Islands.

The short time in which the institution has been in operation hardly authorizes a judgment, as to how far these ends have been answered. But no one who examines it, and sees its practical working, can fail of the conviction that female family boarding-schools must form a very important instrumentality in the work of elevating this nation.

The women remaining as they now are, men, whatever pains may be bestowed on them, can get but little higher; while with every single degree of woman's ascent in the scale of civilization and goodness, you raise man two. The two lessons of chief importance for Hawaiian women to learn, are modesty and industry. Induce these, and every thing is gained—the end of female education at present answered. But a training that does not accomplish this, fails entirely, how much soever knowledge may be communicated, or art learned.

Let an Hawaiian female be only modest and industrious, and she will make a neat and prudent wife, and a better mother than ever Hawaiian boy has had yet. Many such, we cannot but hope, will be made under the management of the teachers of this institution. May God give them wisdom and skill, and permit them to see all, on whom they have bestowed pains, examples of womanly propriety to the females of Hawaii-nei!

It is impossible to see them going in a body to the sanctuary, uniformly apparelled, sitting orderly by themselves, attending, many of them, diligently to sermons, that they may sustain an examination on them, and looked upon with regard and interest by the rest of the congregation, without being convinced that the indirect influence of the institution is beneficial and great. Perhaps it is to be attributed to this, that the common schools in this district are reported the present year more favorably of, and as in a better state than in any other field from which a report is made.

There are twenty-five schools, and eight hundred and eight scholars. I have had the pleasure of seeing them collected at three or four different points for a quarterly examination by the pastor, and *kahu-kula*, (school superintendent.) They are dressed at such times in their best "bib and tucker," which, with the boys, is a shirt and pantaloons, with perhaps a cotton handkerchief over their shoulders for a *kihei;* with the girls, their mother's, or some *makamaka's*, best robe and feather, *lei*, (wreath,) and any thing for a *kihei* they can muster, either a nice white *kapa*, or a breadth of silk, or something figured.

The prettiest thing of all is their flower-wreaths, especially those made of the yellow *ilima.* They string the blossoms on a stem of grass with much taste and skill, and no little patience. With these the girls wreathe their heads sometimes like a turban, and hang them round their necks, which, though they be red-skinned, are sometimes erect and beautiful as that famous one of Mary Queen of Scots.

I like the Hawaiians for their fondness for flowers, or, rather, for decorating their persons with them. It is a pity a custom so innocent in itself should ever have to be discountenanced by their religious teachers. Some have thought it necessary to do so, because wearing of *leis* has been abused to purposes of vanity, and meretricious allurement and display. We can hardly believe, however, that much harm can ensue from putting flowers or feathers to such a use, while the taste is brought thereby into pleasurable exercise, and so far certainly is good.

And while the bonnets of foreign ladies, now and then, perhaps, of missionaries, are seen fluttering with gay ribbons and plumes, it is hardly fair to put a tabu on birds' feathers and wild-flowers for the heads of Hawaiian women. There are ways of wearing them which, it is said, have a vicious meaning, for which church members have been sometimes disciplined; with how much propriety, the good men that have done it, and who may be supposed to know most of native customs and character, are the best judges. Poor human nature is wont to abuse to its injury almost every thing, whether evil or good. But I think the tempter must be brought to an unusual pinch before he would have recourse to so innocent and sweet a thing as flowers, whereby to teach men how to tempt and vitiate one another.

One whom I greatly honor and love says, though not for the world's eye, that

Flowers are books—the sweetest leaves
That Nature's wisdom ever weaves:
And wise and gentle hearts we need,
Their deep and varied lore to read.
Some melancholy lessons, too,
We would not have them hide from view.

And it was the queen of English female poets that sang of the flowers,—

Bring flowers, fresh flowers, for the bride to wear!
They were born to blush in her shining hair.
She is leaving the home of her childhood's mirth,
She hath bid farewell to her father's hearth:
Her place is now by another's side,—
Bring flowers for the locks of the fair young bride!

But farewell for a while to flowers, and to the maidens that wear them, for we are on a horseback excursion of thirty-five miles from Wailuku to the top of

Hale-a-ka-la, The House of the Sun. We make up our party at Rev. Mr. Green's, who resides two thousand feet up the gentle declivity of the mountain. From his house, at five in the morning, we start for the summit of the extinct volcano, eight of us in all mounted, and one native on foot.

To within five miles of the top, as far as an old bullock-pen, into which the Spaniards used to chase wild cattle, the path is distinct and quite good, and the ascent not steep. Thence it is very rugged and stony without any legible track.

> Hills peep o'er hills,
> And Alps o'er Alps arise,

as we advance; and when we think we see and shall soon reach the last, lo! there runs up before us another ridge-like wall, equally distant and high.

At length, by half past ten, we reach the crater's brim, and, dismounting from our tired horses, those of us who have been able to urge them so far, advance to the edge, and there suddenly opens upon us a deep, wide pit, twenty-five or thirty miles in circumference, and two or three thousand feet deep. We counted in it fourteen or sixteen basins of old volcanoes, volcano within volcano, as a wheel within a wheel. There are also two vast openings or sluice-gates in the lava walls, one on the northeast, and one on the southeast, out of which the molten lava and sand once poured down to the sea.

In this great pit a man would be dwarfed to the size

of an infant; and great silver-sword plants, (*ensis argentea*,) as large as a half-bushel, looked, away down on the sides of those volcanic cones, like little white pebbles. Its walls and ramparts are as huge and high, for aught I know, as those "Hell-bounds" in our great English Epic, that kept within the rebel angels. And if a man should once get down there, methinks he would look up oppressed, and feel like Sterne's starling, "I can't get out."

But if the view of the now extinct crater, once rolling its fiery surges, and vomiting from a score of mouths its igneous bowels, was vast and strange, a spectacle of far more grandeur was that immediately presented, as we looked afar over the crater to the northeast and west—a spectacle which neither the tongue, nor pen of angels or men, could ever so describe as to give to any mind an adequate conception of its magnificence and glory.

> "O, 'twas an unimaginable sight!
> Clouds, mists, streams, watery rocks, and emerald turf,
> Clouds of all tincture, rocks, and sapphire sky,
> Confused, commingled, mutually inflamed,
> In fleecy folds voluminous enwrapped."

We had seen for a long time, as we kept ascending, the clouds gathering and rolling up beneath us at a distance of four thousand feet; for, owing to its rarification, the air is incapable of sustaining clouds beyond a certain height, and the principal masses are held at an average elevation above the level of the sea of five thousand two hundred and eighty feet, or one mile.

Now we turned to look from our elevated position of ten thousand feet, and behold! one vast expanse, like a field of purest new-fallen snow, which the wind has rolled in drifts and ridges, covering all the mountain, plain, and sea, and reflecting the sunbeams with a dazzling splendor.

Now and then a place would be rent or excavated in the snowy masses, or the curtain of cloud would be lifted, and the form of the Island of Lanai would be visible away over the mountains of Lahaina, six thousand feet high, and sometimes a portion of the bay and shore of Wailuku, whitened by the noiseless surf.

Then trending off to the horizon, a hundred miles, was the blue Pacific, lifted up ten thousand feet by a familiar optical illusion, to a plane of vision as high as the very summit of Hale-a-ka-la; and rising out of it was the glorious dome of Mauna Loa, on the great Island of Hawaii, its snow-capped summit flashing in the sun like a bank of alabaster. The clouds, and their shadows upon other clouds far beneath, could be seen hovering over the blue abyss, and sometimes they seemed to float in it in separate masses like great icebergs.

The longer one looked, the greater grew the wonder and glory. What with the vast height, the pure, rarified air, the solemn stillness like as in creation's prime, the absence of every thing human and artificial, the smooth envelope of vapor in which every thing below was hid, it was as if we were looking down from some place in the heavens upon the bare convex of the earth; and one of our party remarked, that there was constantly in his mind the description of Milton's angel

> Alighting on the firm, opacous globe
> Of this round world, whose first convex divides
> The luminous inferior orbs, inclosed
> From chaos and the inroad of darkness old.

I fairly wanted to leap down into the soft lap of the clouds, clear as chalcedony, and smooth and white as the breast of an eider-duck; and we thought the sight might tempt the flight of angels from the battlements of heaven, to sport on the bosom of that beautiful sea.

The extent of vision on each of three sides was at least two hundred miles. To the west, the base of the mountain, the bay and plains of Wailuku, the mountains of West Maui, and over them the islands of Lanai and Molokai, as if suspended in the sky, and the great Pacific. To the north, the vast ocean of clouds in mid-air, and of sea below. To the south, looking across the crater, and forty miles over the channel between Maui and Hawaii, could be seen, within an opening of the clouds, the surf-whitened shore of the latter island; and seventy or eighty miles further, towering up in majestic grandeur fourteen thousand feet above the ocean of clouds, were the blue summits of Mauna Kea and Mauna Loa, the former revealing a snow-bank on its top, shining like the battlements of heaven, as seen in the Apocalypse.

The view this side had a reach and immensity of

distance that was indescribably grand. It forms an impression, and fixes an image in the mind, that recurs and visits one again and again, with all the vividness of a dream.*

While we were gazing with delight, now on one side, now on the other, vast masses of vapor began to roll into the crater through the sluice-way on the north, but still so low, that we were between two and three thousand feet above it In descending, we were more than an hour before arriving at the cloudy belt, or having the sun at all obscured.

* We find it said very justly, and from a real experience and a true poetic insight, by a writer in the New York "Independent," as follows:—One who stands upon the summit of Mount Washington, there takes in an idea of vastness, sublimity, and power, which thenceforth is incorporated with his spiritual being, and which will ofttimes dilate his soul when he has returned to the common level of earth. One who stands at the base of Niagara, or peers into its abyss from the overhanging cliff, receives an impression of the grand, the beautiful, the terrible, which thenceforth lives within him, and reproduces itself with its first ecstasy amid all the changes of place and time. One who gazes enraptured upon a beautiful picture, transfers it to the texture of his mind, and, whoever may possess it, he carries it ever with him as his own treasure. One who listens to an enchanting strain of music, thenceforth feels it in every pulse of his soul. One who hears an eloquent oration, is raised by it to a height of intellectual enjoyment to which he oft returns in after-meditation. And though these impressions cannot be conveyed to others in words, their influence is shared through the higher tone of power, of beauty, of love in him who has experienced them. There is, moreover, a peculiar sympathy between those who have received like impressions, which attracts them to each other, and enables them to commune together in that mysterious soul-language which has no outward exponent.

The feelings of a man the first time he gets so far above the limits of human habitation are peculiar and new. One wants to be some time alone, and to give himself silently up to the sight, in order to multiply and deepen by meditation the impressions which it is fitted to produce.

The unfortunate Scotch naturalist, Douglass, who was found dead in a bullock-trap on Hawaii, describing in one of his letters a place on Hawaii somewhat similar to Hale-a-ka-la, very justly remarks, that "were the traveller permitted to express the emotions he feels while placed on such an astonishing part of the earth's surface, cold indeed must his heart be to the great operations of nature, and still colder towards nature's God, by whose wisdom and power such wonderful scenes were created, if he could behold them without deep humility, mingled with reverential awe. Man feels himself as nothing—as if standing on the verge of another world. A death-like stillness of the place, not an animal nor an insect to be seen, far removed from the din and bustle of the world, impresses on his mind with double force the extreme helplessness of his condition—an object of pity and compassion, utterly unworthy to stand in the presence of a great and good Saviour and holy God, and to contemplate the diversified works of his hands."

On the authority of this traveller, there was an active crater on the summit of Mauna Loa, on Hawaii, when he visited it, like this extinct one of Hale-a-ka-la, twenty-four miles in circumference, "five miles square of which is a lake of liquid fire, in a state of ebullition, sometimes tranquil, at other times rolling its blazing waves with furious agitation, and casting them up in columns from thirty to one hundred and seventy feet high. In places the hardened lava assumes the form of Gothic arches in a colossal building, piled one above another in terrific magnificence, through and among which the fiery fluid forces its way in a current that proceeds three and a quarter miles per hour, or loses itself in fathomless chasms at the bottom of the caldron. This volcano is twelve hundred and seventy-two feet deep down to the fire. Its chasms and caverns can never be measured."*

It is a fit employment, when standing on the brink of the giant crater of Hale-a-ka-la, to give one's imagination scope, and attempt to conceive the vast force and intensity of those mineral fires that, ages back, had this for their play-ground and place of disemboguement. With all the helps afforded in the rugged features of the scene, and the visual evidence you have of the terrible volcanic agency that here had sweep, imagination falls far short of the reality. But it gives to the conceptive faculty vividness and amplitude to visit such spots, and to venture out on such imaginary excursions. And a man finds the material he gets there an element of power, sustaining the imagination in a longer flight, and giving its pinions strength and endurance.

* Hawaiian Spectator, vol. II. p. 405.

We were sorry to leave the summit without going down into the abyss.* But that was impossible, unless we would make up our minds to spend the night there, and try the cold and moonlight, for which we were not prepared. We had, therefore, to make the best of our way down before nightfall, carrying with us some plants of the silver-sword, and specimens of a silver geranium, sage, and sandal-wood, picked by the way. Woefully worn and weary, but, through a kind Providence, without any serious accident, we all reached again the hospitable house of our entertainer by six o'clock.

Perhaps, in perusing this account of the spectacle of grandeur and glory presented by the self-sustained clouds of Hale-a-ka-la, some reader may call to mind the expression that burst from the lips of Rowland Hill, as he was viewing some fine scenery in England and Wales :—Oh, if these outskirts of the Almighty's dominion can with one glance so oppress the heart with gladness, what will be the disclosures of eternity, when the full revelation shall be made of the things not seen, and of the river of the City of God! Or that fine passage in one of Luther's Letters—

"I saw lately two signs in the heavens. I looked from my window in the middle of the night, and I saw the stars, and all the majestic vault of God, sustaining

* The bottom of this crater, according to measurements of the U. S. Exploring Squadron, is 2783 feet below the summit-peak, and 2093 feet below the level of the wall.

itself, without my being able to perceive the pillars upon which the Creator had propped it. Nevertheless, it crumbled not away. There are those, however, who search for these pillars, and who would fain touch them with their hands; but not being able to find them, they trouble, lament, and fear the heavens will fall. Again, I saw great and heavy clouds floating over my head like an ocean. I could neither perceive ground on which they reposed, nor cords by which they were suspended; and yet they did not fall upon us, but saluted us rapidly and fled away. And as they passed, I distinguished a splendid rainbow. Slight it was, without doubt, and delicate; one could not but tremble for it under such a mass of clouds. Nevertheless, this aery line sufficed to support the load, and to protect us. So is our rainbow weak, and the clouds heavy; but the end will tell the strength of our bow."

There is yet another and original lesson we learned from our lofty look-out on the House of the Sun; which is this—that it is with Christians, in their travel through the world, their pilgrimage to the heavenly Canaan, as with travellers in climbing the mountains: They must ordinarily pass through a region of storms and belts of clouds, if they will get to the top; and it is seldom or never that they have the clear sunshine all the way. They are willing, indeed, to be drenched in rain and enveloped in darkness, for the grandeur of a storm in the mountains, and to see how glorious is the after sun-gush. And they enjoy the clear weather and reach of prospect from the top all the more, for having gone through blackness and tempest in order to gain it.

Who that has ever climbed with difficulty some commanding mountain, and thence has looked far down upon the zone of clouds that so lately enveloped him, but has felt this? And who has not been well paid, as we were, for the toil and danger gone through in reaching the summit, by the indescribable magnificence of view which then burst upon him, made up, in great part, of those very clouds, that only rained upon him when he was in their bosom, but now show far below him like fields of diamonds, or pavement of chalcedony in heaven's own light?

Even so will it be with the persevering pilgrim, faint, yet pursuing, when he stands on the eminence of Mount Zion above, having safely surmounted all the trials, and perils, and storms of the way. Ah, what glory will break upon him then, if he has been found faithful here; and what a position that will be to stand in and review this life, and find, in the light of eternity, how all things were working together for his good! Excelsior, Excelsior, be my motto, as I mount upward and onward to the City of God, eternal in the heavens!

"And O ye everlasting hills!
Buildings of God, not made with hands,
Whose Word performs whate'er he wills,
Whose Word, though ye shall perish, stands;
Can there be eyes that look on you,
Till tears of rapture make them dim,

Nor in his works the Maker view,
  Then lose his works in Him?
By me, when I behold HIM not,
  Or love Him not when I behold,
Be all I ever knew forgot;
  My pulse stand still, my heart grow cold!"

After this memorable ascent and return from Hale-a-ka-la, our party were all kindly cared for by Rev. Mr. Green at Makawao, including the United States Commissioner, George Brown, since lost, as it is supposed, in a Typhoon, on his return to America by way of China.

In the vicinity of Mr. Green's residence at Makawao is the largest sugar-making establishment at these Islands, except that on Kauai. It belongs to an enterprising and upright American, who has procured a lease from government, on favorable terms, of upward of two hundred acres of excellent land. One hundred and fifty are under cultivation with sugar-cane. He has cast-iron cylinders for his mill, which is turned by oxen. A large part of the fuel for his furnaces is the refuse ground cane. Natives are employed as laborers, at a rate of from twelve to twenty cents per day.

The sugar has to be carted either twelve or eighteen miles to a landing-place, where it sells for three cents a pound. It is clean and well granulated, and much superior in quality to the common West India brown sugar. Much of the cane-juice is not made into sugar, but boiled into syrup or molasses, and sold for eight and ten cents per gallon. It is a much finer article than that which sells in America for thirty and thirty-five cents.

It needs, however, the best thrift and husbandry to keep such an establishment out of debt and make it productive. How long the land will bear cane well without manuring, remains to be seen. The Koloa plantation on Kauai is said to be running out, and no longer to yield a dividend to its holders. Extensive manuring, it is thought, will be necessary in order to keep up its productiveness. The high lands all along the south side of East Maui, from Kahikinui to Haiku, are very fine for farming. It is the region in which most of the Irish potatoes are raised for the ships at Lahaina, and all the wheat raised at the Islands is grown here. Its climate, also, is highly salubrious, and it will yet be the garden of the Sandwich Islands, from which not only whale-ships, but the hotels of San Francisco, shall obtain their supplies.

Were it a *land of brooks of water*, *of fountains and depths that spring out of valleys and hills*, as well as a *land that drinketh water of the rain of heaven*, it would be attractive to foreign settlers above any other district in this group. But, owing to the cavernous and cellular character of the rock, as in every volcanic country, there cannot form reservoirs in the high lands that might be feeders to wells dug lower down; but the rain either at once runs off in some places on the surface, or percolates quickly through and settles to a level with the sea.

Hence there are no wells in Hawaii-nei, except on coral bottoms nearly at a level with the ocean, as at Honolulu, Lahaina, and the mission station on Molokai. The springs from which natives drink all along the sea, especially on the leeward side of the Islands, are so brackish that their water is hardly better than a dose of salts to a man unused to it. Up in the mountains, it is found in pools made by cavities in the rocks.

In returning from Makawao to Wailuku, a distance of twenty miles, you may take a romantic path down to the sea by the way of Haiku, through dells and groves of the silvery *kukui*, and the deep-green moon-leaved *koa*, with its beautiful mimosa-like blossoms. Nearly on a level with the sea, you will cross several long, nicely smoothed artificial furrows, in which the natives used to play at *ulu-maika*, a kind of game of quoits; and you will ride over fine white sand-hills, as pure and crinkled as a drift of new-fallen snow, and as beautiful and barren, too, as any ever seen in Araby the Blest.

One sand-hill in that vicinity has been an old burying-ground or battle-place, now laid bare by the winds. Skulls, having jaws in perfect preservation, with thirty-four teeth sound, (showing that the savage practice of knocking out teeth did not prevail when they were inhumed,) and all the bones of the human body, some of them of gigantic size, lie bleaching all around.

I collected a few for the benefit of comparative anatomy, and rode off with a skull dangling at my pommel, to give to some head-hunting phrenologist; not, however, without certain compunctions as to the propriety of transporting the dead, and separating these *disjecta membra* of our common humanity. Be it that they belong only to the *ignobile vulgus*, or to forgotten savage chiefs, yet are they remnants of a mortal that is to put on immortality, of a corruption that is to inherit incorruption, alike with the guarded bones of the world's proudest kings, whose mausoleum must be a pyramid or structure of marble. Should a passion for bone-worship ever get in vogue here, as in the Old World, the wily priest can metamorphose some of these into good Saint Anthony's, and save the trouble of importation from his tomb in Egypt.

Hamlet's reflections are so natural, though abrupt and moulded by his passion, that every one must have had them in turning up an unknown skull, or observing for the first time the bleaching remains of the dead —"That had a tongue in it, and could sing once. This might be my lord such-a-one that praised my lord such-a-one's horse, when he meant to beg it. Dost thou think Alexander looked o' this fashion in the earth? To what base uses may we return, Horatio! Why may not imagination trace the noble dust of Alexander, till he find it stopping a bung-hole? As thus: Alexander died, Alexander was buried, Alexander returneth to dust; the dust is earth; of earth we make loam: and why of that loam, whereto he was converted, might they not stop a beer-barrel?

> Imperial Cæsar dead, and turned to clay,
> Might stop a hole to keep the wind away:
> O, that the earth which kept the world in awe
> Should patch a wall to expel the winter's flaw!"

As you get into the valley and *vega* of Wailuku, you see numerous remains of old *kihapais*, or cultivated lots, and divisions of land now waste, showing how much more extensive formerly was the cultivation, and proportionally numerous the people, than now. It is so all through this foodful region. From accounts kept one year by Mr. Green, he estimated that the births were to the deaths as one to five; and he says the population has fallen off very greatly since the time he was first settled here.

In the year 1842, in the field of Rev. Lorenzo Lyons, on the Island of Hawaii, out of a population of five thousand six hundred, there were four hundred and thirty-four deaths, and ninety-eight births; or the births to the deaths as one to four and two-sevenths. In the year 1848, the year of devastation by measles, the excess of deaths over births in the whole kingdom was estimated at six thousand four hundred and sixty-five, being an annual decrease of about eight per cent.

If foreigners ever supersede the native race here, they may cultivate rice in the present inundated *kalo*-patches, and without any change. A family of Chinamen are raising it in this valley in considerable quantity. Two crops of rice, it is said, can be realized while one of kalo is ripening alongside of it. Labor expended upon it would, undoubtedly, be better paid than upon the *arum esculentum*, which now constitutes the great staple of Hawaiians. But there must be machinery introduced to thresh and winnow it, and pots to boil it for eating, which few yet possess.

The Chinamen have an Oriental way of getting the grain out of the husk, which is highly characteristic, but hardly to be described. A bed of it, when young and growing, is of a fresh, bright green, that is exceedingly grateful to the eye.

The whole valley of Wailuku, cultivated terrace after terrace, gleaming with running waters and standing pools, is a spectacle of uncommon beauty to one that has a position a little above it. Mr. Bailey's garden, also, at the mission station, irrigated by a brook led out of this valley at a point some way up towards the mountain, is a place by no means devoid of taste and beauty. It is altogether the prettiest missionary's garden in the Islands, and has a considerable variety of plants, fruits, and flowers.

Among these are the passion-flower, the mysteriously shrinking little sensitive-plant, and the splendid night-blooming Cereus, more gorgeous and ample in its corolla than the Magnolia, but chastely beautiful in its color as the most highly prized water-lily. The girls of Mr. Bailey's school show no little taste in combining the flowers into divers wreaths and nosegays, for the adornment of their tables and persons.

We arrived back from Makawao in time to be present at an entertainment which they gave in their dining-hall, under the direction of their manager, Miss Ogden, to the visitors at the station. The half hundred *haumana* (pupils) occupied two tables, twenty feet long. The visitors and resident mission families (of whom not the least attractive portion was twelve happy children) had their places at a middle one. After the guests had all been seated, the ringing of a little table-bell brought in all the girls, neatly dressed and orderly, to their seats. Then they sang a verse of a hymn, followed by a blessing. Supper ensued with great cheerfulness, concluded with giving of thanks and another verse of an Hawaiian hymn.

Afterwards, out on the grassy play-ground, we had blind-man's-buff, and ball, and hide-and-go-seek, with the pretty circle of boys and girls, till we were much more tired, but not less pleased, than they. We should like to keep a child's heart, and spirits, and relish for innocent sports as long as we live. And when the humor suits we will indulge in them, and try to make ourselves and children happy, for all the world. Quod delectat juventutem jucundum est viro—That which delights the youth is pleasing to the man.

VALLEY AND MOUNTAINS OF WAILUKU, MAUI.

# CHAPTER VI.

## SKETCHES OF THE BLIND PREACHER AND THE BIRTH-PLACE OF KAAHUMANU, IN EAST MAUI.

THERE is no light without companion shade:
  There are no griefs which do not herald joys:
In Nature's balance all are fairly weighed,
  And every thing must have its equipoise.
Great Nature is a choral hymn sublime,
  Its melody complete, its octaves true;
Its notes all harmonize, as rhyme with rhyme:
  If there be any discords, they are few;
  And when they cease, the rhythm flows anew.

ANON.

The law of compensation illustrated—Memorials of the first convert to Christianity—His birth and boyhood—Early deformity and loss of sight—Skill in the Hula—Adoption by the court as a buffoon—Abandoned to perish—Dawning of the day-spring—He hears of Christ—He turns to the Pono—The chiefs send for him to make sport—Memorable answer—Journal respecting him—Affecting attitude—Divine sovereignty exemplified—Probation for the church—Record of his examination—First-fruits—He grows and endures—Light breaks—Light is withdrawn—He is thrown upon memory—He hides the Word of God—Acquires extraordinary strength and tenacity of memory—Labors effectively with the missionaries—Is licensed to preach the Gospel—Account of one of his sermons—Power as a preacher—Surprise of the missionaries—Resources of illustration—Ministry in Honuaula—Life and death—We pass and ponder his field of labor—Supposed mental exercises in his blindness—We proceed to Hana—Remarkable road over clinkers—How made, and by whom—After-streams from the volcano—The warfare of a night—Victory to the Ukulele—A chief of the olden time—A dance at Kaupo—Perils by canoe—Sketches of the missionary station of Hana—Natural features and productions—Riding up to the clouds—Cave where Kaahumanu was born—Two strange things in the kingdom of nature and kingdom of grace—A volcanic bathing-house.

THE truth at the head of this Chapter, that there is evermore a law of compensation and equipoise running through all things, has its comment and corroboration in the character and history of a remarkable man, through the earthly scene of whose labors I have been passing, in order to reach the eastern extremity of the Island of Maui.

That man was the first convert to Christianity at these Islands, and the first who received the Christian ordinance of baptism, formally introducing him to the fellowship of the universal Church, under the Christian name of Bartimeus, on the tenth day of July, 1825. His name is on heavenly records, and it is familiar to the ear of Protestant Christendom, as the Blind Hawaiian Preacher, or Bartimeus L. Puaaiki.

The district of Honuaula, in East Maui, through which we have been travelling, was the sphere of his faithful labors as a minister of the Gospel for the four or five years prior to his death in September, 1843. He was born in the densest darkness of Savage Paganism, six or seven years after the death of Captain Cook; and, when buried alive by the hand of his own mother, he was saved, in the providence of God, to be a chosen vessel to bear his name before kings.

He was a neglected and wicked heathen boy; and, between his early addictedness to the use of intoxicating *awa*, his filthy habits, and exposures, with scarcely a rag of clothing, or a hat to shield his eyes from the rays of the tropical sun or wind, he had nearly lost his eyesight before attaining to man's estate. In a brief sketch of him by one of the missionaries, it is said that he was hideously diseased; his beard flowed down to his bosom; his only garment was an old dirty *kihei*, or native kapa, thrown over his shoulders: diminutive in size, he was a laughing-stock of the boys, and was fast wearing himself out in the service of Satan.

"In these circumstances, he attracted the notice of Kamamalu, the favorite Queen of Liholiho, or Kamehameha II., who afterwards died in England. His skill in the *hula*, or native dance, his being a hairy man, and other reasons not easily known at present, recommended him to the favor of the chiefs; not, indeed, as a companion, but as a buffoon. When sent for, he made sport for the Queen and other chiefs, and received in return a pittance of food and of his favorite awa."

On the arrival of the pioneers of the mission at Kailua, in the spring of 1820, Puaaiki was there with the chiefs, but he probably knew nothing of them or of their errand. Having given permission to the missionaries to remain at the Islands for a season, the King and chiefs sailed for Oahu. Mr. Bingham accompanied them, and the blind dancer followed in their train. On arriving at Honolulu, he had a severe fit of sickness. In addition to this, his disease of the eyes became much aggravated; so that, shut up in darkness, and unable to make his accustomed visits to the Queen, he was well nigh forgotten, and in danger of perishing.

"But the time of deliverance to this poor captive of Satan (says the writer of the sketch above referred to) had now come. He was visited by John Honolii, a native youth educated at Cornwall, Connecticut; who, seeing Puaaiki lying in this pitiable situation, was touched with Christian compassion, and spoke to him of the great and good Physician, who alone could heal his maladies and restore his sight. · Puaaiki seemed to rouse up on hearing tidings of so unwonted a character, and he eagerly inquired, 'What is that?' On being again directed to the Lord Jesus Christ, the Physician of souls, he said at once that he would go and hear of him."

As soon as he was able to crawl out of the house, he accompanied Honolii to the place of worship, and heard for the first time the glad tidings of great joy to all people, that the Son of Man had come to seek and to save that which was lost. Nor did he listen in vain; for the Lord, who had shined out of darkness, opened the spiritual eyesight and heart of this blind buffoon, to receive the truth in the love thereof.

The change wrought in him by the Spirit of God soon became known, his connection with the chiefs being one means of making it public. For, soon after the period of his hopeful conversion, the chiefs, having a drunken carousal, sent for Puaaiki to practise the licentious *hula*, as formerly, for their diversion. The answer returned was, "That he had done with the service of sin and Satan, and that henceforth he should serve the King of Heaven."

Though derided, it does not appear that he was opposed in any way, or prevented from seeking instruction; and some of the chiefs themselves, for whom he had made sport, soon after became kindly disposed to the new religion, and all of them, at length, friendly to the Mission.

In the early Journal of the Mission, we find it said of this blind refugee from Paganism, "No one has manifested more childlike simplicity and meekness of heart—no one appears more uniformly humble, devout, pure, and upright. He is always at the house of God, and there, ever at the preacher's feet. If he happens to be approaching our habitations at the time of family worship, which has been very frequently the case, the first note of praise, or word of prayer, which meets his ear, produces an immediate and most observable change in his whole aspect.

"An expression of deep devotion at once overspreads his sightless countenance, while he hastens to prostrate himself in some corner in an attitude of reverence. Indeed, so peculiar has the expression of his countenance sometimes been, both in public and domestic worship, especially when he has been joining in a hymn in his own language to the praise of the only true God and Saviour—an expression so indicative of peace and elevated enjoyment—that tears have involuntarily started in our eyes at the persuasion that, ignorant and degraded as he once has been, he was then offering the sacrifice of a contrite heart, and was experiencing a rich foretaste of that joy which in the world to come will rise immeasurably high.

"He is poor and despised in his person, small almost to deformity; and in his countenance, from the loss of sight, not prepossessing. Still, in our judgment, he bears on him the image and superscription of Christ; and if so, how striking an example of the truth of the Apostle's declaration: *God hath chosen the foolish things of the world to confound the wise; and the weak things of the world to confound the things which are mighty; and base things of the world, and things which are despised, hath God chosen; yea, and things which are not, to bring to nought things that are; that no flesh should glory in his presence!*"

After a suitable probation, and satisfaction given to the missionaries of his preparedness, Bartimeus was received into the church, along with one other, a female. The following is Mr. Richards' record of the examination undergone by this blind Hawaiian, at the time of his admission:

*Question.* Why do you request to be received into the church?

*Answer.* Because I love Jesus Christ, and I love you, and I desire to dwell with you in the fold of Christ, and to join with you in eating the holy bread, and drinking the holy wine.

*Q.* What is the holy bread?

*Ans.* It is the body of Christ, which he gave to save sinners.

Do we, then, eat the body of Christ?

No, but we eat the bread which means his and as we eat bread that our bodies may not die, so our souls love Jesus Christ, and receive him for their Saviour, that they may not die.

*Q.* What is the holy wine?

*Ans.* It is the blood of Christ, which he poured out on Calvary, in Jerusalem, in the land of Judea, to save us sinners.

*Q.* Do we, then, drink the blood of Christ?

*Ans.* No, but the wine means his blood, just as the holy bread means his body; and all those who go to Christ, and lean on him, will have their sins washed away in his blood, and their souls saved forever in heaven.

*Q.* Why do you think it is more suitable that you should join the church than others?

*Ans.* Perhaps it is not, (hesitating.) If it is not proper, you must tell me. But I do greatly desire to dwell with you in the fold of Christ. (Here he wiped his blind eyes.)

*Q.* Who do you think are the proper persons to be received to the church?

*Ans.* Those who have repented of their sins, and obtained new hearts.

*Q.* What is a new heart?

*Ans.* It is one that loves God, and loves the Word of God, and does not love sin, or sinful ways.

*Q.* Do you think you have obtained a new heart?

*Ans.* At one time I think I have; and then I think again, and think I have not. I do not know. God knows. I hope I have a new heart.

*Q.* What makes you hope that you have a new heart?

*Ans.* This is the reason why I hope I have a new heart. The heart I have now is not like the heart I formerly had. The heart I have now is very bad. It is unbelieving, and inclined to evil. But it is not like the one I formerly had. Yes, I think I have a new heart.

These questions were said to be all new to him, and answered from his own knowledge, without ever having committed any catechism.

Once in the church, this blind Bartimeus continued to grow in knowledge, grace, and usefulness. He became a true yoke-fellow with the missionaries, learning constantly at their lips, and communicating what he learned to the people.

In the year 1829, we find it said of him, that he was beginning to recover his eyesight a little, and was making a painful effort to learn to read. A missionary's wife at Hilo in 1830, where Bartimeus then lived as a Christian laborer, collected a few children and taught them the elements of reading. Bartimeus at once applied for admission to the class, but was discouraged on the ground of his blindness, and that the school was merely for children. His reply was, that he was a child, and must insist upon attending. And, by literally *digging*, as it was said—for he was so dim of sight that he used to bury his face in his book—he became able to make out a verse in the Bible.

The disease in his eyes, however, suddenly assumed such an aggravation, that he was forced to abandon his design of becoming a Bible-reader, and to throw himself for Scripture knowledge entirely upon the resources of his tenacious memory. Every text and sermon he then heard were indelibly fixed in his mind, and fragments of Scripture at that time being printed in his native tongue, were made fast in his memory, word for word, chapter and verse, by hearing them read a few times.

"The arrangement of Providence," says Mr. Green, "by which he was obliged to hide the word of God in his heart, was a wise and benevolent arrangement; for he never could have become so eloquent and mighty in the Scriptures as he actually became, had he depended upon his imperfect vision, instead of his extraordinary memory. Still, his example at Hilo as a laborer, putting himself in the place of a little child, learning his letters, and spelling out sentences till he could actually read, was of incalculable value. It was to him, also, a matter of unfeigned delight, that he had been able, though for a short season only, to trace with his own eyes the lines of the Book of God, which he loved more than his daily food."

He labored with great assiduity and delight during the Great Revival of 1837 and '38, when he was publicly ordained to the office of Elder. In 1840, he was duly licensed, upon examination at Wailuku, as a minister of the Gospel in Honuaula, where he labored with great fidelity and acceptableness, up to the time of his decease; returning, every few weeks, to recruit his stores and refill his urn at the missionary granary and well-head, where he was always welcome, at Wailuku.

I have heard Mr. Clark narrate with great interest an account of a sermon which Bartimeus preached there at a protracted meeting, when the King was present, in the evening. His text was Jer. iv. 13: *Behold, he shall come up as clouds, and his chariots shall be as a whirlwind.* He seized upon the terrific image of a whirlwind or tornado, as an emblem of the ruin which God would bring upon his enemies. This image, said Mr. Clark, he presented in all its majestic and awful aspects, enforcing his remarks with such passages as Ps. lviii. 9: He shall take them away as with a whirlwind, both living and in his wrath. Prov. i. 27: And your destruction cometh as a whirlwind. Isa. xl. 24: And the whirlwind shall take them away as stubble. Jer. xxx. 23: Behold, the whirlwind of the Lord goeth forth with fury, a continual whirlwind; it shall fall with pain upon the head of the wicked. Hosea viii. 7: For they have sown the wind, and they shall reap the whirlwind.

Many other passages, also, he referred to, in which the same image is presented, always quoting chapter and verse, till the missionary was himself surprised to find that this image is so often used by the sacred writers. And how this blind man, never having used a Concordance or Reference Bible in his life, could, on the spur of the moment, refer to all those texts, was little less than a mystery. But his mind was stored with the precious treasure, and that in such order, that he always had it at command.

I was never, said our informant, so forcibly impressed, as while listening to this address, with the remark of the Apostle, *Knowing, therefore, the terror of the Lord, we persuade men;* and seldom have I witnessed a specimen of more genuine eloquence.

Near the close of his remarks, turning to the King and his chiefs, he said, Who can withstand the fury of the Lord, when he comes in his chariots of whirlwind? You have heard of the cars in America propelled by fire and steam—with what mighty speed they go, and how they crush all in their way. So will the swift chariots of Jehovah overwhelm all his enemies. Flee, then, to the ark of safety! Here (added Mr. Clark) his appeal to the King and chiefs was bold, and yet persuasive, and, one would have thought, irresistible.

Many more things might be told, and addresses quoted of this blind Hawaiian Preacher, over the field of whose ministry in Honuaula I could not ride, without feeling that it was dignified as with the footsteps of angels, for having been the scene of the labors of this man of God. I praised, as I passed, the compensating sovereign grace of God, who, first choosing so unpromising an instrument as this dwarfed and deformed outcast of humanity, from whom wisdom was at one entrance quite shut out, did so marvellously make up to him the loss of outward sense by inward seeing. The

Oxford lines, attributed, without warrant, to Milton, might have come from him :

I am old and blind !
Men point at me as smitten by God's frown ;
Afflicted and deserted of my kind,
Yet I am not cast down.

I am weak, yet strong ;
I murmur not, that I no longer see ;
Poor, old, and helpless, I the more belong,
Father Supreme ! to Thee.

I have naught to fear :
This darkness is the shadow of thy wing ;
Beneath it I am almost sacred—here
Can come no evil thing.

Visions come and go ;
Shapes of resplendent beauty round me throng
From angel lips I seem to hear the flow
Of soft and holy song.

Two days and nights of continued mule-riding and canoeing from Wailuku, through the bishopric of Mr. Green and the Blind Preacher, have brought us, worn and weary, to the quiet Station of Hana, East Maui, where visitors, or *haoles* of any sort, seldom make their way. It is too inaccessible, and far from any port, for sailors to get to; and the way is too rough and long for common travellers and explorers.

Yet it is a way not devoid of interest and novelty, especially that part of it which runs from Honuaula to Kahikinui and Kaupo ; for it is a road built by the convicts of adultery, some years ago, when the laws relating to that and other crimes were first enacted, under the administration of the celebrated chief Hoapili, in whom was the first example of a Christian marriage.

It is altogether the noblest and best Hawaiian work of internal improvement I have anywhere seen. It is carried directly over a large verdureless tract, inundated and heaved up by an eruption from the giant crater of Hale-a-ka-la; and when it is considered that it was made by convicts, without sledge-hammers, or crow-bars, or any other instrument but the human hands, holding a stone, and the Hawaiian *Oo*, it is worthy of great admiration. It is as great a work for Hawaiians, as digging the Erie Canal to Americans.

A Yankee engineer, to stand on either side of that vast field—and yet, by reason of its pits, and ravines, and blown-up hills, and dislocations, not a field, but a chaos of blackened lava—would be confounded and put to his wit's end to know where to begin and carry a road.

Were the waves of the ocean, in a tempest, when wind and current, or the former swell, were in conflict, to be suddenly congealed to the depth of twenty or thirty feet, and the water below to be then in a moment let off, or vanish, the bed of old Ocean would not exhibit such a rugged, confused, and unnavigable waste as these tracts of broken lava.

Or, as I have seen it somewhere illustrated, if the furious rapids of a mighty river had been turned into ink, and the cold of a winter's day at the poles applied, and every part had become instantaneously congealed in the position where it was just then whirling, tossing, foaming, and tumbling, while millions of flint-like particles, shivered from the mass by the suddenness and intensity of the operation, lay scattered about, it might perhaps present an aspect like that of this old current from a volcano.

In attempting to account for it, it seems sometimes as if a new eruption of intensely heated lava had forced and eaten its way under a tract of solidified matter, and at length, by the expansive force of rarefied gases, and steam, and the vast pressure at its fountain, had suddenly burst, and up-heaved into a million fragments the great superincumbent mass. Then let there follow an indefinite period of earthquake topplings and convulsions, and there might be produced the phenomena exhibited.

Straight over such a tract, crime itself, under the energetic management of Hoapili, has built a commodious road from Honolulu to Kaupo. Like the old man in "The Rime of the Ancient Mariner," we almost "blessed it unawares," as our mules safely trotted or cantered by moonlight over the path it had made. The imaginary bridge that Sin and Death built over Chaos for Satan,—

> Over the foaming deep high-arched, a bridge
> Of length prodigious, broad as the gate,
> Deep as the roots of hell,—

is not to be compared to this real one which Sin has wrought on Maui.

It is made by running two parallel walls about twenty feet apart, then partially macadamizing the space between, and covering it with grass or stubble. For fifteen or twenty miles it runs almost like a railroad, only turning a little now and then to avoid some gigantic boulder, or forced into a zigzag to get over some precipitous ravine, which it would seem as if an impetuous after-stream of devouring fire from the mountain had ploughed and eaten through, till it reached the sea.

We arrived at half past twelve the first night at a village where we thought to have stayed until day; but the *kamaainas* (inhabitants) were all away, and so we had to lay down as we were, supperless, (our man with food having fallen behind,) upon the round-stone floor of the meeting-house. Hard as it was, it would have been a grateful resting-place, but for the warfare of merciless fleas, (*ukulele*,) who, when they found what we were, and what a royal supper they might make on the blood of two *haoles*, set to so fiercely, that, after many vain struggles, we were forced to enter a *nolo contendere*, and leave the honors of the field to our insatiate foes.

We decamped about three, and rode on to Nuu, in Kaupo, where they hospitably entertained and *lomilomied* us, and I drowned several flying detachments of the *ukulele* tribe, by a bath in the sea.

We saw there the high-chief Kealiiahonui, of Kauai,

one of the former husbands of the imperious Queen Kaahumanu, of whom Stewart writes, as far back as 1823, that "he has a handsome face, and, in the classic drapery of a yellow satin *malo*, and purple satin *kihei*, he presents as perfect a model of manly beauty as ever challenged the efforts of pencil or chisel."

Twenty-one years have not altered his fine proportions, nor bent his noble, athletic form, although the classic *malo* and *kihei* have given place to European jacket and trowsers. He was there from the Island of Kauai, to oversee the repair of a schooner of his, which, in the drunkenness of all her company, was not long since run upon the rocks.

Our last stage for the day was to the chief village of Kaupo, as far as mules could go, where we supped and dined all under one, at the house of the teacher, on a boiled chicken. A little rain, after the setting in of evening, made a beautiful lunar rainbow up among the picturesque hills and mountains, so bright as to show its parhelion, or mock-rainbow.

The *kamaainas* of this place seemed much unused to foreigners. Several of the women were abroad with nothing but a narrow native *pau* around the waist. The children of the school, upward of a hundred, were interesting, as they always are. Some of the little barbarians set up a *hula* for my amusement towards evening, which was the first time I had ever seen a native dance. It consisted merely of successive jumps with both feet at once, to a regular harsh sound from the lungs, and occasional slapping or drumming of the hands upon the bare breasts and sides, together with distortions of the countenance and gesticulations with the arms.

At early dawn of the next day, the fierce trade, which always blows at Kaupo, having somewhat abated, we started to go round a range of high *palis* (precipices) by a little canoe. She took a wave, on first launching, from stem to stern, that completely drenched my limbs, and was ever after receiving water over the sides, that kept one of us constantly bailing. It was only about fifteen feet long, and fifteen or sixteen inches deep, and barely wide enough for a man to sit in.

We had seen a man on shore, before leaving, whose foot had recently been bitten short off a little above the ankle by a shark at that place; and the idea of being capsized there was by no means a comfortable one. But through the good care of our God, we passed safely around the *palis*, and, by careful watching on the part of the people where we landed, and of our three paddlers in the canoe, we seized a time between the waves, and were paddled and drawn up high and dry.

Having to climb a precipice, limbered per force our nether limbs, which were somewhat stiffened after a two hours' immersion in brine. A ride of six or seven miles on horseback, after getting on dry apparel, brought us safely to Hana, the former home of my missionary travelling companion, Mr. Rice, where the quiet rural beauty, freedom from dust, and grateful verdure, invite to meditation and repose.

How appropriate and expressive is that Hymn of Nature by Peabody, written, perhaps, in circumstances like those in which we are now surveying the beauties of Creation in the Heart of the Pacific!

God of the fair and open sky!
  How gloriously above us springs
The tented dome, of heavenly blue,
  Suspended on the rainbow's rings!
Each brilliant star, that sparkles through,
  Each gilded cloud, that wanders free
In evening's purple radiance, gives
  The beauty of its praise to thee!

God of the world! the hour must come,
  And Nature's self to dust return;
Her crumbling altars must decay;
  Her incense-fires shall cease to burn;
But still her grand and lovely scenes
  Have made man's warmest praises flow;
AND HEARTS GROW HOLIER AS THEY TRACE
  THE BEAUTY OF THE WORLD BELOW.

The mission history and statistics of this Station of Hana may be given in a few words. It was first taken in 1838, by Messrs. Ives and Conde, with their wives. They labored under the disadvantage which the first occupants at rainy stations have always incurred, of having to live for several years in native grass houses; by which, together with severe missionary labor in schools, the health of Mrs. Ives was so broken, that they were compelled to remove to the dry Station of Kealakeakua, on Hawaii.

Their first houses, also, were consumed by fire, with a great part of their furniture and goods. Two commodious stone dwelling-houses are now erected, and ten or twelve acres of excellent land given by government, are nearly inclosed.

To those who love to be out of the world, and who have health and heart to devote themselves to missionary work, the location presents many attractions. And for those who would like to visit there, a man need not be the son of a prophet to predict a cordial reception, pleasant society, and hospitable fare.

Mr. Rice, who was located here in 1841, to have charge of the schools, and who has himself taught an interesting school of boys, is removed to Punahou, to be devoted there to the children of the mission. He had built a fine house, which he has never occupied, and was just getting ready to labor with advantage. Rev. Mr. Whittlesey and wife have auspiciously entered into his labors; and, with a new teacher, a new religious interest has been awakened among the people.

Mr. Conde is pastor of the native church, which numbers five hundred members, having been organized in 1838 with fourteen. The walls of a new stone meeting-house are commenced, which is to be one hundred and fifteen feet long, and forty-eight wide. Many of the stones are from an old *heiau.* It is to be built by the people and pastor, and by contributions from other churches. The population of Mr. Conde's diocese (which from extreme end to end is sixty miles) is about eight thousand. Seventeen hundred children are in schools. The missionary makes among them three or four tours a year.

The medical wants of the people are many, and to supply them is a great tax upon the pastor. The room where he meets the sick, and transacts business with the natives, he turns, when necessary, into a hospital. If an adult or child comes from a distance, that needs to be treated medicinally, he has a bed spread for them, and there administers proper food and medicine, until they are well or die. It is a practice which at all the stations might save many lives, especially of young children.

But it would necessarily involve an outlay of time and money that can rarely be commanded. A physician, to itinerate between Hana and Wailuku, and the Island of Molokai, is very much needed, and could do great good. If the Board send out celibates, they had better be physicians, who could go untrammelled from station to station, to assist and heal the sick.

The physical features of this region are more like some parts of the windward side of the great Island of Hawaii, than any thing that is to be seen elsewhere in the group. Cascades far up in the mountains, four or five thousand feet, and leaping precipices at once of eight hundred feet; numerous conical, green-sward hills, the work of old volcanoes; gentle slopes and copses, and woody dells; tracts of lava scarcely at all disintegrated, yet covered with a luxuriant growth of grass, wild cane, the *ki*-plant, *wauke*, *noni*, and the *hala*-tree, (pandanus.)

The long leaves of the latter (which is a species of the palm, somewhat like the Palmetto of South Carolina) furnish the material for thatching; and the body of the male tree, which is very hard, and here grows tall and large, is used for posts.

Benignant Nature, on the windward side of these Islands, where there is much rain, soon mantles over the scarred path of an eruption with verdure. Mr. Coan told me that sweet potatoes were already growing in Puna, in the pathway of the lava of 1840; the natives having made basins in some parts of the loose lava, by taking out a few of the stones, putting in a little sand and grass, dropping a potato, and then covering it with dry grass. It soon makes for itself a mold, and shoots out its vines, and they raise* in this way the most mealy potatoes.

These, and upland *kalo* and bananas, are at present

---

* The method of cultivating Sweet Potatoes at the Sandwich Islands may very properly give a hint to agriculturists elsewhere. It answers more nearly to the process sometimes called *mulching*, than to any other practice known in the tillage of England or America. An American horticulturist thus describes the application of a similar process to the cultivation of gooseberries :

" The English gooseberry has always hitherto mildewed here ; and I have been familiar with bushes of the best sorts for many years, without ever being able to gather any perfect fruit.

" I have lately mulched some old bushes which had hitherto borne this worthless fruit. I covered the surface of the ground under them the chief agricultural products of this region, although almost any thing may be made to grow, the soil being a comparatively recent decomposition of lava, exceedingly productive all the way up from the sea-side to the top of the mountain, the ascent of which is here so gradual and smoothly carpeted with green, that you can ride on horseback quite up to the clouds.

Directly opposite the mission premises, which are only forty or fifty rods from the sea, there rises a high volcanic bluff four hundred and fifty feet, being the easternmost point of Maui, called Kauwiki. In a cave at its base, which I have visited, the now world-known Queen Kaahumanu, whose portrait faces the title of this volume, first saw the light, in a time of war.

In one of his preaching tours through this region, before there was a resident missionary, Mr. Armstrong called at this spot, and, from his acquaintance with the facts of history, he very naturally penned his meditations in these words :—"An individual is born at Hana, the very end of the earth, (for the house stood on the very extremity of the island, and not two rods from the water's edge,) of high, but heathen parents; brought up from childhood in perfect familiarity with all that is corrupting, degrading, hardening, and darkening; con-

---

a foot deep with wet, half-rotten straw, extending this mulching as the branches grew.

"Imagine my delight at finding the gooseberries on the bushes so mulched ripening off finely, the fruit twice as large as I have ever seen it before, and quite fair and free from mildew."

sequently, became one of the worst of human kind—haughty, filthy, lewd, tyrannical, cruel, wrathful, murderous, and almost every thing else that is bad. So she lived for perhaps fifty years; and then, while sitting Queen of this nation, feared and flattered by all, the grace of God reached her heart, and she put off the old man, with his deeds. She reigned a few years as a Christian, constraining the very enemies of truth to admire her integrity, her regard for the poor, and her wisdom as a ruler, and died in 1832, praising God and the Lamb."

Some of her last words audible were, as translated, thus :—" I will go to Jesus, and shall be comforted.

Lo, here am I, O Jesus :
Grant me thy gracious smile !"

Well may we say, Wonderful, wonderful, to such an epitome of history as hers was from her cave to her grave! In this remarkable Hawaiian Queen, and the no less remarkable Hawaiian Preacher, we have exemplified at once the moral Heart of the Pacific, as it was and as it is. Two things here are almost equally strange in the Kingdom of Nature and the Kingdom of Grace. One is, that the volcano of depravity should ever have become extinct so entirely, and at about the same time, in those two extreme ends of heathenism, the despot Kaahumanu, and the slave Bartimeus! The other is, how, why, or when the belching volcano, at the foot of which Kaahumanu was born, ceased to burn.

Eruptions of scoria, slag, cinders, and pumice, have evidently issued from both its sides, and flowed over in strata that are plainly marked where they are broken off, on the side next the sea. You descend into one of its craters by a winding way made by earthquake and art in its readily yielding, disintegrated sides; and there at the bottom is a fine covert basin of water for bathing, with a beach of volcanic sand, defended from the outrageous surf by a barrier of lava-rock, against which the sea is ever thundering, and tossing over its giant arms and briny spray.

The top of the cone, in olden time a fort, is now the dormitory of a large flock of sheep and goats, which you may see clambering up its sides every evening, and scampering down in the morning. Sometimes they get tumbled over the precipice into the crater, and are *pau loa i ka make*, as the natives say, or quite used up; that is, taught in the same way that Cowper says he taught the viper in his Colubriad:

> With outstretched hoe I slew him at the door,
> And *taught him never to come there no more.*

In clear weather, a fine view is obtained from Hana to the southeast, across the channel, of the broad-backed Island of Hawaii, distant about thirty miles. Its three great pyramids, or more properly domes, of Mauna Kea on the east, Mauna Loa on the south, and Mauna Hualalai on the west, loom up magnificently in the rising or setting sun.

We were intending to have gone across by canoe,

to see again the mission family at Kohala, and thence over to Waimea by land, to embark in a schooner from Kawaihae either for Lahaina or Oahu. But the sea is not calm enough for natives to venture, and may not be for several weeks. We purpose, therefore, to return to Wailuku by a route yet unexplored by white men, through the colossal crater of Hale-a-ka-la, or the House of the Sun. The Palace of the Sun, therefore, we may next enter, in order to learn what rarities in furniture and equipage are to be found there,

> "Right against the eastern gate,
> Where the great sun begins his state;
> Robed in flames, and amber bright,
> The clouds in thousand liveries dight."

## CHAPTER VII.

### ADVENTURE, ESCAPE, AND ARRIVAL AT MOLOKAI.

He that in venturous barks hath been
  A wanderer on the deep,
Can tell of many an awful scene,
  Where storms forever sweep.
O God! thy name they well may praise
  Who to the deep go down,
And trace the wonders of thy ways,
  Where rocks and billows frown!

Mrs. Hemans.

We embark in the double canoe—Sudden catastrophe—Men swept overboard—A special providence—How we are saved—A traveller's hymn—Emotions of gratitude and impulses of obedience—Behavior of the natives—Effect of familiarity with danger—Remark of Butler—The psalm of life—The fatal sequel of another disaster—Conflict with the sharks—They win the day—The raft rises—Few escape—We gain the reef—Lagoons for fish—How to make abstract numbers concrete—Reefs described—Spiritual analogies and lessons derived—Rules for the navigator—The Divine Pilot—Ocean of futurity—Site of the Molokai Mission—Head-quarters of Æolus—A missionary's grapery—The two vineyards, natural and moral—Division of labor—Church and school—Industrial enterprise—The maids of Molokai—Native costume versus the foreign—Court fashion and rules of dress—The queen's way of conformity—Criticism on the fashionable habiliments of the sex—Honest remonstrance and satire by Dana.

A change in my route little expected, finds me at another island, seventy miles by canoe from Hana, instead of ranging through the crater of Kale-a-ka-la. To Him, whose unseen mighty arm defends and upholds us, when we can take no care of ourselves, be all the praise that our grave has not been made upon the coral bottom of the deep, between Molokai and Maui.

We left Hana about half past seven in the morning, with nine men, in the large double-canoe belonging to the Molokai missionary station. The wind was very strong, nearly aft, and the canoes light, so that with main-sail, and a kind of fore-stay-sail, we shot around the windward side of East Maui with great swiftness, admiring the numerous cascades that leap into the ocean from those precipitous lava cliffs.

When, however, we had encompassed the island to the point of departure for Molokai, and were about one-third of the way across the channel, or six miles from land on either side, so tremendous a wave and gust of wind struck our canoes as nearly to capsize them, throwing the windward canoe almost out of water, and the leeward under, and instantly carrying three men overboard from my side.

Though the waves had been all along very high, and frequently breaking over the forward part of the canoes, so as to keep the men bailing, yet, from confidence in the skill of the natives, I did not apprehend much danger; and, having been very sea-sick, was dozing at the moment of the disaster, one hand being made fast to a rope and the frame-work of a mat-screen that was put up against the wind, the other arm around my life-preserver.

Alarmed by the shock and cry of the natives, and a dash of salt water, I opened my eyes upon the scene of disaster just as the men were rolling off before me into the billowy deep. I have seldom or never looked danger so full in the face—

> Danger, whose limbs of giant mould
> What mortal eye can fixed behold?

By instinctively catching with my loose hand to the plank that constitutes the raised platform between the canoes, the life-preserver slipped from me after the men, but I was enabled to hold on till the canoes nearly regained their equilibrium, in the trough of the towering wave. It was unaccountable, except on the ground of that Special Providence which Scripture and experience unite in proving, that we were not irrecoverably swamped and lost, and our canoes torn asunder. Our deliverance surely was not owing to the bubble that bore us, for its thin sides would have burst but for the bands of the Almighty, and left us helpless

> To sink into the depths with bubbling groan,
> Without a grave, unknelled, uncoffined, and unknown.

But, in God's goodness, something better was before us. Our men quickly rallied from the first stunning of surprise and terror; the wrinkled and bronzed old native, our captain, acquitted himself nobly after his first fearful AUWE, a howl of lamentation and terror peculiar to Hawaiians, which no one that has once heard ever forgets. Little as I could say to them in their own tongue, that little was cheering, and my hands I could use for bailing.

Sails and mast were soon taken down; the canoe, sunk nearly to the water's edge, was hove-to and lightened of its load of water, and two of the missing men soon got aboard, through their matchless skill in swimming. But we had gone so far to leeward of one of them, that it was good part of an hour before we could work up to him against the heavy sea.

At length, however, the men tied all the rope in the canoe to one of the light *wili-wili* rollers, and one of them launched out with it to meet the struggling swimmer; and they were soon both safe aboard, exclaiming upon the *pomaikai o ke akua* (the goodness of God) in their deliverance. In fifteen or twenty minutes more, the life-preserver was recovered, and a book which I had supposed lost, was found in the bosom of one of the men that had been overboard, he having caught and kept it there all the while he had been in the water. I shall keep it as a prized memorial of this narrow escape.

The canoe being got under way again with diminished canvas, two hours more of anxious sailing, with a boisterous wind and heavy sea, brought us to an opening in the coral reef which extends along the inward side of the island; and I breathed more freely as we ran through the surf, and swept into comparatively still water, where we ran before the wind again for ten miles with great velocity, till we reached the station, gladly greeted by friends that had been feeling no little anxiety on our behalf.

It was only *He who commandeth and lifteth the stormy waves, who holdeth the winds in his fists, who measureth the waters in the hollow of his hand,* that brought us through peril to dry land, in those frail hollowed logs.

'Tis to His power we owe our breath,
And all our near escapes from death.

I never repeated those lines of Addison and Wesley with more significancy—

When by the dreadful tempest borne,
  High on the broken wave;
They know Thou art not slow to hear,
  Nor impotent to save.

When passing through the watery deep,
  I ask in faith His promised aid,
The waves an awful distance keep,
  And shrink from my devoted head.
Since Thou hast bid me come to thee,
  Good as Thou art, and strong to save;
I'll walk o'er life's tempestuous sea,
  Upborne by the unyielding wave.
Dauntless, though rocks of pride be near,
And yawning whirlpools of despair.

To sing rightly "The Traveller's Hymn," one needs to have met with "hair-breadth escapes by flood and field," to have seen the kind interpositions of Providence, and to have felt underneath him in peril the arm of Omnipotence. We meet with a thousand deliverances that we never know of, from straits and perils that we do not see, both in our natural life, and in the moral and religious life of our souls as pilgrims through a world of shipwrecks, temptations, pit-falls, and snares. What watchful, recollective pilgrim is there, that in the observance of providences, and the habitual review of life, is not often singing with thankfulness and grace in his heart,—

A thousand deaths I daily 'scape,
  I pass by many a pit;
I sail by many dreadful rocks,
  Where others have been split.
Whilst others in God's prisons lie,
  Bound with affliction's chains,
I walk at large, secure and free
  From sickness and from pains.

One such preservation from palpable peril as that we have now experienced, makes the full heart feel deeply God's goodness, and if not sadly hardened, or far out of the way, to gush with unusual emotions of gratitude and impulses of obedience.

It is good for a Christian, or any man, to be arrested and made thoughtful by such exposures and providential deliverances, that *he may consider his latter end, and the measure of his days, what it is, to know how frail I am*, and to ask himself, Am I ready for the surprise of death? Out of sight, it is too apt with us to be out of mind; and a man needs to be often met with startling providences, in order to make him realize his own exposedness, and to enforce the practical necessity of being ready; for let death once come, and,

Ready or not ready—no delay;
Forth to his Judge's bar he must away.

And yet it is a melancholy fact, account for it as we

may, that familiarity with danger and death seldom produces a softening, monitory effect, except upon the mind of a Christian, but rather induces a moral hardiness and effrontery, that steels the mind against lessons of mortality, and casts an ominous gloom upon the prospects of the soul.

There is a remark of Butler in the "Analogy," which I have never seen exemplified except in the case of those, whose habits have been formed as the children of God. It is this—that at the same time our own exposure to danger, and the daily instances of men's dying around us, *give us daily a less sensible passive feeling or apprehension of our own mortality*, such instances greatly contribute to the strengthening a practical regard for it in serious minds; that is, to forming a habit of acting with a constant view to it.

Let me never get so obtusely used to danger and death, as not to mind it; but may I always live looking upward and recollective,

"As ever in my great Task-master's eye;"

calmly self-possessed and ready, through faith in my Lord, for his summons, whether it shall come in sunshine or storm, in a form grateful or appalling to the natural man. Death will then have no sting, the grave no victory. And a sepulchre in the sea, till the sea give up its dead, will be as safe and easy, as to die among kindred, and lie peacefully under the sod, till the morning of the resurrection.

A true poet has interpreted, in the Psalm of Life,

what the heart of the young man said to the Psalmist, and what is often brought to remembrance by the escapes and vicissitudes of our mortal pilgrimage:

> And thou, too, whosoe'r thou art,
> That readest this brief psalm,
> As one by one thy hopes depart,
> Be resolute and calm.
> O fear not in a world like this,
> And thou shalt know ere long—
> Know how sublime a thing it is
> To suffer and be strong.
> Let me, then, be up and doing
> With a heart for any fate ;
> Still achieving, still pursuing,
> Learn to labor and to wait.

The channel we have crossed, and all the passages between these Islands, are often the scene of disasters in native canoes. A Frenchman attached to the French sloop of war Bonite, on a visit to this Archipelago in 1836, tells the following story, which we have heard for substance also from a missionary:

One day, a native, accompanied by his wife and two small children, put off in a canoe from the northern point of Lanai, with the design of landing on the southern part of Molokai, a distance of seven or eight leagues. When he had put to sea the weather was fine; but suddenly a dark cloud blackened the sky, a gale commenced, and the sea became very rough. For a long time the skill with which the Islander guided his frail skiff in the midst of the waves preserved it from being wrecked; but at length a sea broke the outrigger, and the canoe capsized.

The children were too young to be able to swim. He seized them at the moment when the sea was about to swallow them up, and placed them upon the canoe, which, being made of light wood, floated, although bottom up. Then he and his wife, swimming at its side, undertook to urge it along to the nearest shore; they being then near the middle of the channel.

After many hours of fatiguing exertion, and when they had almost reached the shore, they met a very strong current, which urged them back into the open sea. To struggle against the force of the current would have been to expose themselves to certain death; they therefore decided to direct their canoe towards another part of the island. Yet the night came on, and they began to feel cold.

The woman was the first to complain of fatigue; but the desire so natural to escape death, and the sight of her children, whose life depended upon the preservation of her own, gave her courage, and she continued to swim near her husband, pushing the canoe before them. Soon the poor children became fatigued; for they could not long cling to the round and polished surface of the canoe without a continued effort, and they were also chilled with cold. At length they relinquished their hold, and fell, one after the other, into the sea.

Their parents seized them and placed them again upon the canoe, striving, at the same time, to encourage them. But their little hands could no longer retain their grasp, and the sea engulfed them for the third time. It was no longer necessary to think of preserving the canoe; the parents, therefore, took the children upon their backs and swam towards the land, which was scarcely visible in the darkness.

An hour later, the woman discovered that the child which she was carrying was dead, and she broke forth into bitter lamentations. In vain did her husband persuade her to abandon the child and to take courage, pointing out to her the shore, which now seemed near. The unhappy mother would not separate from her lifeless child, and she continued to carry her precious burden until she felt her strength nearly exhausted, when she told her husband that she must die, for she could swim no further; yet, notwithstanding her husband's earnest entreaties, she would not relinquish her burden.

He then endeavored to sustain her with one hand and to swim with the other; but nature could not prolong the struggle, and she disappeared beneath the waves. The husband continued to swim on in sadness, the desire to save his surviving child alone keeping him up. At length, after many hours of unspeakable hardship, and when almost dead himself, he reached the shore. But it was only to fall senseless upon the sand, when he discovered that the darling boy on his back was dead.

In this condition he was discovered at daybreak by some fishermen, lying on the sand. By their attentions he revived, but died soon after from grief and suffering, having been in the water eighteen hours.

It was only a few years ago, in a part of Polynesia further south than these Islands, that a company of chiefs and people, thirty-two in number, were passing from one island to another, in a large double-canoe like that in which we have just escaped such peril. They, too, were overtaken by a wind, the violence of which tore their canoes from the horizontal or curved spars by which it will be remembered, in our previous description* of a double-canoe, that I have said they are united. It was in vain to endeavor to right them or empty out the water, for, without out-riggers, they could not prevent their incessant overturning.

As their only resource, therefore, they collected the scattered spars and boards, and, with the help of cord taken from the wreck, they constructed a raft, on which it was barely hoped they might drift to land. The weight of the whole number, however, who were collected on the raft or hanging to it, was now so great as to sink it below the surface, so that those upon it often stood above their knees in water. Hence of course they made little progress towards land, and they soon became exhausted with fatigue and hunger.

In this defenceless condition they were attacked by a number of prowling sharks. One after another was seized and devoured by the rapacious monsters, or

* Island World of the Pacific, p. 248.

pulled away by them, until three or four only remained; and the raft, lightened of its load, rose to the surface of the water, and put them beyond the reach of the terrible jaws of their destroyers. Delivered thus from the sharks, the few that survived were providentially carried ashore by the current and tide, to tell of the dreadful deaths of their fellow-voyagers.

Ourselves happily saved from such a conflict, and no lives lost in our disaster, we have been circumnavigating the Island of Molokai, and with comparative safety, on the reef; observing how the coast is all along lined with immense fish-ponds of salt water, to the extent of twenty-five or thirty miles. These are made by merely walling-in many acres of the coral reef on the seaward side, and then stocking them with spawn and little fish.

Beyond these the reef extends still half a mile or more, with its shallow whitened water, and then there is a crest of foaming breakers, made by the impetuous waves striking upon the outside of the reef. Beyond, the white caps foam and glisten all the way across the boisterous channel, ten miles wide, to Maui; which you must pass in a frail canoe, in order to get again into the range of the world.

The lagoons for fish were made under the despotism of ancient times, and are capable of affording a very great supply. When Rev. Lorrin Andrews was teaching arithmetic to the first class at Lahainaluna, there was one man studying the notation table rather brighter than the rest, and of a practical turn, who could not see, for the life of him, what was the use of such high numbers, over a hundred thousand or million. Up to this he could get along very well, making them in some way concrete.

But one day, as he was reckoning units, tens, hundreds, thousands, &c., "Stop," said he, "I've got it: it will do for the head-man of Molokai to reckon his fish by." His millions had become concrete, and notation was ever after as plain sailing as through the smooth water on the reef of his native Molokai.

This reef has furnished me an instructive analogy, which I cannot forbear presenting. When we stand upon the shore, on a level with the reef, and look far away seaward, over the water with which it is covered like a vast lagoon, we cannot tell what are its dimensions or limits, where there is deep water or where it is shoal. But when we climb one of the steep mountain-sides, and look down from that commanding elevation upon the wide reef, and the still wider boundless ocean all around, it is then that we can see clearly where the reef begins and where it ends; where the surf breaks, and where the blue sea-line begins; and we can distinguish even the different hues of separate fields of coral, and the outline thereof below the surface, through the different shades of the water in which it is all hid.

Just so, in a whale-ship at sea, the man at the main-top-mast head is always the first to discover when the ship is entering shoal water, from a change in the color or shade of the all-surrounding fluid, only discoverable at first from that great height.

And in illustration of the same it may be added, that once, on a calm, clear day, when at a point twelve hundred feet above the level of the Mediterranean Sea, on the top of the Rock of Gibraltar, I recollect to have seen at its base some Genoese fishermen dragging their nets, and exposing their persons in the water, all unaware of the dangerous vicinity of three huge prowling sharks, which could be seen with wonderful clearness through our spy-glass, swimming around the rocks underneath, and seeming to us every moment as if they would dart up and seize the unsuspecting fishermen.

Now the spiritual lesson we have learned from all is this: that, in order to have a just view of the trials, and temptations, and perils of probation; of the points of safety and of danger, and the limits of each, and the lines where they meet, and the gracious providences that are ever stepping between us and destruction, we must stand on the eminence of Mount Zion above. From the top of some commanding cliff in Eternity we must be able to look backward over the troubled sea of this life, and onward upon the calm ocean of Eternity into which it has passed, before we can judge justly of its hardships and encounters, and the Divine meaning of them, or perceive the greatness and goodness of our often miraculous deliverances, or estimate aright the skill and wisdom of the Divine providential Pilot that never quits our helm.

Must we not, then, quietly leave the management of these precious barks of immortality to infinite Wisdom and Love, navigating through faith alone, by quicksand and breakers? What else, indeed, can we do, when the Unknown Future to which we are bound, is to all men what the Equatorial Coast of the Brazils is to the mariner, who makes his land-fall just at night, in the rain and howling wind, and sees the dense clouds gathering heavier and blacker, and the lurid lightnings flashing with louder thunder over those vast regions dimly before him, somewhere in the deep shades of which he is to find a port?

We must wait till the morning of the resurrection for the clouds to clear away and the sun to shine, sailing, meanwhile, by faith's chronometer, just as that navigator must lay-to and stand off, or go sounding on his dim and perilous way by lead and line, till the night and storm are past, and sunlight opens to him the glories of Nature in the tropics, even as the resurrection dawn will to the faithful soul the glories of Eternity.

That glorious but now unknown world of the future, along with its other revelations, will disclose the good that is now doing by the Missionary Station planted at Molokai. It is very near the sea, on the level land between the shore and the mountains. This interval of arable land is from one-quarter to half a mile wide. Valleys that might be made fertile, run up further between the hills, in one of which a better site than the present was chosen, and buildings commenced. But they were torn down by a creature of Governor Adams, to whom the land belonged. It would have been far preferable to the present spot, as further removed from, and yet giving a much finer view of, the sea, and as being partially screened, also, by the hill-side from violent blasts.

If Hawaiian mythology had had a god of the winds, his excellency would certainly have been assigned to Molokai, where the trades could have rocked him from New Year's morn to Christmas eve. He must have had his table in some one of those huge holes to windward, or he could hardly eat the meat of his sacrifices before it would have been blown out of his teeth. The trades rush by here as if they had just broke prison from the cave of Æolus, and were flying away at the top of their speed, afraid of being caught.

For a man to keep his breath, or his hat on, in riding against them, he must have a long wind and little head; two conditions that so seldom meet in the same person, that most who come here at first lose both. And it is well if their patience does not go, too, in waiting, wind-bound, a time to get away. Pleasant society and hospitable fare will, however, generally prove a good antidote and hold-fast to the latter.

Notwithstanding the uniformly high winds, Rev. Mr. Hitchcock, one of the missionaries, has succeeded in training a fine grapery, by erecting a high screen towards the northeast. We are now luxuriating on the delicious fruit, whose flavor is almost equal to the *uvas* of Andalusia. Wine is made from it to supply the communion-table; or, rather, an unfermented syrup, which, diluted with water, forms a more fitting element for the Supper than either alcoholic wine or simple water.

The number of communicants here is somewhat over six hundred, in a population roughly estimated at about five thousand. They have the best-made meeting-house (excepting the Bingham stone church in Honolulu) that I have seen in Hawaii-nei. The material is stone, three long windows in each of the two sides, doors in the two ends and side facing the sea, a gallery in the end opposite to the neatly made pulpit, for the choir, with two small windows for light and ventilation.

The walls are one hundred feet long, fifty wide, and eighteen high to the ceiling. The roof is of thatch, and in the old Dutch style, thus saving gable-ends, which it is not easy here to make secure, and at the same time look well, of stone.

In the process of building it, the people have contributed five hundred dollars in cash, besides getting the timber from the mountain, procuring and burning the lime, plastering the walls, and putting on the roof.

In June of 1850, there was acknowledged from the Molokai church,* by the Treasurer of the American

---

* The entire contributions on the Island of Molokai, for the year 1850, are as follows :—

Board, the sum of five hundred and seventeen dollars and fifty cents, to constitute several persons in America

---

| | |
|---|---|
| Support of Pastor | $420 00 |
| Kohala Meeting-house | 102 00 |
| Monthly Concert | 501 50 |
| French Protestant Missions | 23 00 |
| Relief of the Poor | 40 00 |
| Church-bell at Kalaupapa | 166 00 |
| Repairing Meeting-house | 120 00 |
| Materials and Labor, at cash | 400 00 |
| Repairing Pastor's House | 25 00 |
| | $1,797 50 |

Here is a lesson in liberality that deserves to be studied. It will assist in doing this, to know that the population of the island is less than 3500, and to call to mind how few years it is since they began to emerge from the deep poverty of barbarism. Look now at the various items. Consider especially that noble one for rebuilding the prostrate house of worship at Kohala, and also the avails of the monthly concert. Here are respects in which we may bring ourselves into comparison with them; for the appeal in behalf of that afflicted church reached us, and what we gave the last year at the concert is also on record. But let us not content ourselves with mere admiration of their "good works," but, "provoked by their zeal," let us "sow bountifully," that He who "loveth a cheerful giver" may in turn "make all grace abound towards us."

The whole amount of contributions at all the Islands for the year 1850, is $7213.14. This includes $237 for the French Protestant Mission. The most of it given from "their deep poverty." Truly, "the grace of God bestowed on them" has "abounded unto the riches of their liberality." See how expansive is their benevolence; how heartily they responded to that appeal from France, thus showing their ability to distinguish between the nation that would crush them, and those in that nation who were one with them in Christ; yet not the less giving an example of a noble superiority to national prejudices. At the same time, let it be observed that they do not forget to "provide for their own;" and that they open their hand liberally to assist their pastors in the calamities that befall them.—*Journal of Missions, March,* 1851.

and the Sandwich Islands members of the American Board of Commissioners for Foreign Missions.

The congregation here is ordinarily five or six hundred, well dressed and decorous in behavior, seated generally on rude settees. The most interesting and hopeful part of the congregation are, as always, the children and youth, of whom the proportion here is probably greater than in any other field in these Islands. There are twelve hundred in the day-schools, and all of them are required to be present at the Sabbath-schools.

At the Station are three different classes on the Sabbath, in the *Ai o ka la*, or Daily Food: children in the morning, adults at noon, and a class of unmarried young persons just before the sermon in the afternoon. The singing of the native choir is very respectable, without any help from the pastor, being trained by a graduate from Lahainaluna.

The resident missionaries are called invalids, but they perform an amount of labor (at least the pastor) in preaching, pastoral care, and supervision of schools, that would be deemed quite enough for robust well men at home.

Miss Brown has a school of eight or ten girls, whom she is teaching to card and spin cotton, and to weave and knit.* It is hoped they will learn by it a habit of

* The common schools of Molokai have been generally organized after an industrial plan, for purposes of utility, and to instil the principles and habits of industry in Hawaiian youth; and the following is the substance of their report for 1850, which may exemplify what is doing

industry, and a fondness for work, so as not to be willing hereafter to loll and to lounge, like most Hawaiian women, who, in civilization, intelligence, and all the proprieties of social life, are far below the men.

When you see a company of young Hawaiian girls, from ten to fourteen, with bright, sparkling eyes, faces

---

by practical working missionaries, in the line of educational and social improvement at the Heart of the Pacific:

The schools are divided into male and female departments. The female department meets in the morning for regular school at half past eight, and continue at their books till half past eleven. At twelve the male department meets for the same purpose, and continue at their studies till three P. M. During the afternoon, the girls, under lunas chosen by themselves, engage in light suitable work for those who wish to employ them, and at prices agreed upon between the lunas and the employer.

This money is kept by said luna till the end of the quarter, and then equally divided among the members composing the division.

The males, on the contrary, begin work at daylight and work till about eleven, when the first bell rings for them to prepare for school. This plan has now been in operation several years, and, it is thought, with excellent results.

On Molokai are 929 scholars in all; from these deduct for Catholic scholars, who do not generally have a working department, 76, leaves the number 853. These 853 scholars have, during the year 1850, received for their labor the nice sum, in cash, of \$1556.56¼.

Of this sum, the station school at Kaluaaha has earned \$490.25. This is exclusive of sums earned by the scholars in their own time after three P. M.

The number of scholars at Kaluaaha is 206, making the average earning of each child in the school \$2.38; but if we take from that number the 60 or 70 scholars who are too small to work, we shall find that each working scholar has really earned over \$3.25.

The 76 Roman Catholic scholars have only reported \$9.50 as the proceeds of their labors.

full of sportiveness and glee, and their forms expanding like rose-buds, you wish they might always look so, and you think what a pity it is they should ever become the gross, sensual creatures that so many of them turn into in a few years.

There is needed at every station, to operate upon Hawaiian females, a school like Mrs. Coan's at Hilo, or the Female Seminary at Wailuku: to teach them notions of propriety, to form habits of industry, and to make them suitable as wives and mothers. Multiply such schools, and they would do incomparably more than all the silly orders of the Cabinet and King for the ladies to appear only in tight dresses and corsets.

On the score of modesty alone, to say nothing of its economy and comfort, the present dress of Hawaiian females, something like a lady's loose morning-gown, is both decorous and comely. The hasty rage which some foreigners seem to have at once to Europeanize and make court-like the Hawaiian government and dress, is, we cannot help saying, alike unwise and ridiculous. If it does not swamp the nation, annihilate whatever is distinctively Hawaiian, and give paramount ruinous ascendency to foreign interests and influence, it will be strange.

It is said the Queen was once disciplined in the church for drinking *awa*. But she alleged, on trial, that she was drinking it to reduce her portly person to the fit of the tight dress prescribed by the tyranny of court-fashion.

Now we say, give strait-jackets to maniacs, and leave corsets and small-clothes to the rouged harlots of the Opera; but for the women of Hawaii, both modesty and taste would be less offended to have them resume something like the old heathen costume of the *pau* and *kihei*, than to be squeezed into the garb of Paris belles.

The highest authority in America for taste and purity in all that appertains to woman—to woman as she is and woman as she should be—has said of the fashionable modern habiliments of the sex,—

Your dress has made the form by nature given,
Unlike aught ever seen in earth or heaven.
Where, girl, thy flowing motion, easy sweep,
Like waves that swing, nor break the glassy deep?
All hard, and angular, and cased in steel!
And is it human? Can it breathe and feel?
The bosom, beautiful of mould, alas!
Where, now, thy pillow, youth? (But let it pass.)
And shapes in freedom lovely?—I will bear
Distorted forms, leave minds but free and fair.
'Tis all alike conventional: the mind
Is tortured like the body, cramped, confined:
A thing made up, by rules of art, for life;
Most perfect, when with nature most at strife:
Till the strife ceases, and the thing of art,
Forgetting nature, no more plays a part;
Sees truth in the factitious;—pleasure's slave—
Its drudge, not lord; in trifles only grave.
With etiquette for virtue, heart subdued,
The right betraying, lest you should be rude;
Excusing wrong, lest you be thought precise,
In morals easy, and in manners nice;
To keep in with the world your only end,
And with the world to censure or defend;

To bend to it each passion, thought, desire;
With it genteelly cold, or all on fire,
What have you left to call your own, I pray?
You ask, What says the world, and that obey;
Where singularity alone is sin,
Live uncondemned, yet prostrate all within.
You educate the manners, not the heart,
And morals make good breeding and an art.

R. H. Dana.

Sandwich Islands Double Canoe.

# CHAPTER VIII.

## THE CORAL MASONRY AND CORALS OF MOLOKAI AND OTHER PARTS OF THE ISLAND WORLD OF THE PACIFIC.

"THERE, in the furthest deserts of the Deep,
The coral worm its architecture vast
Uprears, and new-made islands have their birth."

Curious work of Zoophytes—Sub-marine gardens described—Living specimens exhibited—Letting a crab out of prison—How the corals grow—Theory for the formation of a coral island—The tumuli of a buried continent—Evidence of a re-elevatory process—Geological phenomena not accounted for—Observations of Williams, the martyr of Eromanga—Effect of electricity in precipitating the particles of lime in sea-water—Instances adduced—The part it may have in the formation of reefs—Views of Sir David Brewster examined—Mixture of fancy and fact—Experiments of Peyronnel—Philosophical analysis—Secrets of Nature's laboratory—Results of coral architecture—Astonishing amount of matter solidified—Observations of Captain Flinders—Conditions necessary to the perfection of coral—The coral builders watched—Work described—Banks reared—World-matter—Half-way Island—Coral formations of Rimatara—Honolulu reef—Mediterranean and Red Sea coral—Rate of growth—Effect of light—Agents that reduce it—Indian Ocean coral—Appearance of a reef between the tides—Millions of worms observed—Facts gathered from navigators—Coral of prose and of poetry—Moss corals by the microscope—Zoophytic tribes classified by the Geologist of the U. S. Exploring Squadron—Scientific deductions—Fejee Island reefs described—Vast size of individual specimens—Notices of the Kingsmill group—Vast depth of soundings off the reef—Uses of coral—Natural and æsthetic ends served.

THE island of Molokai is well worth a traveller's visiting, despite the risk of crossing that boisterous channel, for the curious and beautiful corals he may get there, and the near view he may have of the living coral-beds, in all their sub-marine luxuriancy. You may go out upon the reef in a canoe, and sail over the gay gardens, and in only a foot or two of water, may gather some of the most exquisite specimens of marine animalculic vegetation ever seen.

The kinds, too, are uncommonly unique and various. In one mass, and disengaged at a single reach and effort of the arm, there will sometimes be five or six different species of this wonderful formation cemented together.

The colors are various, and sometimes exquisite. Now and then you can point out a piece to a native, and he will bring it up all blushing with purple or blue, which you would give any thing to preserve in a cabinet with that delicate Tyrian tint. Sometimes it is like colored confectionery crystallized, with all the hues of the rainbow. But the tints of sunset clouds are not more fading and evanescent than the rosy blush of those beautiful sea-flowers, when once plucked from their aqueous bed.

It is only the coralline forms, or the different ways in which those ingenious little architects make their coral groves to grow, that can be preserved. And then those little radiations and branches are so brittle, and the microscopic finish of the crystalline structure is sometimes so nice, that in washing off the extraneous matters, and packing them up for friends at home, you are almost sure to break and mar the most perfect specimens.

It is very curious to observe how a family of corals will grow together and intermarry, till you can trace the pedigree from sire to son, through a coral ancestry for many generations. There is a species which the natives call *ana*, of which one of the missionary boys here has a rare specimen to send to one of his brothers in America.

The *ana* grows somewhat like the head of a mushroom, on a flower-stalk put forth from the parent stock. If you call it a flower, its petals are innumerable white scales, growing erect, and separate each from its bed like the seeds of a sun-flower. These are of all sizes, from that of a button to the crown of a hat. The specimen referred to is a family tree, the trunk bearing its infant and youthful sprigs, of appropriate sizes through adolescence to maturity, when some of the adult *anas* are having little miniature grandsons of the third generation.

The theory which avers that corals do not grow vigorously in less water than two or three fathoms, is quite disproved by the growth at Molokai. We have seen and collected some fine living specimens, where the water was not more than two feet deep, and where the reef must be sometimes laid bare in low water.

In a specimen obtained by Mr. Andrews, only a few days ago, there was found snugly inclosed in one of the cups formed by the little branches locking in with each other like locked hands, an interloping crab. There he was, nicely caught and encased by the growing coral, as between the palms of two locked hands, precisely as toads are sometimes found in rocks, or the solid heart of trees. How long he had been imprisoned there by the busy little builders upon those immense reefs, we could not tell; but the boys thought it must have been in some Rip Van Winkle sleep, if such things ever happen in the life of crabs.

Coral is most abundant on the leeward of the Islands, and the larger reefs are only found there. It is said to be ascertained by observation, that a uniform temperature of at least seventy-six degrees is most favorable to their growth. The great thickness of the reefs is supposed to be caused by the gradual and long-continued subsidence of the original shelf of coral, while the surface is maintained at the same level as at first by the unceasing additions made by the polypes.

According to this theory, the islands of Polynesia once formed a vast equatorial continent, which, through volcanic agency as its probable cause, has subsided, and left the present islands as grave-stones to commemorate its former existence.

Be this as it may, besides the overflow from volcanic eruptious, a re-elevatory process must have been going on for ages in the islands of Hawaii, in order to account for the existence of well-defined coral, on this island of Molokai, for instance, five hundred feet above the present level of the sea.

The same has been found, also, according to Mr. Andrews, on Maui; and natives say that on one of the mountains of Kauai, four thousand feet above the sea, there is a bed of coral and coral sand, and in it a spring of water.

On the road from Lahaina to Wailuku, there is lava three or four hundred feet above the sea, covered with a deposit of lime from one-eighth to half an inch in thickness, as if made by successive coats of whitewash, precisely as I have frequently seen stones at the sea-side coated with carbonate of lime, which is, undoubtedly, a precipitate from the sea-water.

In ravines, and on the sides of precipices where the strata of successive volcanic eruptions are broken off, there is often to be found a perpendicular vein of carbonate of lime, that seems to have run into fissures, or to have been deposited there when in a state of solution, from what source it is not easy to tell. That it is lime cannot be doubted, for I have frequently seen it effervesce at pouring on sulphuric acid. There is also, on this island, one thousand feet above the sea, a locality of a mineral, very like to white flint, and which one might suppose to be crystallized coral, though it will not effervesce with the strongest acids.

While on the subject of corals, it is in place to mention an inference which Williams makes in his Missionary Enterprises, in regard to the formation of corals, from the fact of their being carbonate of lime always in solution with salt water. His remarks are, that, "as corals are carbonate of lime, and as they are found to exist only in warm climates, where, by the process of evaporation, there is abundance of materials supplied for these insects to build with, instead of secreting the substance, or producing it in any other way, they are merely the wonderful architects which nature employs to mould and fashion the material into the various and beautiful forms which the God of nature designed it should assume. In the Museum at Liverpool, among the specimens of coral, there is a branching piece of coral which is a calcareous crystal, formed in the evaporating house of the salt-works of the King of Prussia."

So, in regard to sea-shells, instead of saying that the animals secrete the calcareous coverings which they inhabit, he thinks that they emit or secrete a gluten, to which the calcareous particles adhere, and thus form the shell. Let there be a chemical precipitation of the minute calcareous particles floating in sea-water by any means, and there might be formed a reef; agreeably to the experiment, in which the passing of a stream of electric fluid through water having calcareous and silicious particles in solution, produces stones.

The lightning of tropical regions, and the electric fluid engendered by sub-marine and other volcanoes which abound in the South Seas, may thus produce an effect adequate to the formation of those wonderful and invaluable structures. This is a much more rational theory to account for the existence of the immense coral reefs and coral islands of the Pacific, than that alluded to above, which supposes them wholly the work of saxigenous polypes or lithophytes.

The so-called saxigenous, or rock-making polype, builds *upon* the reefs, and cements his singular tree-imitating structures to them; but this agency, we cannot but think, is altogether inadequate to the formation of immense islands. The more solid and compact texture of the coral rock, often stratified, would also lead one to ascribe to it a different origin from the corals, whose exact and beautiful cellular structure evinces an animal agency as plainly as the honeycomb of a bee-hive.

It is therefore quite unnecessary to suppose the calcareous coral rocks either secreted by insects, or the exuviæ of the insects, or the dead bodies of the insects themselves; but they are simply carbonate of lime precipitated from the sea-water which holds its particles in solution, mixed and cemented together with broken shells and pieces of corals. The coral, properly so called, (that which is to be seen in museums and cabinets,) is what is built upon this rock as a foundation, by the coral insect.

These observations made on corals as seen in the beds where they grow, at the Sandwich Islands, and recorded on the spot, have induced me to compare the results thus obtained with what has been written on this subject by certain late authors.

In a recent article from the North British Review, by Sir David Brewster, he says:—"Our readers, no doubt, are aware that the coral rocks which form islands and reefs hundreds of miles in extent, are built by small animals, called polypus, that secrete, from the lower portion of their body, a large quantity of carbonate of lime; which, when diffused around the body, and deposited between the folds of its abdominal coats, constitutes a cell, or *polypidom*, or *polypary*, into the hollow of which the animal can retire. The solid thus formed is called a coral, which represents exactly the animal itself.

"These stony cells are sometimes single and cupped; sometimes ramifying like a tree, and sometimes grouped like a cauliflower, or imitating the human brain. The calcareous cells which they build remain fixed to the rock in which they began their labors, after the animals themselves are dead. A new set of workmen take their places, and add another story to the rising edifice. The same process goes on from generation to generation, until the wall reaches the surface of the ocean, where it necessarily terminates.

"These industrious laborers act as scavengers of the lowest class; perpetually employed in cleansing the waters of the sea from impurities which escape even the smallest crustacea; in the same manner as the insect tribes, in their various stages, are destined to find their food by devouring impurities caused by dead animals and vegetable matter in the land.

"Were we to unite into one mass the immense coral reefs, three hundred miles long, and the numberless coral islands, some of which are forty and fifty miles in diameter; and if we add to this all the coralline limestone, and the other formations, whether calcareous or silicious, that are the works of insect labor, we should have an accumulation of solid matter which would compose a planet or a satellite—at least one of the smaller planets, between Mars and Jupiter. And if such a planet could be so constructed, may we not conceive that the solid materials of a whole system of worlds might have been formed by the tiny, but long-continued labors of beings that are invisible!"

Now here is a mixture of fancy and fact, which a single personal inspection of a coral reef by the learned theorizer would have very considerably modified. He would become satisfied, I think, that the great reef itself, as it appears at the Sandwich Islands, so far from being the work of insect labor alone, is the basis which Nature herself lays, in the way before referred to, by the precipitation of carbonate of lime, through electrical agency, from sea-water, for the coral insect to build upon, and garnish with his beautiful structures. This basis, it is true, is increased from time to time by the decay of the coral fabrics, but it is never reared by them alone from the depths of the sea.

Coral was generally deemed a vegetable substance until the year 1720, when M. de Peyronnel, of Marseilles, commenced and continued for thirty years a series of observations, by which he ascertained the coral to be the production of a living animal of the polypi tribe. The general name of *zoophytes*, or plant-animals, has since been applied to these marine insects, though sometimes called lithophytes, or stone-plants. They occur most frequently in the tropical seas, and decrease in number and variety as we approach the poles.

"The various species of these animals (says Dr. Milner, Gallery of Nature, p. 381) appear to be furnished with minute glands, secreting gluten, which, upon exudation, convert the carbonate of lime in the ocean, and other earthy matters, into a fixed and concrete substance, twisted and fashioned in every variety of shape.

The formation of coral is one of those chemical processes in the great laboratory of nature, which the skill of man has not enabled him either to imitate or to comprehend; but the fact is clear, that large masses of solid rock are formed by those diminutive living agents, sea-workers, toiling and spinning to the music of the waves, whose constructions are capable of resisting the tremendous power of ocean, when most agitated by winds and tempests, and ultimately become a secure habitation for man himself."

The coral substance appears to bear the same relation to the insect, as the shell of a snail or of an oyster does to either of those animals, without which they cannot long exist; and it is upon the death of the animalcules that their separate structures become firmly knit together by some mysterious cement, and serve as the basis for the erections of fresh races, which, as they die off, increase the growth of the firm and solid fabric.

> "Millions of millions thus, from age to age,
> With simplest skill, and toil unweariable,
> No moment and no movement unimproved,
> Line laid on line, on terrace terrace spread,
> To swell the heightening, brightening, gradual mound,
> By marvellous structure climbing towards the day.
> Each wrought alone, yet all together wrought,
> Unconscious, not unworthy instruments,
> By which a hand invisible was raising
> A new creation in the secret deep.
> Omnipotence wrought in them, with them, by them;
> Hence, what Omnipotence alone could do,
> Worms did."

Captain Flinders, while surveying the coasts of New

Holland, examined the coral formations in process there; and his remarks seem to me to give the true theory of coral reefs, if there be added the fact of the natural precipitation of carbonate of lime from the sea-water in which it is held in solution, and the formation of the cement by electrical agency and heat.

"It seems to me," he writes, "that when the animalcules, which form the coral at the bottom of the ocean, cease to live, their structures adhere to each other by virtue either of the glutinous remains within, or of some property in salt water; and the interstices being gradually filled up with sand and broken pieces of coral washed by the sea, which also adhere, a mass of rock is at length formed. Future races of these animalcules erect their habitations upon the rising bank, and die in their turn to increase this monument of their wonderful labors.

"The care taken to work perpendicularly in the early stages, would mark a surprising instinct in these discriminative creatures. Their wall of coral, for the most part, in situations where the winds are constant, being arrived at the surface, affords a shelter, to leeward of which their infant colonies may be safely sent forth; and to this, their instinctive foresight, it seems to be owing that the windward side of a reef, exposed to the open sea, is generally, if not always, the highest part, and rises almost perpendicular, sometimes from the depth of two hundred, and perhaps many more fathoms."

Commander Wilkes, of the United States Exploring

Squadron, sounded only one hundred and fifty fathoms off from the perpendicular coral cliff of Aurora Island, but found no bottom with a line of that length.

To be constantly covered with water seems necessary to the continued existence and activity of the coral animalcules. It cannot, indeed, be perceived that they are living at all, except in holes upon the coral reef itself that are below low-water mark, where we have often watched the progress of their rising structures, when we could not detect with the closest inspection the busy little builders themselves; yet imagination has been busy in tracing their work as Æneas was, under the cloud, at young Carthage:

> Miratur molem Æneas, magalia quondam;
> Miratur portas, strepitumque, et strata viarum
> Fervet opus.

Almost as fast as they build, the coral sand, always suspended and washed about in sea-water, fills up the little cells, and pores, and interstices of the minute masonry, while broken remnants of dead coral and other matter thrown up by the sea are caught and cemented to the growing wall, and form a solid mass with it as high as the common tides reach. When that limit is attained, and the surface of the reef is now out of, or even with the water, the labor of the coralligenous zoophyte is over, the sea gradually recedes, the rampart rises, the limed debris or fragments upon it, being now rarely covered with water and dried by the sun, lose their adhesiveness and become brittle remnants, forming what is called sometimes a *key* upon the top of the reef, from the Spanish *Cayo*.

This new bank is, of course, not long in being visited by sea-birds; salt-plants take root upon it, branches of floating sea-weed are caught and entangled by it; muscles, and crabs, and echinuses, and turtles, and krakens, perhaps crawl upon it and leave their shells, and a soil begins to be formed. By and by a cocoanut, or the drupe of a tropical Pandanus, is thrown ashore; land-birds light on it and deposit the seeds of shrubs and trees, and augment it, perhaps, with a layer of guano. Every high-tide, and still more, every gale, adds something to the bank in the shape of matter-wrecks, organic or inorganic. At length appears the blue hummock of a tropical island, and last of all comes man to take possession, cast there by Providence, and glad not to have the sea his grave, or in quest of discovery and gain.

I have repeatedly seen and stepped upon progressive and unfinished parts of creation like this, where, as traced by a poet-observer of the Processes of Nature—

> The atom thrown from the boiling deep,
> The palm-tree torn from its distant steep,
> The grain by the wandering wild-bird sown,
> The seed of flowers by the tempest strown,
> The long kelp forced from its rocky bed,
> And the cocoanut, on the waters shed,—
> These gather around the coral's lee,
> And form the isle of the lonely sea.

There is an island in Australia called Half-way Island, from the fact, we believe, that nature does not yet seem done with it, or to have finished its creation; yet above the reach of the highest spring-tides or the wash of the surf in the heaviest gale. A navigator who has visited it says, that he distinguished in the coral rock which forms its basis, the sand, coral, and shells formerly thrown up and cemented together by the lime always held in solution by sea-water. Small pieces of wood also, pumice-stone, and other extraneous bodies which chance had mixed with the calcareous substances when the cohesion began, were inclosed in the rock, and in some cases were still separable from it without much force.

We have observed the same at the lonely South Pacific island of Rimatara, over whose verdure-clad coral remains we once had a joyous day's ramble. The same is true, also, of other reefs at the Sandwich Islands, where, as at Honolulu for instance, blocks of it are quarried from exposed parts, and used for building purposes, (to which it is well adapted,) besides being burned into lime.

From an admirable work on corals, published in the Scientific and Natural History series of the London Tract Society, and containing a number of very accurate wood-cuts, representing different species of coral polypi and corallines, we learn that coral is found in different parts of the Mediterranean and Red Sea, not only attached to rocks, but also to movable bodies, as stone vases and fragments of lava. It is also discovered at different depths, but thrives best in a warm and sunny aspect. Light operates powerfully in its growth, and its deposition by the living creature is by no means rapid.

It is thought to require eight years for a stem of Mediterranean or Red Sea coral to obtain the average height of ten or twelve inches, in water from three to ten fathoms deep; ten years if the water is fifteen fathoms; twenty-five or thirty years if the water is a hundred fathoms; and at least forty years if the depth is one hundred and fifty fathoms.

It is more beautiful in shallow water, where the light reaches it, than where an immense body, absorbing most of the luminous rays, deprives it of their curiously modifying influence. Having attained its full growth, it is soon pierced in every part by worms, (which attack even the hardest rocks,) loses its solidity, and but slight shocks detach it from its base. The polypi perish, and the coral stem, by attrition with the sea-worn pebbles, as it rolls along, is soon reduced to powder, or coral sand.

Captain Hall says of the reefs in the seas about Loo Choo, Indian Ocean, what I have often heard American whalemen say of those in the Mozambique channel, which is the region of ocean most prolific in curious shells, that when the sea has left a reef for some time between the tides, it becomes dry, and appears to be a compact rock, exceedingly hard and ragged. But no sooner does the tide rise again, and the waves begin to wash over it, than millions of worms protrude themselves from holes on the surface, which were before quite invisible.

"These animals (he says) are of a great variety of shapes and sizes, and in such prodigious numbers, that in a short time the whole surface of the rock appears to be alive and in motion. The most common of the worms was in the form of a star, with arms from four to six inches long, which it moved about with a rapid motion in all directions, probably in search of food. Others were so sluggish, that they were often mistaken for pieces of the rock; these were generally of a dark color, and from four to five inches long, and two or three round.

"When the rock was broken from a spot near the level of high water, it was found to be a hard, solid stone; but if any part of it were detached at a level to which the tide reached every day, it was discovered to be full of worms, of all different lengths and colors: some being as fine as a thread, and several feet long, generally of a very bright yellow, and sometimes of a blue color; while others resembled snails; and some were not unlike lobsters and prawns in shape, but soft, and not above two inches long."

Probably it was with the minute description in mind of some closely observing navigator in Eastern seas, that the accomplished author of the finely conceived Poem called "The Pelican Island," adds this as a sequel to the coral-forming process which he has been most accurately describing:

A point at first
It peered above those waves; a point so small,
I just perceived it, fixed where all was floating;

And when a bubble crossed it, the blue film
Expanded like a sky above the speck:
That speck became a hand-breadth; day and night
It spread, accumulated, and ere long
Presented to my view a dazzling plain,
White as the moon amid the sapphire sea;
Bare at low water, and as still as death,
But when the tide came guggling o'er the surface,
'Twas like a resurrection of the dead:
From graves innumerable, punctures fine
In the close coral, capillary swarms
Of reptiles, horrent as Medusa's snakes,
Covered the bald-pate reef. Then all was life,
And indefatigable industry:
The artisans were twisting to and fro
In idle-seeming convolutions; yet
They never vanished with the ebbing surge,
Till pellicle on pellicle, and layer
On layer, was added to the growing mass.
Ere long the reef o'ertopped the spring-flood's height,
And mocked the billows when they leapt upon it,
Unable to maintain their slippery hold,
And falling down in foam-wreaths round its verge.

There is a variety of coral, of microscopic minuteness in its structure, of which the naturalists Ehrenberg and D'Orbigny have discovered hundreds of fossil species; and their minute shelly cases enter into the composition of chalk-beds, compact mountain limestone, the sea-sand of Europe, the Mauritius, the Sandwich Islands, and the sands of the Libyan desert, even.

Some idea of the minuteness of these fossil moss corals may be formed from the fact, that in the finest levigated whiting multitudes are present, without having suffered change in the preparation of the chalk.

Only let the microscope be employed, and a mosaic-work of moss-coral animalcules may be seen, of varied and beautiful forms, on the chalk-coating of the walls of a room.

The best way of observing them is to place a drop of water on a delicate film of mica, and to add to it as much fine chalk-powder as the top of a penknife will take up. Spread this out like a very thin layer, then drain off the water, and with it the floating particles; when the layer is quite dry, coat it over with pure Canada balsam, holding it, while this is being done, over a spirit-lamp. Then the powder, examined through a microscope, will be found chiefly composed of minute cells, the relics of moss corals.

Since the publication of the Annals of the U. S. Exploring Squadron, and especially the late volume of its Geology, by James D. Dana, Geologist of the Expedition, science has no lack of materials for describing and classifying the various species of coral zoophytes, their localities, modes, and probable times of growth. The facts furnished by this Expedition are almost innumerable; and in the superb quarto volume on Geology they are arranged in such a felicitous scientific order, (though, from the vast amount of original matter, necessarily diffuse,) as to afford the coral naturalist all the information he could desire.

The author's own deductions are clear and philosophical, and being derived from no partial knowledge of facts, they constitute a most valuable exhibition of the conclusive and comprehensive logic of Modern Science. His view of the formation and growth both of reefs and corals agrees substantially with that presented above, and derived from our observations around the Island of Molokai.

His description of the inner reefs in the Fejees might answer almost equally well for this island. Examples are common there where, as in the account I have given of our ten miles sail upon the Molokai reef, a remote barrier incloses as pure a sea as the ocean beyond, and the greatest agitation is only such as the wind may excite on a narrow lake or channel. Over the surface there are many portions still under water at the lowest tides; and fine fishing sport is afforded on them to the natives, who wade out at the ebb-tide with spears, pronged sticks, and nets, to supply themselves with food

"The lover of the marvellous may find abundant gratification by joining in such a ramble. Among coral plants and flowers, with fishes of fantastic colors —star-fish, echini, and myriads of other beings, which science alone has named, fit inhabitants of a coral world—there is on every side occasion for surprise and admiration. Generally, the rock of these inner reefs is composed of coral, which stands as it grew, less fragmentary than the outer, but united by a solid cement. Upon its surface the limits of the constituent masses may be often distinctly traced. The corals grow underneath the surface in solid hemispheres; but when the surface is reached the top dies, and enlargement only goes on at the sides.

"Some individual specimens of Porites, in the rock of the inner reef of Tongatabu, were twenty-five feet in diameter; and Astreas and Meandrinas, both there and in the Fejees, measured twelve to fifteen feet. The platform resembles a Cyclopean pavement, except that the cementing material between the huge masses is more solid than any work of art could be.

"Sometimes the barrier reef recedes from the shore, and forms wide channels or inland seas, where ships find ample room and depth of water, exposed, however, to the danger of hidden reefs. The reef on the northeast coast of New Holland and New Caledonia extends four hundred miles, at a distance varying from thirty to sixty miles from shore, and having as many fathoms of depth in the channel. West of the large Fejee Islands the channel is in some parts twenty-five miles wide, and twelve to forty fathoms in depth. The sloop of war Peacock sailed along the west coast of both Viti Lebu and Vanua Lebu, within the inner reefs, a distance exceeding two hundred miles.

"A barrier reef, inclosing a lagoon, is the general formation of the coral islands, though there are some of small size in which the lagoon is wanting. These are found in all stages of development: in some the reef is narrow and broken, forming a succession of narrow islets with openings into the lagoon; in others there only remains a depression of surface in the centre to indicate where the lagoon originally was. The most beautiful are those where the lagoon is completely inclosed, and rests within a quiet lake. Maraki, one of the Kingsmill group, is one of the prettiest coral islands of the Pacific. The line of vegetation is unbroken, and seen from the mast-head it lies like a garland thrown upon the waters.

"When first seen from the deck of a vessel, only a series of dark points is descried, just above the horizon. Shortly after the points enlarge into the plumed tops of cocoanut-trees, and a line of green, interrupted at intervals, is traced along the water's surface. Approaching still nearer, the lake and its belt of verdure are spread out before the eye, and a scene of more interest can scarcely be imagined. The surf, beating loud and heavy along the margin of the reef, presents a strange contrast to the prospect beyond—the white coral beach, the massy foliage of the grove, and the embosomed lake, with its tiny islets. The color of the lagoon water is often as blue as the ocean, although but fifteen or twenty fathoms deep; yet shades of green and yellow are intermingled, where patches of sand or coral knolls are near the surface; and the green is a delicate apple shade, quite unlike the usual muddy tint of shallow waters.

"These garlands of verdure seem to stand on the brims of cups, whose bases rest in unfathomable depths. Seven miles east of Clermont Tonnere, the lead ran out to eleven hundred and forty-five fathoms (six thousand eight hundred and seventy feet) without reaching bottom. Within three-quarters of a mile of the southern point of this island, the lead at another throw, after running out for a while, brought up in an instant at three hundred and fifty fathoms, and then dropped off again and descended to six hundred fathoms without reaching bottom. The lagoons are generally shallow, though in the larger islands soundings gave twenty to thirty-five, and even fifty and sixty fathoms."

In observing these vast walls of coral masonry, and in studying the diversities of coral upon them, and the curiously modified forms of beauty they assume, it is natural to ask, What ends do they serve? and what is all this outlay of beauty for? It were a good answer to say, in the words of the Psalmist, when he was attempting to uncover and describe some of the curious processes of Nature:—*O Lord, how manifold are thy works! in wisdom hast thou made them all.*

Aside from the manifest utilitarian ends they serve in building* up beautiful oases from the bed of ocean, as places of habitation for man and beast, and then affording the material in such exhaustless affluence out of which art may construct temples for God's worship and palaces for man's abode, we say of them, as we can of all things in God's Universe, what one of the most eminent American authors has written in the Poem entitled "Factitious Life:"—

> THESE are Earth's uses:—God has framed the whole,
> Not mainly for the body, but the soul,
> That it might dawn on beauty, and might grow
> Noble in thought, from Nature's noble show;

* See Note B.

Might gather from the flowers an humble mind,
And on Earth's ever-varying surface find
Something to win to kind and fresh'ning change,
And give the powers a wide and healthful range;
To furnish man sweet company where'er
He travels on—a something to call dear,
And more his own, because it makes a part
With that fair world that dwells within the heart.
Earth yields to healthful labor meat and drink,
That man may live—for what? To feel and think;
And not to eat and drink, and like the beast,
Sleep, and then wake and get him to his feast.
Over these grosser uses Nature throws
Beauties so delicate, the man foregoes
A while his low intents, to soft delights
Yields up himself; and, lost in sounds and sights,
Forgets that Earth was made for aught beside
His doting; and he woos it as his bride!

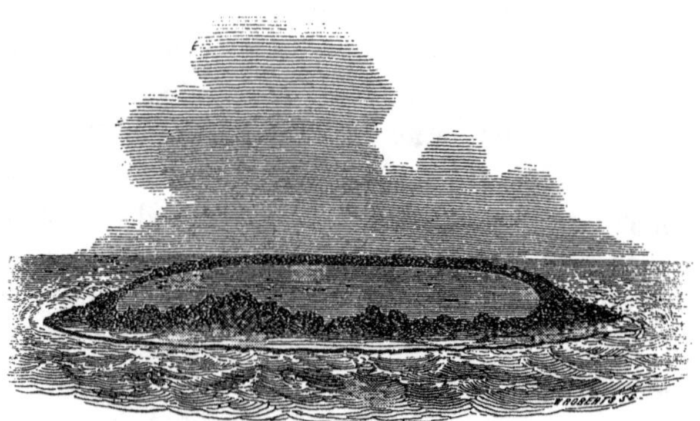

Circular Coral Reef and Lagoon.

## CHAPTER IX.

### REMINISCENCES OF LAHAINALUNA, AND SKETCHES OF THE FIRST HAWAIIAN COLLEGE.

Suave, mari magno turbantibus æquora ventis,
E terra magnum alterius spectare laborem.

LUCRETIUS.

Sweet, from a post of safety, to review the labors and virtues of other men beyond the seas.

We recross the Molokai channel by canoe—Sketch of an Hawaiian College—Internal economy and discipline—Origin and history—Faculty and course of study—Intention of the founders--Ability and usefulness of the first graduates—Laws ahead of morals—Wisdom not always married to the wise—Prudence not limited to the prudential—A revolution in progress—Signs of the times—Entente cordiale—Natural differences of opinion among missionaries—A pastor's expedient to sound the knowledge of his flock—Great difficulty of being simple enough in the exhibition of truth—Remarkable answers of natives—Heathen destitution of common ideas—Consequent inappreciation of Scripture—Similar experience of missionaries in the east—Remarkable cases in proof—Fruits of the great revival—Reasonings of practical men—Sources of correct information—How to find the meridian of truth—Illustration from the working of longitude by lunars.

It is one of the most grateful recollections of the tour we have been making through the Hawaiian Heart of the Pacific, that a providential passage across the rude channel between the islands of Maui and Molokai, consigned me over to the very cordial hospitalities of Lahainaluna. The location there of the Mission Seminary, containing one hundred and thirty or forty lads and young men, the college-like aspect of the main building, and frequent sounds of the bell, summoning to some exercise, all invest the place with a literary air that is not to be found elsewhere at the Sandwich Islands.

Persons connected with the Seminary, and the families of the teachers, are the sole residents. It is far enough removed from Lahaina to be retired, while the town and shipping are all in sight two miles below. The panorama it commands of sky, ocean, and island, with their overhanging clouds, especially from a point still higher up the mountain, where Mr. Dibble himself built a house, is very extensive and grand. Four different islands and the magnificent expanse of the Pacific are always there, and sometimes, on a clear day, you can discern Oahu, seventy miles off to the northwest, and Hawaii, still further to the south.

There are three dwelling-houses for teachers, besides a commodious stone printing-house, and the College edifice, which, including its wings, is one hundred and forty feet front, and between thirty and forty feet deep, of two stories high, with attic and cupola. The students' quarters are two ranges of adobe and grass-houses, a little to the south of the College. A brook is always flowing in front, lining itself with verdure, and a row of thrifty trees more than repays, with grateful shade and green, the pains bestowed upon them.

The internal conduct and discipline of the Institution is much after the form of Colleges in America. The students study at their rooms, and recite by divisions. Afternoons, from two to supper-time, are devoted to cultivating food, and other labor, for which they are compensated in clothing, at fixed rates. Meals are at a common table.

The expense of food is about two cents a day for one person, or seven dollars and thirty cents per year. Clothing, including mats and sleeping kapas, amounts to nearly the same. Books, stationery, and other incidentals, make up the whole to about twenty dollars per year, for which sum, given by any Church or Sunday-school, constituting a scholarship, the faculty will educate a man for the ministry.

The faculty officiate by turns at morning and evening prayers. A church is constituted within the institution, of which Mr. Dibble, during his life, was pastor. Twenty-five of the students were members. They have frequent religious meetings by themselves, and worship in a body in the chapel on the Sabbath. The departments of instruction and executive administration are three.

Rev. Mr. Alexander had the department of Mathematics, Natural Philosophy, and Astronomy, and the immediate oversight and discipline of the students. Rev. Mr. Dibble had the department of Mental and Moral Science, Theology, and History. Rev. Mr. Emerson that of Languages, Geography, Composition, and Oratory, and the management of the manual labor department. He was also pastor of a church at Kaanapali, twelve miles distant, numbering one hundred and thirty-one members. They have had to prepare their text-books in each department, a work which, from the outset, has been one of no small magnitude.

This institution has now been in existence twenty years. It was commenced in 1831, under the care of Rev. Lorrin Andrews, and had to wade along several years through a dismal swamp of embarrassments, accidents, and contracted means. The Res angustæ domi, so often the lot of literary Men, is generally, too, the portion of Literary Institutions, during the period of their infancy. This was eminently true of the early days of the High School, as it was then called.

But the sons it reared in those days, like the offspring of honest poverty, have turned out practical and robust men, the main stay of Common Schools, many of them apt to teach, industrious, and faithful. Of one hundred and fifty-eight graduates, living in 1842, eleven only were reported as not usefully employed, or immoral. Seventy-three were church members, and nine officers in the church.

Up to the year 1849, the Seminary, with all its permanent dwelling-houses and appurtenances, cost the American Board about seventy-seven thousand dollars, and it is now adopted by, and given over to, the Hawaiian Government, and is to be sustained hereafter by Government funds alone, but on essentially the same plan as heretofore. Up to the present time of its being made over to the Government, it has sent forth two hundred and forty-one graduates, and it now has one hundred and fifty-six under-graduates, as shown by the last catalogue.

It is a good investment for the church, at compound interest; and the day, I trust, is not far distant when it will be rendering a dividend of well-educated assistant missionaries and medical practitioners for Hawaii-nei, and all the other islands of Polynesia, who will not need an annual shipment from foreign lands to supply their wants; who will be of common kith and kin, and habits with the people to be instructed, and by whom their languages may be easily acquired, being, like their own, dialects of the one great language that is spoken throughout Polynesia. But in order to this, it must be more liberally endowed and better furnished, and the range of study must be more extensive and thorough.

The plan of study, and the length of the course, have been somewhat modified in order to meet the increasing necessity for the acquisition of English. It has been determined that scholars of very little promise be dismissed from the Seminary at an early date; and that at the close of the first three years, all who do not give special promise of future usefulness be dismissed: That the English language be not taught in the Seminary till the close of the three first years of the course, when all the members of the class, who shall not be dismissed, are expected to enter upon the study of the English, as a prominent branch; and that the whole course, including the study of Theology, be extended from eight to twelve years: That to teach successfully the English language, is a work that will require the time and strength of one teacher.

We are well persuaded that this is not all that will be necessary in order to secure an available knowledge of English, which is becoming so much an object of desire on the part of Hawaiians. Boys must be taught it at the preparatory station schools, and be drilled in it all through the course of their education, till the sciences can be learned in it, as in the Seminary at Batticotta, and its treasures of knowledge be made accessible to the Hawaiian teacher and preacher.

It will be a much cheaper and surer way of enlightening the Hawaiian mind, than to attempt to introduce any thing but the very elements of English science and literature in an Hawaiian dress. Natives, to be competent teachers, and preachers, and civilians, must know something more than these, and otherwise than through the medium of a translation.

Besides, it is only by a knowledge of English that Hawaiians can compete with foreigners, and fill their own offices of government. The kingdom is inevitably departed from them, and men of other blood rule over them, unless they learn to write and wrangle, and make treaties in English, and present qualifications to office, as clerks and scholars, equal to those of supplanting foreigners. The wise among them are beginning to see this, and to inquire, What are we coming to? And they are urgent, above any thing else, for themselves and their sons to learn the English.

It is not the least of the advantages of the excellent school of young chiefs at Honolulu, that they are receiving their instructions, and learning to converse and transact business in the language which threatens to conquer theirs. The policy of it, to say no more, is as wise as that of certain States in a former age, that, in order to avoid subjugation to ancient Rome, adopted, as far as possible, her customs and laws, and put themselves in safe alliance with the mistress of the world.

It is easy to see that the mistress-tongue both of the Continental and Island-World of the Pacific, as well as Atlantic, is to be the accommodating and all-supplanting English. They who perceive it among the Hawaiians desire therefore to master it beforehand, as the best way to keep from being denationalized and mastered by it.

In the constitution and laws of the Mission Seminary at Lahainaluna, it is declared to be a definite object to train up and qualify school-teachers for their respective duties, to teach them, theoretically and practically, the best method of communicating instruction to others, together with a knowledge of the arts, usages, and habits of civilized life, with all their train of social blessings. It is, then, a thing to be wondered at, and for the Government to be ashamed of, that it has done no more than it has for a Seminary that has so noble an object, and that is itself doing so much for the well-being of the nation.

As an offset to the unnatural thing of charging the Mission duties on goods imported for their own family consumption, (which was once done, but now we believe is not,) Government ought at least to have endowed or supported an English Professorship long before this, and so to have been doing something in a line with Christian benevolence towards paying the nation's debt to the churches of America.

In 1842, of one hundred and fifty-eight persons then living, who had been members of the Seminary, thirty-five were officers of Government, one hundred and five teachers of the public schools. By general consent, the influence of the Seminary has been highly beneficial to the Hawaiian people; and it has a claim upon the national treasury which will not be any longer overlooked, provided only it be replenished by the indemnity asked of Great Britain, and by the twenty thousand dollars so ingloriously extorted by the French, and other damages sustained in the outrages under Admiral Tromelin. The usual yearly appropriation from the treasury of the Mission has been two thousand five hundred dollars. To the Boarding-schools at Hilo and Wailuku, eight hundred dollars each.

In its early days, when this Institution was struggling for existence, its pupils were nearly all adults with families, and they had to support themselves while getting an education. The perseverance and stability of character, which was both a prerequisite to, and an effect of such a discipline, made them trusty and able men, whose services have been of great value to the nation and the cause of Christ. All those that have graduated younger and unmarried of late years, have not turned out so well.

Nor is it to be expected that youth just set free from the close restraints and vigilant keeping of a life in school, should behave themselves always so properly as sedate men, who had sown their wild oats years before, and who went out to places of usefulness with characters tried and established, and their domestic relations fixed.

It would be strange, indeed, if the spirit of the young colt should not sometimes break out with newly enjoyed liberty; and stranger still, if young men taught the value of property by an apprenticeship of seven or eight years, should not be sometimes found covetous and greedy. But these are evils necessarily incident to the working of a good system, and tell nothing against it, any more than do the infirmities and faults of Christians against Christianity, which yet are the husks that swinish men do eat.

If the nation is to be permanently elevated and enlightened, some of its youth must be educated and disciplined in such an Institution as this is meant to be. If some, upon whom pains and expense are bestowed, prove worthless, it is only what experienced men expect, and does not blind their eyes to the good that has been done, or quench their hopes for days to come.

There have been some painful disclosures of immorality at Lahainaluna, that have resulted in the dismission of eight or ten of the students, and the purging out of some of the old leaven. But their offences, though flagrant, were such as (if we are not mistaken) would hardly have caused expulsion from a New England College.

In a community like that at these Islands, where the laws are so much ahead of the morals, and where the religious teachers are endeavoring to form a public sentiment of abhorrence towards vice, it is perhaps necessary that offences against purity should be punished more rigidly than they would be, were there more of positive virtue and less of vice. But we cannot help saying with the Roman poet, "*Quid leges*, (and, we might add, *quid pœnæ*,) *sine moribus?*"

> Of what avail are laws and penalties,
> Unless there be a virtuous moral sense,
> A public conscience to frown upon
> And render immorality disgraceful?

The faculty would be much relieved and aided in the guardianship and discipline of the Seminary, and a great deal of moral mischief would doubtless be prevented, if they had a suitable man to be entirely devoted to its secular interests, and to inspect the youth in their hours of relaxation, labor, and rest. But either the right man has been always wanting, or to the ruling Missionary Board in America it has not seemed proper to send one.

Wisdom eighteen thousand miles off, and legislating like a mother-country over her colonies at the Antipodes, is necessarily far from being perfect. It has all the disadvantage of a lever of the third power, the fulcrum at one end, the weight to be raised at the other, and the power to be applied between the fulcrum and resistance; so that the weight being so much further from the centre of motion than the power, the difficulty of raising it is increased rather than diminished.

Thus, the Prudential Committee of the American Board of Commissioners for Foreign Missions is the fulcrum, like the ground to a man trying to raise a long ladder; the missionaries the other side of Cape Horn are the man's arms lifting, and the poor people of Hawaii, the long and heavy arm of the ladder to be raised. Now, if the fulcrum could be moved nearer to the weight, and the lever turned into one of the first power, it would work to much greater advantage.

This is in fact practically being done in the present movement towards independency of the Hawaiian churches; for the lapse of time, and the extraordinary blessing of God upon missionary operations at the Sandwich Islands, are now bringing to pass a revolution, which is seen in the late separation of a number of missionaries from their pecuniary relation to the Board, and their consequent independency, and in the adoption by Government of the College at Lahainaluna.

This will both relieve the treasury of the Board, and supersede the necessity of much cis-Atlantic management and counselling on the part of the Secretaries of the Board, who will soon be able to forego or renounce all other relations to the Pacific Mission churches, except such as the American Home Missionary Society sustains to its churches in the West.

In the language of the Committee, "they seek to facilitate the independent settlement of the members of the Sandwich Island Mission, as pastors and teachers at the Islands, and to place those who cannot yet obtain a living on the same footing with our home missionaries. And they expect by this means to enable and induce the missionaries generally to remain at the Islands with their families, and thus insure, through the divine blessing, a Puritan basis for the community, whatever it shall be, which is to exist on those Islands."

In the event of an American Protectorate, at the request of the Hawaiian government, or of annexation to the United States, (one of which measures would seem to be almost indispensable for the protection of these Islands against the insults and aggressions of the French,) the future Sandwich Island community must be substantially an American community, moulded to a great degree by American missionaries. It is therefore a matter of congratulation to the philanthropist who looks to the future good of the human race, and to the patriot who would rear an intelligent and Christian nation in the Heart of the Pacific, that the foremost men at the Sandwich Islands are, or have been, missionaries, actuated by one prevalent desire, the perpetuation and improvement of the Island race, whether pure or mixed.

In this the missionaries all agree. But familiar intercourse with the different members of the Hawaiian Mission, while it has made known an excellent spirit of concord and fraternal esteem between its members, has also caused me to be acquainted with some natural differences of opinion on things pertaining to the conduct of missionary operations, and the enlargement and discipline of native churches.

Some are of opinion that it is best to keep one door of the church always open, and make sure of admitting all the sheep by it, and afterwards to eject all the goats, as they are discovered, by a back door. Or, as others express it, that they must keep a little stream running through the church, in order to keep up their congregations, and save some from going to the Catholics.

Others, on the contrary, of the conservative stamp, argue that the Church being the practical exposition of Christianity, there is danger of its losing respect and moral power by a great many dismissions and excommunications—that more harm is done by getting into the church a good many hypocrites, than by keeping out of it a few good Christians—that a church of twelve truly regenerated is worth more, for good, than a church of twelve times twelve, a good part of them deceivers or self-deceived.

They contend that some who are admitted to the church do not know enough to be Christians. It has been thought that in a church at one time of one thousand professed converts on the Island of Oahu, there were hardly ten Christians. Its pastor informed me that of forty young persons admitted not until six months after he hoped they were Christians, there were only two or three that had not been disciplined for lewdness, and become worthless and depraved. The difficulty which some conscientious men find in satisfying themselves of the suitableness of candidates for the church is very great, such are the darkness and ignorance of a heathen mind.

When Mr. Alexander, one of the Lahainaluna teachers, was a pastor, and used to visit his people sixteen years ago, on the Island of Kauai, from house to house on week-days, he told me that he has often taken one single truth of Scripture and turned it over and over this way and that way, racked his brain for illustrations, and explained it in diverse forms, and then has asked a question to try how far the mind was instructed, and found, to his grief, that the person knew nothing at all—did not appear to have received a single correct idea.

Then he would return and go through again the same process of explaining and simplification, at length ask again some test question, and finding, as before, they seemed to have apprehended nothing, would have the melancholy query to put to himself, What do they know of my sermons?

Frequently, when the people would come to tell him their *manao*, (thought or mental exercise,) as that their sins were as many as the sands upon the sea-shore, or as the stars of the sky, or the leaves upon the trees, or the fish in the sea, he would interrupt them by some question, to which they, saying over in their minds their *manao* lest they should forget it, would not be able to give any definite answer, but would be stumbled and balked by the simplest inquiry about the nature of salvation.

Ask them again, sometimes, how they were to be saved, and they would answer, by praying—by breaking off sin—seldom by faith in Christ. "Do you sin now?" "No." "Do you not have evil feelings?" "I used to, but don't now."

Their answers were not always out of the way, but

frequently witty and to the point. As Mr. Alexander was once asking some of his people about depravity, and how they would express their moral state, he was aptly answered, We are all like rotten eggs. Some of the first inquirers at the Islands said to the early missionaries, "My heart is dark: you are light, and must enlighten it." Another, "My heart is a wilderness, you must cultivate it." Another, "My heart is a lamp, you must fill it with oil." Another, "My heart is a dry field, you must water it."

So an old man in the interior of Africa, when his people were asked by the missionary whether they would not like to be taught the truths of God's word, replied that "they were like men lost far off in the bush, and in darkness, unable to find their way out.* The

* The experience of a thoughtful pagan shrouded in the dense darkness of heathenism, yet feeling after God, is strikingly exhibited in the talk of a Bechuana, called Sekesa, with a missionary from whom he had been hearing the Gospel:

"Your views, O white man, are just what I wanted and sought for before I knew you. Twelve years ago I went, in a cloudy season, to feed my flock along the Tlotse, among the Malutis. Seated upon a rock, in sight of my sheep, I asked myself sad questions; yes, sad, because I could not answer them. The stars, said I, who touched them with his hand? On what pillars do they rest? The waters are not weary; they run without ceasing, at night and morning alike; but where do they stop? or who makes them run thus? The clouds also go, return, and fall in water to the earth. Whence do they arise? Who sends them? It surely is not the Barokas (rain-makers) who gave us the rain, for how could they make it? The wind—what is it? Who brings it, or takes it away, makes it blow, and roar, and frighten us? Do I know how the corn grows? Yesterday, there was not a blade to be seen in my field. To-day, I return and find something. It is very small; I can scarcely missionary seemed a kind friend meeting them, and offering to conduct them home."

The missionaries, to a man, testify to the extreme difficulty of preaching simply enough for the Hawaiian mind. Doubtless many sermons, especially from young missionaries, quite fail of giving instruction because

---

see it, but it will grow up like to a young man. Who can have given the ground wisdom and power to produce it? *Then I buried my forehead in my hands.*

"Again I thought within myself, and I said, We all depart, but this country remains; it alone remains, for we all go away. But whither do we go? My heart answered, Perhaps other men live, besides us, and we shall go to them. A second time it said, Perhaps those men live under the earth, and we shall go to them. But another thought arose against it, and said, Those men under the earth, whence come they? Then my heart did not know what more to think. It wandered. Then my heart rose and spoke to me, saying, All men do much evil, and thou, thou also hast done much evil. Woe to thee! I recalled many wrongs which I had done to others, and because of them my conscience gnawed me in secret, as I sat alone on the rock. I say I was afraid. I got up, and ran after my sheep, trying to enliven myself; but I trembled much!"

In like manner a certain man on the Malabar coast had inquired of various devotees and priests, how he might make atonement for his sins. At last he was directed to the following means: He was to drive iron spikes, sufficiently blunted, through his sandals; on these spikes he was to place his naked feet, and walk 250 coss, (about 480 miles.) If through loss of blood, or weakness of the body, he was obliged to halt, he might wait for healing and strength. He undertook the journey; and while he halted under a large shady tree, where the Gospel was sometimes preached, one of the missionaries came and preached in his hearing from these words: "The blood of Jesus Christ, his Son, cleanseth us from all sin." While he was preaching the man rose up, threw off his torturing sandals, and cried aloud, "This is what I want—This is what I want;" and he became a lively witness that the blood of Jesus Christ cleanses from all sin.

they give too much, and are deficient in a reiterating simplicity. Many of the commonest ideas, too, which we have from very childhood, natives are utterly destitute of.

Tell an Hawaiian that we are God's because he made us, and it is no reason at all to them, for they have all along till now been in the habit of making canoes, cultivating food, manufacturing kapa, and the like, and having it immediately taken away from them by their chiefs; so that the making of a thing by no means with them constituted ownership. So to preach to them from the text in which God challenges honor from the paternal relation which he stands in to men, "If I be a father, where is mine honor?" makes little impression, because they are a people among whom the filial relations and duties have been hitherto so little regarded.

In like manner, to tell them God loveth whom he chasteneth, and scourgeth every son whom he receiveth; that he chastens them in love as a father does the son in whom he delighteth, is to say what they cannot appreciate, and know nothing of, for they never punish *their* children, but when they are *huhu roa*, that is, mad.

And here I am reminded of what an English missionary says of his similar experience in the East. "They (the natives) have the most expressive terms for sin and holiness, and the duty of worshipping, and they will hear you with approbation while discoursing vaguely on these qualities, and yet they attach no proper meaning to the terms, and will totally misunderstand you. While discoursing on sin, they will think you mean *insulting a Bramin*, or *killing a cow*, or some such thing; and while on holiness, that you mean *making offerings to their idols*, or *going on pilgrimages*, and performing some acts of external self-mortification. With such notions as these in regard to sin, and holiness, and repentance, and worship, they can hardly be said to have a conscience, and you have yet to form, or rather to mould, one within them."

But all this to the contrary notwithstanding, and maugre all that may be said on the dark side of native character and piety, we are sure that they have learned a great deal of the Gospel at the Sandwich Islands, and that multitudes among them have felt its power. And we have noted the memorandum, (whether right or wrong,) that the older missionaries grow, and the more thoroughly they become acquainted with native character, and the language, the more they have of charity.

Mr. Alexander, when pastor of the church at Waioli, on the island of Kauai, admitted one hundred and twenty, and he fears that may have been too many. "Not (he says) that the Gospel has been preached in vain—I believe that there are not a few sincere converts; but I have discovered such a disposition in the people to make the attainment of church-membership a paramount aim, that I have felt like adopting the sentiment of the great Apostle to the Gentiles: Christ sent me not to baptize, but to preach the Gospel."

Other pastors, equally conscientious and engrossed with preaching the Gospel, were admitting at the same time (the period of the Great Revival) hundreds, and even thousands, in the hope that they were the children of God, and believing that a place in his church was their right.

Mr. Hitchcock, the laborious missionary on Molokai, testifies in regard to that work thus: "A greater number of the fruits of that revival give little or no evidence of conversion, than do the same number of those who were received before. And may not the same be said of great revivals, in general, in every part of the world? I have not the means of determining how much the cases of discipline in this church exceed those of the same size in the United States. Probably the excess may be considerable. In estimating, however, the amount of the work of the Holy Spirit, the truth will not be come at by mere comparisons in numbers.

"It must be remembered that the converts here were taken from the lowest depths of ignorance and moral debasement, and many, yea, all of them, have lived in habits of falsehood and many other overt sins, until such habits have become a second nature to them. All those powerful influences which co-operate with the grace of God in restraining converts from sin in our native land, are wholly wanting here. Let it be supposed, for a moment, that all those who entered the church as fruits of any great revival in New England, have been destitute of parental influence, destitute of conscience, destitute of any true sense of the worth of character, and having lived to the moment of their conversion in the midst and in the practice of licentiousness.

"It is easy to perceive that, even allowing them to have been true converts, many more cases of discipline might, and probably would have occurred in those churches, than can be expected to occur now. What we have supposed of the converts in such a New England revival, is fact with converts at the Sandwich Islands. The fact, therefore, that cases of sin and disorderly conduct are more frequent here than there, does not prove that the work of the Holy Spirit, or that the number of real conversions here, has been less than there; or that the proportion between real and false conversions in the Sandwich Islands revivals, is less than in those occurring in civilized lands.

"Taking into account all the unfavorable circumstances of the members of the church of which I have the care, their great ignorance, the limited range of their ideas, the irresistible influence of the example of their ungodly friends and of society in general, the force of early education and habits of sin, their extreme poverty, idleness, and aversion to thinking, and numerous other adverse influences; the grace of God, in enabling them to walk as consistently with the Gospel as they do, seems to me more evident and conspicuous than it does in churches where there are vastly greater attainments in holiness, but where adverse influences do not exist, and where there are ten thousand precious influences acting in a direct line with that grace."

I have quoted thus at length, because these remarks,

and the whole communication from which they are extracted, contain a better view of Hawaiian churches and revivals than could be given by any man not a missionary. To the same purport is an earnest letter from Mr. Coan, in the same number of the Missionary Herald.*

It has often appeared to me that truth is to be arrived at from comparing the differing views and statements of different men, very much as a ship's longitude is obtained in working lunars. The labor lies in applying rightly the numerous corrections, now on this side and now on that. There are the first, second, and third corrections, with their proportional logarithms. There are the corrections of the sun's and moon's altitudes, for parallax and refraction, and the height of the observer above the sea.

There are the corrections of declinations, and distances as calculated in the Nautical Almanac at the meridian of Greenwich, for the meridian of the ship. And then there is the correction for the seconds of the moon's horizontal parallax, and the correction for equation of time, and other things, all of which are to be exactly applied, and the variation tables carefully consulted, before the navigator can find his real place. And even then it is rarely that he gets it by a lunar nearer than ten or fifteen miles.

So, in gathering truth from the observations and reports of men, you have to take into account the place,

* Vol. xxvii., p. 105.

and profession, and leanings of the observers. You must compare and correct for the differences of mental parallax and altitudes made by observers from different points of view. You must note, if possible, the aberrations from the fixed meridian of truth, when to be added and when subtracted. The various deflections and increase or diminution made by prejudice are to be ascertained. The dip of the mind's horizon is to be noted, and the different degrees of refraction made by the differences in men's ordinary intellectual atmospheres, whether clear or foggy. There is a correction to be made according as you find the observers to be short or long-sighted, and as they have the eye of an eagle or that of an owl.

And finally, there is an allowance to be made in the representations given, according as they think you will use and steer by their observations or not. And, after all, if you have patience and skill to apply all the corrections, or are so happy as to be able to do it by intuition, even as rare geniuses are said sometimes to solve mathematical problems, yet it is not certain that your result will be absolute truth. And it is seldom that a modest man will peremptorily challenge another's assent to his own particular conclusions.

While the author of this work is far from challenging assent to his reasonings and inferences from things at the Sandwich Islands, either as presented in the present volume, or in "The Island World of the Pacific," he both asks and expects a belief in his facts, which he has certified to be accurate and true, and concerning which he affirms only what he well knows. Conclusions may be mistaken, but facts are fixed and reliable. From the facts carefully given throughout these pages, let our readers draw their own conclusions as to the civilizing* power of the Gospel, the relative values of the Merchant and the Missionary, the results of their united labors, and the prospects of humanity for time to come in the HEART OF THE PACIFIC.

* Several laws have been recently passed by the Hawaiian Government, to promote the cause of Education; among them, one giving the proceeds of certain lands for educational purposes; an annual tax of two dollars, on each male subject, has been imposed, for the same general purpose; and a fine of one dollar is exacted of every child who absents himself from school, and a fine of *five* dollars, if the absence is the parents' fault. Under the fostering care of Government, and the encouragement of the missionaries, school districts are now formed all over the Islands, and school-houses have been erected even in the most remote and inaccessible places.

## CHAPTER X.

### SANDWICH ISLANDS LITERATURE AND LETTER-WRITERS.

As there are two wants connatural to man, so there are two main directions of human activity pervading, in modern times, the whole civilized world; constituting and sustaining that NATIONALITY, which yet it is their tendency, and more or less their effect, to transcend and to moderate—namely, TRADE and LITERATURE.

S. T. COLERIDGE.

Number of printed works in the Hawaiian tongue—Literary contributions of natives—Newspapers in the vernacular—An original work on Hawaiian history—Installation of native ministers—A collection of old meles—Translation of an original song on the creation—Specimens of Cupid's epistolography—Letter from a damsel of Lahaina—Others from students of the Seminary—Samples of the Hawaiian madrigal—A letter from the Hilo school-girls—Others from teachers in Kohala—Curious vernacular idioms—Letters from men of Hawaii to a society of ladies in America—Comments and correspondencies—Unique epistle from a native teacher—Ingenuous working of regenerated minds—A study for the philosopher—A trophy of triumph for the Christian—Other specimens of Hawaiian literature—Cheering proofs of progress.

IT is natural, while at the spring-head of Hawaiian learning, at Lahainaluna, to say something upon the subject of Hawaiian literature. This, indeed, has yet but little to boast of as purely its own. But, aside from the entire Scriptures, there have been translated and compiled by the missionaries, within a period of less than thirty years, upwards of eighty different works.*

* M. Barrot, a French Catholic writer, having taken occasion to censure the missionaries at the Sandwich Islands for not printing more books in the Hawaiian language, upon "the progress of industry or science," and a less number upon "religious subjects, such as commentaries

8*

Those are now serving for reading, reference, and class-books, from the primer of A-B-C-darians, up to the text-book of students in theology.

---

on the Bible, catechisms for the use of the natives, and hymn-books," the editor of the Honolulu Friend thus replies:

Whether the American Missionaries have been particularly censurable in this respect, we leave our readers to infer by perusing the following catalogue of publications issued from the American Mission press previous to 1845:

Elementary Lessons.
Decalogue and Lord's Prayer.
Scripture Doctrines.
Thoughts of the Chiefs.
Sermon on the Mount.
Hawaiian Hymns.
First Book for Children.
Universal Geography.
New Testament.
Fowle's Child's Arithmetic.
Animals of the Earth.
Catechism on Genesis.
Geometry for Children.
Tract on Marriage.
Sacred Geography.
Geographical Questions.
Bible-class Book.
Colburn's Arithmetic.
History of Beasts.
Lama Hawaii, newspaper.
Hawaiian Almanac.
Vocabulary.
Compend of Ancient History.
Union Questions.
Colburn's Sequel.
History of Beasts for Children.
Hawaiian Teacher.
Child's Teacher.
Daily Food.
Hawaiian Grammar.
First Reading Book for Children.
Tract on the Sabbath.
Maps of U. Geography.
Scripture Chronology and History.
Hymns, revised and enlarged.
Hymns, with Tunes.
Linear Drawing.
Little Philosopher.
English and Hawaiian Grammar.
Tract on Popery.
First Teacher for Children.
Tract on Astronomy.
Maps of Sacred Geography.
Sixteen Sermons.
Tract on Lying.
Attributes of God.
First Book for teaching English.
Moral Science.
Key to Colburn.
Heavenly Manna.
Hymns for Children.
Hawaiian History.
Colburn's Algebra.
Anatomy.
Scripture Lessons.
Mathematics, Geometry, Trigonometry, Mensuration, Surveying, and Navigation.
Tract on Intemperance.
Bible-class Book, vol. 2.
" " vol. 3.
Keith's Study of the Globes.
Volume of Sermons.
Sandwich Islands Laws.
English and Hawaiian Lessons.
Keith on the Prophecies.
Dying Testimony of Christians and Infidels.
Bailey's Algebra.
Reading Book for Schools.
Messenger, semi-monthly.
History of the Sandwich Islands in English.
Hawaiian Bible.
Child's Book on the Soul.
Natural Theology.
Nonanona, newspaper.
Articles of Faith and Covenant.
Church History.
Moral Philosophy.
Pilgrim's Progress.

A good many of them have been prepared by the teachers of the Lahainaluna Seminary; one of the objects of which is declared to be to disseminate sound knowledge throughout the Islands, embracing general literature and the sciences, and whatever may help to elevate the people from their present ignorance and degradation, and cause them to become a thinking, enlightened, and virtuous nation.

Another object of kindred consequence, is to educate young men of piety and promising talents, with a view to their becoming assistant teachers of religion, or fellow-laborers with the missionaries, in propagating the Gospel of Jesus Christ among their destitute and dying countrymen, and throughout all the islands of Polynesia.

These objects are being steadily accomplished. In fulfilment of the first end, besides acting as teachers and filling important places in the government, the graduates are doing something towards making books and forming a national literature. They have had not a little to do in framing the present Hawaiian code of laws, and their communications to the Kumu Hawaii, Nonanona, and Elele, three native newspapers, have been numerous and often pithy.

It was members of the Seminary, also, who furnished the written matter from which Mr. Dibble compiled the

---

We regret our inability to place beside this catalogue the list of publications issued from the Catholic press. We have never met with but two or three small publications printed at that press, and they were *most strictly confined to the peculiar tenets of the Romish Church.*

volume called Moolelo Hawaii, or Hawaiian Annals, which has been the groundwork of two of the Histories since written in English. A valuable article on the Decrease of Population was furnished by the intelligent native, David Malo, now a licensed preacher of the Gospel. Several of the Lahainaluna graduates have been licensed also from time to time as Evangelists. And in December of 1849, there was seen the first instance of the ordination and installing of a native minister, as the independent pastor of the Congregational Church at Kahuka, island of Oahu. This was in the person of Rev. James Kekela, a graduate of the Seminary, at which he was for several years a beneficiary of James Hunewell, Esq., of Charlestown, Massachusetts.

The first teacher at Lahainaluna, Rev. L. Andrews, has in his possession a mass of old Hawaiian *meles* (songs) which he gathered and wrote down with much care from the mouths of natives. They are somewhat after the style of the old Greek Rhapsodists, and they are said, by competent judges who have seen them in manuscript, to be good specimens of the decent sort of unwritten Hawaiian Literature, containing the curious jumble of Hawaiian mythology, and all the Norse-like fables of their giant kings and gods. But like the talk of Gratiano in the play, it is all an infinite deal of confused nonsense and nothing. All that's worth preserving is as two grains of wheat in two bushels of chaff; you shall seek all day ere you find them; and when you have them, they are not worth the search.

A later *mele*, on the creation, by Ke-Kupuohi, an old

chief woman of Hawaii, composed after having read, for the first time, the first chapter of Genesis, Mr. Andrews translated, as follows:

A MELE ON THE CREATION.

God breathed into the empty space,
And widely spread his power forth,
The spirit flying, hovered o'er;
A spirit 'tis, a shadow of what is good,
A *shadow of heaven* is the Holy Spirit.

His power grasped the movable, it was fast,
Fast was the separating mass, lest it should move;
It moved not, God made it fast:
It was fast by the power of His will.

The earth became embodied,
The islands also rose, they rose to view,
The land was bare of verdure,
And desolate the earth.
'Twas earth alone;
Earth also was man,
'Twas God that made him,
By him also were all things made.

He caused to grow the verdure;
The earth was decked with beauty.
He adorned with flower the shrubs:
Beautiful was the earth
From the hand of God.

God made this wide-extended heaven;
He made the heavens, long, long ago;
He established the heavens a dwelling-place;
He dwelt alone, Jehovah by himself,
The Spirit with him.

His power created multitudes,
Thousands, myriads, numberless,
Until the heaven was full, and full the earth;

Filled with righteousness, with power, with goodness,
With glory, with holiness, with mercy;
Great were all his works.

Through God's abounding goodness,
Vast are the extended heavens,
Great are the heavens and the earth,
Great are the mountains, and the sea;
The work of God alone,
And his alone the power.

He fixed the sun his place;
But the islands moved, moved the islands,
With sudden, noiseless, silent speed;
We see not his skilful work:
God is the great support that holds the earth.

One of the graduates of the Seminary wrote an ode, a sort of funeral elegy, on the death of a son of Dr. Judd, a translation of which is inserted in Mr. Jarves' History of the Sandwich Islands, that is truly touching and beautiful. Some others have occasionally appeared elsewhere that possess considerable merit.

I have been not a little amused with perusing some intercepted letters that passed at one time between sundry lads of the Lahainaluna Seminary, and certain of the lasses of Lahaina. They are too good specimens of the Hawaiian madrigal, and of an Hawaiian's sensibility to love, to pass unnoticed. We transcribe some extracts, taken down as Rev. Mr. Alexander, the missionary teacher, was interpreting them for our amusement. The first is from one of the damsels of Lahaina, to her lover, up at the Seminary.

Love to you, who speakest sweetly, whom I did kiss. My warm affections go out to you with your love. My mind is oppressed in consequence of not having seen you these times. Much affection for thee dwelling there where the sun causeth the head to ache. Pity for thee in returning to your house, destitute as you supposed. I and she went to the place where we had sat in the meeting-house, and said she, Let us weep. So we two wept for you. And we conversed about you.

We went to bathe in the bread-fruit yard: the wind blew softly from Lahainaluna, and your image came down with it. We wept for you. Thou only art our food when we are hungry. We are satisfied with your love.

It is better to conceal this; and lest dogs should prowl after it, and it should be found out, when you have read this letter, tear it up.

FROM ONE OF THE LADS, BOKI.

Love to thee, thou daughter of the Pandanus of Lanahuli. Thou *hina hina*,* which declarest the divisions of the wind. Thou cloudless son of the noon.—Thou most precious of the daughters of the earth.—Thou beauty of the clear nights of Lehua.—Thou refreshing fountain of Keipi.—Love to thee, O Pomare, thou royal woman of the Pacific here. Thou art glorious with ribbons flying gracefully in the gentle breeze of Puna. Where art thou, my beloved, who art anointed with the fragrance of glory? Much love to thee, who dost draw out my soul as thou dwellest in the shady bread-fruits of Lahaina. O thou who art joined to my affection, who art knit to me in the hot days of Lahainaluna!

Hark! when I returned great was my love. I was overwhelmed with love like one drowning. When I lay down to sleep I could not sleep; my mind floated after thee. Like the strong South wind of Lahaina, such is the strength of my love to thee, when it comes. Hear me; at the time the bell rings for meeting, on Wednesday, great was my love to you. I dropped my hoe and ran

* Supposed to mean a beautiful flower that grows on the tops of the mountains, where sea and land breezes meet.

away from my work. I secretly ran to the stream of water, and there I wept for my love to thee. Hearken—my love resembles the cold water far inland. Forsake not thou this our love. Keep it quietly, as I do keep it quietly here.

### A THIRD FROM ONE OF THE STUDENTS.

Love to thee, by reason of whom my heart sleeps not night nor day, all the days of my dwelling here. O thou beautiful one, for whom my love shall never cease. Here also is this—at the time I heard you were going to Wailuku, I was enveloped in exceeding great love. And when I heard you had really gone, great was my regret for you, and exceeding great my love. My appearance was like a sick person who cannot answer when spoken to. I would not go down to the sea again, because I supposed you had not returned. I feared lest I should see all the places where you and I had conversed together, and walked together, and I should fall in the streets on account of the greatness of my love to you. I however did go down, and I was continually longing with love to you. Your father said to me, Won't you eat with us? I refused, saying I was full. But the truth was, I had eaten nothing. My great love to you, that was the thing which could alone satisfy me. Presently, however, I went to the place of K——, and there I heard you had arrived. I was a little refreshed by hearing this. But my eyes still hung down. I longed to see you, but could not find you, though I waited till dark. Now, while I am writing, my tears are dropping down for you; now my tears are my friends, and my affection to you, O thou who wilt forever be loved. Here also is this: consent thou to my desire, and write me, that I may know your love. My love to thee is great, thou splendid flower of Lanakahula.

Now we have no hesitation in saying that these lovelorn products of Lahainaluna and Lahainlalo, meant for the eye of the loved alone, but accidentally brought to my inspection, will compare favorably with many a sonnet, of world-wide notoriety,

"Made to his mistress' eyebrow,"

by the poet-lover, in lands of chivalry and song. They are the strictly natural, unsophisticated, and therefore by no means silly effusions of the youthful Hawaiian mind, under the liquescent process of that almost universal mental solvent, of which Coleridge says,

All thoughts, all passions, all delights,
Whatever stirs this mortal frame,
All are but ministers of love,
And feed his sacred flame.

Perhaps it is hardly fair to make such a use of intercepted Hawaiian madrigals, but they will have interest for the curious and the philosophic, as well as for the swelling heart of youth, because they prove, if nothing else, how the human mind, under the sway of the passion of Love, as well as under the teachings of Religion, expresses itself after the same way, and evinces the same phenomena, whether in polite Greek, or protean English, or simple Hawaiian.

Let us now compare with these sui generis specimens of Cupid's Epistolography at the Sandwich Islands, the following epistles from the same part of the world elicited by only the ordinary sentiments of sincere friendship, gratitude, and Christian esteem.

HILO, HAWAII.

Love to you, Mr. C——. Great is our love to you, in consequence of our dwelling together so pleasantly at Hilo here. Therefore, for our love to you, we have made a *palule* for you.

We remember all your words, and your commands. It is our mind to keep them all.

This also.—We are living together pleasantly and in peace, we school-girls of Mrs. Coan. If you should hear we are doing those things which are not right, then your heart would be heavy.

This also.—We remember our pleasant walks with you in Hilo.

Will you pray much that we may live in the peace (literally, cool shade) of our Lord?

By the waves and the winds of the ocean is borne this our thought of love to thee.

From the girls of the Boarding-school at Hilo.

By me,
KALAMA.

KOHALA, HAWAII.

Love to you, Mr. C——. This is my thought of love to you. I declare it to you on this white paper, and with this black ink, that it may be carried on the wing of the wind. Great love to you, in whom is the Spirit of God. This is what I know of you. You have given us a bell for our meeting-house.

These are some also who have assisted us in building our house; the King, whose is the kingdom, gave only sixty dollars; and the Governor of this island gave only forty dollars, and the members of the church have given only their ninepence and their twenty-five cents! But your present is a bell! That is like—how many dollars? Therefore my love for you has burst forth, and I have thought to write to you. Great indeed is your love for us!

Our meeting-house is finished. It is thatched with *ki*-leaf on the sides and ends, and with cane-leaf on the roof. It is filled with seats, and most of it is floored with boards; a little remains.

This also I declare to you. There is trouble in the church. Some of the brethren have been drinking sour potato and smoking tobacco. By-and-by, perhaps, the punishment of God will fall upon us of Kohala, if we do not run into Him for shelter. The people of Kona and Kau were guilty of this sin before, and God is punishing them. There is a great famine there, and after years, or months, perhaps, so it will be here. The beginning of this evil was with the land-officers. This it is that I declare to you. Tell to us some of the wonderful things done in your land. My thought is finished.

By me, a pupil of E. Bond's when you were here in Hawaii.

PAHIA.

KOHALA, HAWAII.

Great love to you, Mr. C——, our father in the truth. Love and blessing to you because of your love to us and your great kindness. Because also of your stirring up the brethren in the United States to that which is wanting to our new meeting-house in Kohala.

We are very happy in having received it, (i. e. the bell,) and in hearing its voice—a strange voice! Ended now are the old things. The horn (shell with which they formerly called to meeting) is nothing now! for here is the bell!

Concerning the bell my word is done.

Here is this new thought. I declare it to you. Blessed are we in having obtained a new meeting-house! It is an excellent house! It has a floor of boards, nice windows, and is full of good seats. All our wants are now supplied in this house.

Here is this new thought, too. We have a singing-school here in Kohala now; there are a great many pupils. By-and-by, perhaps, we shall understand this good work. If the pupils are attentive they will know well. That's done.

This, too, is another thought. The brethren are awaking. A great many now attend meetings on the Sabbath and on other days. Some who had fallen into this sin and that sin, have returned again.

This is my very last thought to you. Love and peace be to you in the Lord Jesus. I remember you in my prayers to God for you, because of illness in your body, and because of our meeting here in Kohala. And I praise God, too, that he has given both to us and to you blessings for our bodies and our souls; to us a teacher and the Sabbath, His word and good things a great many.

I, with respect,

KILAKAU.

From a number of other curious and original manuscript specimens of the Epistolary Literature of the Sandwich Islands in my possession, I select the following to a society of American ladies, friends of the Rev. Mr. Bond, who had sent out to him a box of ready-made clothing for the use of his school-boys. Their short way of naming their teacher is not from any want of politeness or of reverence, but is peculiar to the nation.

Hawaiians generally know nothing of the titles Mr. and Madam, or of Christian and surnames united. Thus, in speaking to or of Rev. Mr. Thurston, they would say *Kakina*, the nearest sound to Thurston they can utter. And so of his wife they would say Kakina-Wahine, the woman Thurston, or Thurston's wife. This is curt enough, and there must be great advance in the arts of civilization before they will come to Rabbi, Rabbi. The expression "great, perhaps," may be taken, if the reader please, to indicate that they meant to keep clear of all flattery, and not to speak positively, where, after all, a very moderate degree of love might have sent the garments. It will be noticed that they know when they have done, a thing that cannot be always said of either speakers or writers.

Love to you, Ladies of Hallowell, in America. Great is your kindness to us, in giving us the pantaloons for ourselves, and the shirts also. We are now clothed in the garments you have so generously given us, the boys in this High-school of Kohala. Great, perhaps, is your love towards us, and therefore have you sent us these fine garments. Love to you all, from the greatest to the least of you. This thought is done.

Here are some of the things we are doing in Bond's school:

We rise early in the morning, wash our faces, and go to meeting, (our morning prayer-meeting;) and when we return, we read in the Holy Bible. At the ringing of the bell, we go into school; and when school is out, we eat; and afterwards go to work. We have finished one half of the garden and the paths. The work we have done looks very nice, and the many things also growing in the garden are beautiful.

Here is another thought for you. What kind of a country is yours? Very good, perhaps, and pleasant, and not hot; and the living there, too, is agreeable, perhaps.

This thought is finished.

By me,

KEKIPI.

IOLE, KOHALA.

Where are you all, Ladies of Hallowell, in America?

Great is my joy and my desire for the good work done in your country, and for the undertakings there, and for the building up of the kingdom of Jehovah. This, also, for your aiding us with pantaloons and shirts. You are very generous, we should say. That is your character. Bond has given them to us who dwell in these mean houses and in these tattered garments.

This is the reason of our miserable houses and clothes—the dark-heartedness of our fathers. They did not know the God of heaven, but they worshipped lying gods. They knew not Jehovah, the God that made heaven, and earth, and all things. Therefore is the ignorance of the present race of people in these Islands. Because also of their great unbelief, and their prayers made with the mouth only. They have not prayed with hearts confessing to God.

Here, also, is a thought—to tell you of the labors of our teacher. These are a great many, stirring up the church, teaching in the teachers' school, and in the Sabbath-school, and in the High-school of Kohala, Hawaii.

My letter is finished.

By me,

KALAMA.

There is much meaning in one of the sentences of this last writer, who is an assistant teacher with Mr. Bond: "Because also of their great unbelief, and their prayers made with the mouth only; they have not prayed with hearts confessing to God." Alas! of how many is it too true, elsewhere the world over, in the words of that Scripture: *This people draw near me with their mouth, and with their lips do honor me, but have removed their heart far from me, and their fear towards me is taught by the precept of men.*

But have removed their heart far from me! Missionaries are tried with this in the native churches, and it grieves them deeply. But the foreign piety at the Islands has much more of the professional and heartless in it, than that which is native-born. There are certain professors of religion who, with a name to live, do show in their walk so little interest in any thing that pertains to life and godliness, that one can hardly believe otherwise than that the heart of their religion is quite eaten out, or dried up. They have a state of the spiritual being like marasmus or atrophy of the body.

If their piety has not completely run out and washed away, you cannot feel any pulse to prove they have a heart left; and the principle of spiritual life, if by bare possibility it do yet exist, is so feeble and low, that they are little better than dead.

Hence, though living in the midst of a people just emerging from heathenism, where the results of the Gospel are so benignly shown, and owing their own safety and well-being to that Gospel, they yet manifest no interest in the missionary's religious work, are never seen at the monthly concert or any prayer-meeting, give nothing for the propagation of religion among Hawaiians, have no love for the souls of natives or uncivilized humanity anywhere, and would willingly see the whole race melt away, and their place supplied by a stock they could have more complacency in.

The same is true of some visitors, and yet more transient residents at the Islands, professing piety. They do not make themselves acquainted with the nature, the trials, or the rewards of missionary work. They share in missionaries' hospitality, and avail themselves of their aid in travelling from place to place, but have little or no sympathy with them in their cares and efforts to Christianize the people.

They see them at their homes generally comfortable and happy, sometimes forming some of the happiest domestic circles in the world. But they do not enter at all into their motives as missionaries, their anxieties, harassments, responsibilities, toils, and cares. They see in the natives a great deal that is offensive, squalid, and still heathenish.

Heathenism, barbarism, and the state of nature, when

you come to be in contact with them, are stripped of all the romance that is apt to invest the life and work of a missionary afar off; and those persons not having either depth of piety, or love for souls, or sufficient of riddance from selfishness, to become interested like the missionary in the personal work of instructing and converting them, are actually, in practice, less engaged in the cause of missions than they were in America. And very likely they may go home and have less sympathy for missionaries, less charity for heathen converts, and less regard for the great enterprise of the world's evangelization, than they had before visiting this most highly favored missionary field.

But is it with good reason? No! but because having eyes they see not, having ears they hear not, neither do they understand or appreciate missionary work, native character, or the allowance that is to be made for early training, and the modifying effect even upon true experimental piety, of old bad examples, usages, habits, and polluting associations.

I write not without a meaning and a reality of fact in the mind's eye, and I cannot help recommending such persons to anoint their eyes with the eye-salve of truth and charity, that they may see; to get the crust of worldliness and vanity rubbed off from their religious sensibilities, which is so apt to form here, and to resort earnestly to the medicine of God's word and prayer, in order to work off from their systems the poison of scandal, which both travellers and residents have been heretofore wont to imbibe at the Sandwich Islands.

I close this chapter of unique Hawaiian letters with one more from a native teacher, of whom Mr. Bond says in forwarding it, "The writer is a fine young man, one of our most promising teachers. His own entirely was the thought to write you, and, according to his request, I translate hastily the epistle."

The spirit of piety it breathes, and the vein of Christian simplicity that runs through it, make it well worth preserving. And could all my readers see the original communication, in its clear, legible handwriting, and in a vernacular which, but for the missionaries, would still have been kept sealed to all but oral expression, they would wonder, even more than men do now, at the strange misrepresentations of some persons that the Hawaiians are not a Christian people.

It is a matter of thankfulness that our honored American missionaries there resident, are too strongly rooted both in the confidence and affection of the American Church and nation, for the slanderous aspersions upon the results of their labors to be for a moment believed. The success of the Missionary enterprise, as demonstrated at the Sandwich Islands, is beyond a doubt; and there are thousands of hearts devoutly thanking God for it every day, and praying fervently that the same glorious results may be realized everywhere.

HALAULA, KOHALA.

Love to you, Cheever, who hast sent your love and good wishes to us. Your letter was received by Bond in November, and on the Sabbath after the Sacrament of the Lord's Supper, the brethren of this church in Kohala heard of it. Bond declared it to us, and also the famine in Ireland and Scotland, by which men have died.

This I declare to you: it is a hot season with us in Kohala. The ground is very dry because of the sun, and has been so these seven months. Yet we are not greatly distressed for food. The water in the streams is dry. God has indeed granted us a few drops of water from the cloud-place, and the food is benefited thereby. The food, however, is scanty—very little. Even in kalo lands, where there is always water, the kalo-patches are drying up, and the potatoes near the streams.

The Chinaman's sugar-cane near Bond's house is fed up to cattle. It is entirely dry. The Chinaman thinks he shall leave Kohala. That thought is done.

Your aloha, (the bell,) here it is with us who are here. It calls us on Sabbath, Wednesdays, and Saturdays; but here is our fault: we do not obey its voice; children and parents who go to meeting. Bond said, "When the bell rings let all come in;" but we do not so; some go in a little while after the bell has done ringing, and some stay out. For all meetings it calls us with its ringing voice. It can call us as far as three miles. Bond's scholars do not have to blow the conch-shell with their mouths now.

Your love it is that rings constantly; pulled by the hand, it sounds.

Much love to you, because of your good counsel to us in the work of the Lord. Great was my love to you when I heard from Bond this declaration, "Cheever sends love to you, brethren of Kohala. He says he shall not forget you who live here." Then this was my thought to you—Thou art sweet honey to my mind; as cool refreshing water from far among the hills.

Pray to God for us, you and the brethren, that we may not come into distressing famine and death, as we have heard about the suffering in Ireland and Scotland; but that we may prosper, as does the country of your birth. That great country aids Great Britain with love, and according to the greatness of intelligence in your land, in carrying to them without avaricious motives. That just consists with God's word, Matthew v. 45—"That ye may be the children of your Father which is in heaven; for he maketh his sun to rise on the evil and on the good, and sendeth rain on the just and on the unjust;" and 1st Timothy vi. 17, 18—"Charge them that are rich in this world, that they be not high-minded, nor trust in uncertain riches, but in the living God, who giveth us richly all things to enjoy; that they do good, that they be rich in good works, ready to distribute, willing to communicate."

Your people have shown love for man, for the spirit-thing. Great indeed was my joy in hearing about it. Great is my love for those who are dying in such distress. We have prayed in monthly concert for the perishing, and have pledged ourselves to aid them. God will bless those whose country is distressed by famine. May he grant them a fruitful soil, that food may grow abundantly, even as the United States has contributed in behalf of Great Britain.

Love to you, my friend, in the cause of the Lord Jesus Christ. Pray for us just as we do for you. With Jesus is everlasting love. Amen.

By me,

JOHN WILLIAM KAILIHALAPIA.

Now we challenge the production of any thing in the early annals of nations, more demonstrative of the genuineness of their evangelization, than such ingenuous, childlike workings of the native Polynesian mind, in the first generation after it has come forth in its grave-clothes, as it were, out of the utter darkness of heathenism! The course of Divine Providence and grace, in the regeneration of the Sandwich Islands, is a subject for adoring wonder, gratitude, and praise; and the developments of the intellect, as well as of the resources of the Islands under the benignant, productive, yea, creative influences of the Gospel, should be matter of deepest interest, even to the mere philosopher.

Witness, also, the following from six native female converts at the Sandwich Islands, accompanying a bed-quilt by them made and sent to the New York Home for the Friendless:

KALUAALAO, October 29th, 1849

Our love to you, good people, who live in the great city of New York. This is our writing and request unto you, that you give unto those persons dwelling in the House of the Friendless, and orphans, this small gift, which we send unto you.

This is our gift, that we give unto you, one bed-quilt. This is our gift, and with it, we send the love of our hearts unto you, in whose hearts such love has sprung up, for the friendless ones and the orphan children. We are but few who have joined in this work, but having heard from our teacher what you were doing, we met together, and made a quilt for you to help you in your good work for the Friendless and the Orphans.

No one prompted us to do this thing, we did it of our own accord. It was not the rich, it was not our chiefs, it was not our teachers, that commanded us to do this; no, it was from the overflowing love of God in our hearts that compelled us to do it; it was of our own free will. We are not rich who do this, in this world's riches, but have been made rich by the Holy Spirit of God, as we hope, and therefore we wish to aid you in your good work.

Yours truly in behalf of the others,

W. KALUNA.

Of a later date is the following, acknowledging the gift of a Communion Service, consisting of four flagons, twelve plates, twelve goblets, and two baptismal fonts, for the two churches in Hilo and Puna, under the pastoral charge of Rev. Titus Coan.

HILO, HAWAII, July 29th, 1850.

*Salutations to H. T. Cheever, our friend in the Lord, and servant of the Most High God:*

We remember you on account of our associating with you at the time you abode with our minister, viz., T. Coan. You were one who desired to lead the children of God at Hilo, to wit, the church of Hilo, island of Hawaii.

Express thou our love to thy disciples, viz., the brethren in the Lord Jesus. Their love and beneficence have come to us. Like your seeing our faces, so is your giving to us the articles necessary for the Supper of the Lord, in your true love to us from the heart.

The love of God first flowed from his people dwelling in America, in the year 1820. They conceived their thought and labor without doubting, in seeking to pluck us out of the raging heat of death. They endured patiently, that wandering spirits might return to the place of rest. Their work has been great from the time of the arrival of the first American missionaries, Bingham, and others, until the present time, the year 1850. At the time of the arrival of the missionaries, we were living in the blackness of hearts, and in sins so exceeding great that they cannot be expressed on this paper for shame and pollution.

The exceeding love and benevolence of American brethren towards us is now most manifest, according to the words of Paul, 1st Cor. xiii. 8–13.

Of the life-declaring Apostles whom they sent, first in the year 1820, one, Whitney, nearly perished in the ocean. He fell into the sea; one threw him a board from the ship, by which he escaped, and obtained the vessel.

They have been patient, that their mission might be fulfilled. Two of them, Bingham and Richards, were greatly cursed by opposing foreigners, not for the evil of their works—they labored correctly—the wicked opposed them for righteousness' sake, lest their mischievousness should be known.

Through their patience we are now living in peace. Some

taught by them, have taken up labors to benefit the kingdom. Some have been governors, magistrates, collectors, school-superintendents, school-trustees, sheriffs, lawyers. Some regulate their own affairs. Every tree produces its own specific fruit, according to the words of Jesus Christ.

That stranger and this stranger have brought hither the things which are for his own profit to bring, and these little Islands are now replenished with things useful to man's body. But this company (missionaries) have brought hither an everlasting treasure, a good thing which excels all good things which our eyes have seen.

Previous to the year 1820, our houses were dark for want of oil. Then we obtained oil without wick, the thing to ignite the lamp; but through the kindness of God which was made to spring up within these true friends, they sent us some wicks to kindle our lamps, and they now burn, and thus until 1850 their burning has increased.*

As the abundance of your love for the souls of the wild goats upon the mountains of the Hawaiian kingdom, so will be the greatness of God's love and blessing on you. As your thought is on this church, so, indeed, is our pastor and true friend—not slothful—patient amidst all the evils of the way: and this his unslothfulness will be a capillary attraction to draw the souls of this people to everlasting life.

Through the constant care of all your friends in this Hawaiian kingdom for us, the nation is good, truly dwelling in blessedness and peace.

In the name of the church at Hilo, I am your affectionate brother,

S. KUPANEA.

---

* This figure may seem obscure. The idea is this: The *oil* brought in 1820, was the grace or love of God in the *hearts* of the missionaries. The *wicks* which came afterwards, were books, preaching, schools, etc., which helped the oil to shed light through all the dwellings of Hawaii.

Other parts of the Island World of the Pacific have furnished the materials out of which it were easy to compile another chapter of Polynesian Literature; but the following must suffice as a specimen of their direct and clear way of expressing themselves in letters, in groups of islands further south than the Sandwich.

It will be seen that their rhetoric comes to the point very soon, turns corners very sharply, and stops short when they have done. The communication is from a New Zealand Chief, and occasioned by the death of a governor who had been sent out there by the British Crown.

### NEW ZEALANDER'S LETTER TO VICTORIA.

Good Lady Victoria, how farest thou? Great is my love to you, who are residing in your country. My subject is, A governor for us and the foreigners of this island. Let him be a good man. Look out for a good man, a man of judgment. Let not a troubler come here. Let not a boy come here, or one puffed up with pride. We, the New Zealanders, shall be afraid. Let him be as good as this governor who has just died. Mother Victoria, let your instructions to the foreigner be good. Let him be kind. Let him not come here to kill us, seeing that we are peaceable. Formerly we were a bad people, a murdering people; now we are sitting peaceably. We have left off the evil. It was you appointed this line of conduct, and therefore it is good to us. Mother, be kind.

From me,

WEROWERO.

## CHAPTER XI.

### RIDE AROUND THE ISLAND OF OAHU, AND NOTES BY THE WAY.

*Portia.*—Good sentences, and well pronounced.

*Nerissa.*—They would be better, if well followed.

*Portia.*—If to do were as easy as to know what were good to do, chapels had been churches, and poor men's cottages, princes' palaces. It is a good divine that follows his own instructions: I can easier teach twenty what were good to be done, than to be one of the twenty to follow mine own teaching. The brain may devise laws for the blood, but a hot temper leaps over a cold decree.

*Merchant of Venice.*

We return to Honolulu—Festivities of the anniversary of Independence—Effect upon public morals—Natural hankering after the leeks and flesh-pots of heathenism—Converts from paganism now and in the apostles' day, one and the same—Comparison instituted—We mount for Kaneohe—Visit by the way to the country villa of the king and chiefs—Work, trial, and reward of the pastor at Kaneohe—Mistaken timidity in admitting to the church—Arguments for and against—Corroborative views of Isaac Taylor—Practical working of an open church polity and a close one contrasted—Going to Egypt for the corn of scandal—Much ado about nothing—Leonato to Antonio—We halt at Waialua—Contrasts of natural scenery—Kaneohe the supposed pit of an old volcano—Toilsome descent—Picturesque view from its brink—Face of the country between the two stations—Hospitality of a teacher at Hauula—Deportment of natives met with on the way—The stale charge of hypocrisy considered—No new thing for religion to be pressed into the service of selfishness—Examples of double dealing in the Pacific, by foreigners—Prevalent forms of self-deception among the natives—Causes assigned—Treatment of cases when discovered—Rigor of church discipline—The usages of the church an education for Republicanism—The future Republic of the Pacific—A prophecy ventured.

One night's sail of seventy miles in the little government schooner Victoria, transfers us from the college of Hawaiian youth at Lahainaluna, Maui, to the island of Oahu; where we find the king and his court keeping the annual feast on the anniversary of the giving back to him his kingdom by the good Admiral Thomas. Those festivities were rather inconsiderately prolonged through three days, and cost the government much money, besides leading to more waste and dissipation on the part of individuals, and giving too free rein to the sensual mind of a people just getting up from the long debauch of heathenism.

The pastors at Honolulu found a strong current of worldliness and sensuality setting there some time after the feast; and there was a revival of a species of heathenism, for which some church members even had to be disciplined. The common people, after the example of their rulers, feasted themselves in squads.

They would get together, pray, then eat and drink, sing meles, (old native songs,) and indulge in other excesses; and there was a strong hankering after old heathenish pleasures, which they would like to baptize with a Christian name; like some of the love-feasts of the Corinthian and other converts, where *one was hungry and another drunken;* at which *they counted it pleasure to riot in the day-time; feeding themselves without fear, sporting themselves with their own deceivings, having eyes full of adultery, and that cannot cease from sin.*

Without the Gospel, men everywhere, be they savage or civilized, are constantly tending downward. And when this tendency seems arrested, and some steps have been taken upward, there is still a gravitation in the sensual mind towards evil, which has to be watched against and counteracted, if we would keep an individual or a people progressing. Human nature, it is remarked by Taylor, in his "Ancient Christianity," however much it may have been raised above its ordinary level in particular instances, has always quickly subsided, and been substantially the same in every age and country.

Ancient and modern heathenism are of much the same type. The one in the Apostles' day had little to boast over the other in this. It took longer to purge out the old leaven from some of the primitive churches; and many of the converts then (it is manifest from Paul's own epistles) were not at all more stable—we doubt if as much so—or spiritually-minded, than some of the converts in these days at the Sandwich Islands.

A favorite ride and walk of twelve miles north from Honolulu, brings the traveller on Oahu to Kaneohe, one of the three out-stations on this island, of which the population, by the late census, is twenty-one thousand three hundred and sixty-three. You turn out of town on an excellent road near the large adobe and grass meeting-house of the Rev. Lowell Smith, belonging to the second church of Honolulu. The scenery of the Nuuanu Valley, with all its cultivated *kalo*-beds, cascades, cottages, and romantic mountain sides, is highly beautiful and unique.

Stewart's Journal of a Residence at the Sandwich Islands has made it familiar to many readers. And there is no one who has ridden through it up to the "Pali," but can testify that his glowing description has no more than done it justice.

About five miles up the valley, we stopped at a large unfinished house belonging to the king, in a grove of ancient koa-trees, where the chief boys and girls were rusticating a while with the family of their missionary teachers. They make an exceedingly well-behaved and happy company. All of them, to the number of sixteen, talk English with considerable fluency; and their entire aspect and bearing reflect much credit upon the fidelity and tact of their amiable guardians. The king is fond of riding up there, and takes great pleasure in the school, often expressing his sense of its utility, and wishing there had been such a school for him when a lad.

Rev. Mr. Parker, of Kaneohe, a patient missionary there for sixteen years, up to 1850, was greatly tried when I knew him, with the stupidity, the sensual tendency, and the disposition to deceive among his people; and he was consequently very slow in admitting to the church. He was of opinion then that the stone Meeting-house which he had built by dint of hard labor, some help from other native churches, and the savings of his own family, would in two Sabbaths be crowded to more than its capacity, if he should have a meeting of those out of the church, propound a few of them for admission, and call another meeting of inquirers.

They would think the *kumu* is now opening the *puka* (door) of the church, if not of heaven, and would run from every quarter to get in. There was a revival movement in his district in the year 1844, but out of a company of three hundred inquirers he admitted but five, because he feared their hypocrisy, and thought he could have more hold of them out of the church, but as instructed candidates for it, than when in.

Since that period there has been another religious awakening in his district, from which more fruit was cautiously gathered into the church; and the Minutes of 1848 show that there have been received in all into the Kaneohe church, by profession and certificate, from the time of its formation, three hundred members.

With all deference to the principles and conscientious fears of the pastor there, and of a few others who think like him, I cannot help expressing the opinion that a very close and rigid policy, as the rule of admission to Hawaiian churches, is a mistaken one. To say nothing of the propriety of using all suitable means to keep up a congregation, in order that a missionary may not preach to bare walls, we argue that if a man preach the true Gospel of Christ, and pray sincerely for a blessing, and there appear at times good evidence of the presence of the Holy Spirit, it is but reasonable to believe, in the absence of strong evidence to the contrary, that this same Divine Agent completes the work of regeneration in many souls that seem earnestly feeling, it may be, groping through thick darkness after God.

And when, as at all missionary stations, through ignorance and imperfections, both in him who judges, and in those whose conversion is to be judged of, the evidence of certainty cannot be had, we do not think that the fear of receiving some hypocrites should keep a minister from admitting to the church a goodly number of those who seem to have been wrought upon by the Holy Spirit, who profess repentance and faith, who pray and abandon outward sins, and who desire to be taken into the fellowship of saints.

Isaac Taylor very properly remarks in the History of Fanaticism, that "the duty of those, whether they be the few or the many, to whose hands are intrusted ecclesiastical powers, is not that of a Rhadamanthus. Responsibility does not stretch beyond natural powers, and it is quite certain that men have no power to search each other's bosoms; nor should they think themselves charged with any such endeavor. The pretender and the hypocrite belong always to Divine jurisdiction; the Church will be asked to give no account of them, so long as they successfully conceal the fatal fact of their insincerity. Let but a community be more or less extended in its sphere, be pure in manners—PURE, not sanctimonious; let the Scriptures be universally and devoutly read by its private members, and honestly expounded by its teachers; and in this case it will be very little annoyed by the intrusion of heretical or licentious candidates."

If they are not so embraced and taken care of in the Church, they are liable, weak and unsteady as the undisciplined mind is, to wander and stumble as sheep without a shepherd, to fall at length into darkness and sin, to lose patience and hope, and cease praying together, and to fall, perhaps, into the clutches of the Man of Sin.

Rather than that this should ensue with any of God's elect, or that any who are truly seeking him should be balked and lose their souls, it were better that many wolves in sheep's clothing get within the consecrated ground of the Church. The conversion of spurious professors here is by no means so doubtful or difficult a thing as when they get into the churches in America; and at the worst, they can be turned out when discovered.

The state of things at Kaneohe, and at the next station of Waialua, is confirmative of these views. Many have become slack and indifferent, and have left off going to meeting, saying the way to the church is long, and have given up heart, and hope, and effort altogether.

The Catholics have a priest not far from there, and he has gained some, together with the control of one hundred of their children, not because they really think the Popish way is the right way, but because, by their own confession, they are tired of waiting upon their kumu, (teacher,) and have an itching desire to be sprinkled and housed in some church, with a lurking belief—by no means unknown to wiser minds in Christian lands—that somehow they are more likely to be saved in the Church, than unbaptized out of it.

It is natural there should be a difference of opinion as to how such cases are to be prevented, or treated when found, among a people with whom a profession of religion is so popular. No one can deny that the whole subject of admitting to the Church is beset with difficulties. Perhaps the more conscientious and orthodox the pastor, the greater will be his quandary.

It is but fair that those who are interested in and support missionaries, should be made acquainted as far as possible with their trials, and what they have to contend with, the deceit and hypocrisy of native character, the degradation and vileness of the native mind. If the dark side of native character, and the dark aspect of native churches, have been heretofore* too much withheld from the public, as some think, there is more reason that both sides should be given now, in order that erroneous views may be corrected, and the truth arrived at by comparison, so far as it can be ascertained by those who are not on the spot to see things as they are, and as no reports can possibly exhibit them.

---

* Travellers who visit missionary establishments sometimes contribute to existing errors. If they write in favor of them, they wish to do it to some purpose; they wish, of course, to be popular, in an age which asks for new and exciting matter from the press. Hence we have seen books professing to give the state of things at the Society, Sandwich, and even Marquesas Islands, written in a style of extravagance, adapted rather to gratify than to inform the reader. There are other travellers who fall into the other extreme. It is a point with them to show that the missionary enterprise does no good; that it impoverishes and depopulates the Islands, and that the natives who survive its pestilential influence are made more idle, filthy, and vicious. The reader needs not to be informed that it is an old usage among men to comfort one's own conscience, by an effort to lay its guilt on the back of another. Neither does the public, we presume, need to be informed that if any one goes down into Egypt after the corn of scandal—the sins of missionaries—he will find the stewards of the granaries on board his craft before he can anchor, and the sack filled, and the money also returned in the sack's mouth—at so cheap a rate do they supply the wants of their brethren.—*Hawaiian Spectator,* Vol. i. p. 99.

Therefore we have been always ready, in these pages, to state facts as they have fallen in our way, and to make it known when we differ as to how difficulties should be surmounted, and trials met; at the same time not forgetting the proverb which says of grief ironically, that every one can master it but he that hath it; nor letting slip one of those sayings of Shakspeare's heroine which I have put at the head of this chapter, I CAN EASIER TEACH TWENTY WHAT WERE GOOD TO BE DONE, THAN TO BE ONE OF THE TWENTY TO FOLLOW MINE OWN TEACHING.

We can easily point out faults and errors in others, and commend them to patience and fidelity in suffering and duty; but it is quite another thing always to act in just the right way ourselves, or to be and to do what we recommend wisely to others. How finely does Leonato say to Antonio in the drama of Much Ado About Nothing—

Brother, men
Can counsel, and speak comfort to that grief,
Which they themselves not feel; but, tasting it,
Their counsel turns to passion, which before
Would give preceptial medicine to rage,
Fetter strong madness in a silken thread,
Charm ache with air, and agony with words;
No, no; 'tis all men's office to speak patience
To those that wring under the load of sorrow;
But no man's virtue, nor sufficiency,
To be so moral, when he shall endure
The like himself: therefóre give me no counsel.
My griefs cry louder than advertisement.
I pray thee, peace: I will be flesh and blood;
For there was never yet philosopher,
That could endure the tooth-ache patiently;

However they have writ the style of gods,
And made a pish at chance and sufferance.

There is seldom seen, even in Hawaii-nei, where the extremes of fruitfulness and aridity often meet, a greater difference in the external aspect of two places, than appears at the present time between Kaneohe and Waialua, at which latter missionary station we have now arrived in the course of our travels around Oahu.

At Kaneohe, directly around the mission premises, and all the way up to the lofty precipice which breaks it off from the Valley of Nuuanu, on the Honolulu side, there are grassy knolls, running brooks, and green meadows of great fertility, alternating within the compass of ten or fifteen miles. There is good evidence that the entire district was once a volcanic crater. It is hemmed in on all sides, except seaward, by lofty basaltic and lava precipices, just like the sides of Hale-a-ka-la. Nothing can be more picturesque and charming than the first view you get of it from the brow of the Pali.

There you stand, if the fierce rush of the trades will let you, at least two thousand feet above the diversified grassy basin below, and look away over the rich landscape of calm sunshine and shade, blended by distance into a mellow unity, along the aspiring cliffs, and off "o'er the waters of the dark blue sea," till they rise up in the distant horizon to a level with the plane of your eye.

The descent is so long and difficult by a zigzag in the almost upright wall of the Pali, like the celebrated Estroza Pass in the island of Madeira, that one has to take the best heed to his steps who will go down there. And if a man's rectus and vasti muscles, the semitendinosus and biceps flexor cruris, do not ache after it, it must be because his legs are made without them.

When once fairly down, the way to the station, four or five miles, is clear over the greensward; and you look back with wonderment at the vast walls and ramparts, of which no power less than volcanic could have been the architect, or could ever have rent from them, and sunk to nearly a level with the sea, the great subjacent plain over which you are passing

The way thence to Waialua is forty miles to the westward, along the sea, often on the beach. At the point where you emerge from what may be called the great crater of Kaneohe, the precipice is cut off plumb down to a level with the sea, making a wall on your left of eight or ten hundred feet perpendicular height. There are several villages to be passed through where the Catholics are numerous.

Fish-ponds are fenced-in all along, and there are many little bays and bights of the ocean which, together with the grassy and gentle line of the coast, form an unusual variety in Hawaiian natural scenery, and a fine contrast to the deep cuts and bold mountains further inland. The country on all that side of the island is well watered, and holds out many inducements for settlement to Hawaiians; yet the population is but five thousand, and that decreasing.

I stopped to rest and bathe at a place called Hauula,

where a line for the teacher from Mr. Parker, procured me entertainment as readily as if I had been an envoy of the king. He at once unsaddled my horse, and put him to grass, broke me a stalk of sugar-cane, baked a fowl and potatoes, and entertained me an hour with a simple, easy hospitality, while I used up all the Hawaiian I ever learned, and maltreated a good deal more, in answering and asking questions.

On the way from his house, I fell in with companies of native men and women, some of whom mistaking the traveller for a sailor, by a pea-jacket spread upon my saddle, behaved themselves in a way which proved two things—both what sort of indecencies are agreeable to the foreigners with whom they generally have to do, and that they deport themselves very differently before a man whom they believe to be not a missionary, nor a missionary's friend, and one who *is*.

I might probably have learned more had I stopped, and had I thought it quite right to play the part of the character they took me for. This I could not do for three reasons: First, the knowledge that a man's own feelings and state of mind are very likely to become, even against his will, those of the man whose actions and words he imitates. Second, real truth and virtue are unwilling to dissemble, and feel disgraced, like a chaste virgin, to be taken for what they are not. Third, because an honest man hates deception in any form, and feels conscience-struck and sorry ever to allow it, or not frankly to show what he is.

Knowledge of Hawaiians, or of any other persons,

gained in such a way, would be too dear bought, and one had better remain in ignorance than get it at such a sacrifice. The lawfulness of deceit for a good purpose was held by some of the Fathers, and along with cunning priests to tend the loom, it may be said to have woven the pall of night that covered the Dark Ages. It is held by Romanists still. But an honest man and a Protestant possesses in his bosom a light of conscience, that puts to the blush such a maxim of time-serving expediency.

He knows, (says Coleridge with his usual earnestness,) that by sacrificing the law of his reason to the maxim of pretended prudence, he purchases the sword with the loss of the arm that is to wield it. The duties which we owe to our own moral being, are the ground and condition of all other duties; and to set our nature at strife with itself for a good purpose, implies the same sort of prudence as a priest of Diana would have manifested, who should have proposed to dig up the celebrated charcoal foundations of the mighty Temple of Ephesus, in order to furnish fuel for the burnt-offerings upon its altars.

You hear nothing oftener in the mouths of irreligious foreigners, than that missionaries don't know the natives, that they don't act out before *them*, and that they are great hypocrites. Now we think the missionaries might know it by this time, through being told of it so often, if not by their own observation. And the truth is, they *do* know it well, and mourn over it, and endeavor to keep on their guard against it.

But they are not so ignorant of history or other men, as to believe hypocrisy, and falsehood, and double-play peculiar to Hawaiians. Hypocrisy is not monopolized by Hawaiians, nor will it die out of the world with them. They cannot be called a community of hypocrites with any more propriety than a foreigner should call the people of the United States so, because in the first steamboat or railroad-car he might take passage in, he should see posted up in large letters, LOOK OUT FOR ROGUES AND PICKPOCKETS.

Other barbarians, both the instructed and uninstructed, evince as much deceit as these Hawaiians, and most of them more; and I have little doubt that the history of the intercourse of white men, of Anglo-Saxons, and Anglo-Americans with these islanders and those of the Pacific generally,* would reveal more falsehood, treachery, and double-dealing on their part, and lead an unprejudiced mind to the conclusion that there was at

* The author of the bold Polynesian romance entitled "Typee," very properly remarks that the enormities perpetrated in the South Seas upon some of the inoffensive islanders well-nigh pass belief. These things are seldom proclaimed at home; they happen at the very ends of the earth; they are done in a corner, and there are none to reveal them. But there is, nevertheless, many a petty trader that has navigated the Pacific, whose course from island to island might be traced by a series of cold-blooded robberies, kidnappings, and murders, the iniquity of which might be considered almost sufficient to sink her guilty timbers to the bottom of the sea. It may be asserted without fear of contradiction, that in all the cases of outrages committed by Polynesians, Europeans have been at some time or other the aggressors, and that the cruel and blood-thirsty disposition of some of the islanders is mainly to be ascribed to the influence of such examples.

least as large an infusion of these amiable qualities in *their* composition as in that of the red-skinned race.

Hypocrisy and deception do not belong pre-eminently even to savages, but to human nature. They are not the monopoly and trade of barbarians merely, but they are diffused as widely as the human race. Perhaps they stand out more glaringly on the page of history, than any other vices to which men are subject.

Especially has religious hypocrisy been exhibited wherever religion has been known, the former being, as it is often remarked, a homage paid to the latter, of which, indeed, it only proves the reality and excellence, just as counterfeit dollars and doubloons in circulation prove that there are real ones too, for no one would take the pains to counterfeit that which was not valuable and did not exist.

And if religion has in all times, especially in highly civilized countries, been made the stalking-horse and shoeing-horn to selfishness, whereby unprincipled men have ridden into place and power, why should it be thought strange that many of the Hawaiians, among whom religion has become popular, and a passport to reputation and confidence—why is it strange that *they* should be found running after it, and assuming its semblance, in order to get its good?

If bad men in other lands have so often made it the cloak of sinister designs, why is it wonderful that in Hawaii-nei natives should now and then be found trying to wrap it round their rottenness, in order to hide the gaping sores of their moral corruption, as well from their own eyes as from the sight of others!

I believe this latter use is less often made of religion here than elsewhere. When Hawaiians profess repentance and faith, and act the hypocrite, it is either as self-deceived, or that they may get the favor of their minister, and entrance into the Church as a means of grace and salvation—very seldom (if we are not mistaken) as self-known deceivers, wearing the characteristic mark of hypocrisy, and in order to cover up and carry on some ulterior design.

Often, as in all societies, after the committal they have made of themselves has led them to break off outward sins, and they are safely housed in the Church, and the novelty and excitement of their new estate and relations has worn off and become stale, then iniquities prevail against them, their corruptions return too strong to be resisted by unregenerate human nature, they yield and are disclosed to themselves and their brethren as having been "hypocrites," if that term be preferred to self-deceived and deceivers, which in this case it certainly means.

If there be not immediate repentance upon the disclosure of guilt, such persons are cut off. If there be, they are suspended for a time, till it is clear what they are, and then, if giving good evidence, they are restored; if not, excommunicated. Who will say that this is not right? or who can point out a better way?

It may be remarked here, that the usages and discipline of the Christian Church are doing for Hawaiians what the same causes did for the founders of New England, that is, preparing them for self-government and republicanism. As the Republican State in New England found its germ in the Republican Congregational Church which preceded it; and as the principle of individual equality and representation, first practically exemplified in the constitution of the Church, was thence transferred to the constitution of the State, in like manner is the present generation of Hawaiians in a process of training, under its religious teachers, for civil liberty.

The result will doubtless be to develop the capacity of self-government, and in due time to rear a flourishing Republic in the Heart of the Pacific. A virtual colony as it will then be from the United States, founded by American Christianity and American Commerce united, and linked, as it will speedily become, to our Pacific and Atlantic seaboards by steamer and telegraph, it may suitably be adopted into the sisterhood of American States.

Hawaiian Senators and Representatives may ere long take their seats in the Capitol, at Washington, with members from Minnesota, Utah, Deseret, New Mexico, and Santa Fé. The Star of Hawaii may yet blaze in the flag of the American Union; and the sons of her present missionaries, together with native-born Kanaka Maole from the Island Heart of the Pacific, may yet mingle in debate on the floor of the American Congress, and the voice of Senatorial eloquence from the luxurious tropics may yet awaken echoes from the hardy North. May propitious Heaven speed the augury!

And may that happy consummation of universal brotherhood among all the nations be soon realized, of which Edmund Burke said in his place in the British parliament: I believe, my lords, that the sun, in his beneficent progress round the world, does not behold a more glorious sight than that of men, separated from a remote people by the material bounds and barriers of nature, united by the bond of a social and moral community.

## CHAPTER XII.

### SIDE VIEWS OF HAWAIIAN CHARACTER AND DESTINY.

*Polonius.*—If circumstances lead me, I will find
Where truth is hid, though it were hid indeed
Within the centre.—
'Tis too much proved, that with devotion's visage,
And pious action, we do sugar o'er
The devil himself.—*Hamlet.*

Relative position and fortunes of the posterity of Shem and Japheth—Practical bearing upon the labors of missionaries—The ground principle of success—Variety of talents called into exercise—How to be beloved and useful—Study of books, versus the study of human nature—Something had and something wanting at Waialua—A maxim gathered from observation—Management of cases of casuistry—A common weakness commented upon—Difference of behavior between sentimental and genuine sorrow—The acting of a fine mind when sin or grief-stricken, and that of a coarse mind—The Hawaiian infirmity illustrated by a fact—The pea-hen everywhere—Native volubility and destitution of shame—Charities of the Waialua church—A manual labor school—How established and why abandoned—We journey to Ewa—A successful experiment at self-support—Remarkable proof of disinterestedness—Progress reported—Honor to whom honor is due—Fact and cause of the nation's decay—Alarming statistics—Report of a committee on moral reform—Responsibility of foreigners who have fed the national vice—Moral strength of the government now and formerly—Suppression of vice the duty of magistrates—Plea of virtue and humanity—Sophisms of the selfish and impure—Righteous reasonings of the duke in the moral play of Measure for Measure.

THE future of nations and of individuals is absolutely known to Omniscience only. The issues and destinies of ages to come, God alone can explore, on whom they depend. A guess beyond the present, or a rational judgment of the future by the past, is all that the wisest of uninspired men can venture. There are thinking men of the race now dominant in the world, who judge that all the nations of the earth descended from Shem, (including the Indians of North and South America, the races of Oceanica, and the kingdoms of the East,) have already reached that point of degradation or of fixedness observed by ethnologists, from which neither individuals nor nations are disposed of themselves to rise, and from which the Most High is seldom disposed to raise them. They are to be irrecoverably absorbed,—according to the prophecy, God shall enlarge Japheth, and he shall dwell in the tents of Shem—in the posterity of that son of Noah to whom Europe was given.

Be it that many of them as individuals may be converted and saved, they cannot survive much longer as nations. The decree has gone out against them—prophecy must be fulfilled. Embracing Christianity will not save them from decay, though it may save their souls. They have sunk too low, and have become diseased too mortally, to be raised and live. Repentance comes too late for their national salvation, as to a man who has ruined his constitution by excess, past the sanative reach of reform. The process of extermination before the favored posterity of Japheth, is too far under way, and too surely predetermined, to be arrested now.

Now, how much soever of theoretic truth and Scripture evidence such opinions may have for their basis, yet, when much dwelt upon, and constantly compared in the mind with all facts that look that way, it is hardly possible that they should not blunt the edge of appetite for missionary work, and disable the sword-arm for nervous thrusts at the powers of Pagan darkness.

The mind will be naturally reasoning—My labor here is comparatively hopeless and of little account; how much better to be expending my energies for immortality upon the race of Anglo-Saxons that is to live and inherit the earth, than upon a degraded people that are soon to die out and become extinct, and their memorial to perish with them!

Such reasonings, like the notions Satan started in Paradise, when he sat

> Squat like a toad, close at the ear of Eve,
> Assaying by his devilish art to reach
> The organs of her fancy, and with them forge
> Illusions, as he list—

disturb and divert the mind from its proper work;

> Thence raise distempered, discontented thought,
> Vain hopes, vain aims, inordinate desires,
> Blown up with high conceits, engendering pride.

It is no more possible for a missionary, than for a clergyman in service elsewhere, to pay the debt to his profession which Lord Bacon says every professional man owes, *nisi noctes atque dies in hoc studio consumat.* All his days and nights must be given to studies and employments that have a steady bearing upon his great work, and tend either to enlarge his capacity, or augment and burnish his intellectual armor, or to throw the light of his individual reason and experience upon the duties of his profession, for the benefit of others.

It is not, indeed, for one man to say to another how

much or how little he may diverge from his main pursuit, or whether literary diversions be compatible or not with the duties of a missionary. We can only lay down the general principle, that both ministerial and missionary work demands the entire energies of those who are dedicated thereto. In order to be at all eminent or successful, experience has proved that the man must be totus in illis. *Give thyself wholly to them—Make full proof of thy ministry—Do all the work of an evangelist*—is the charge of the Apostle. To divide the strength is to weaken it, and one's profession inevitably suffers.

Examination of the yearly minutes of the Hawaiian Mission, and a bird's-eye view of the business they lay out for themselves, every one or two years at general meeting, as well as the personal inspection of them at their several stations, would satisfy any one that there is no chance in Hawaii-nei for laziness. There is work enough, both professional and miscellaneous, to keep them all busy; and there is full exercise, in one way or another, for all gifts and talents, inventive, administrative, executive; teaching, preaching, organizing, building, improving in every way.

Some of the missionaries excel in preaching, and some in teaching; others, again, in translating and book-making; and others in devising and constructing new ways and means of operation upon the native mind, whereby it shall develop and educate itself.

Some pastors, by reason of their impulsive, sanguine temperaments, strong faith, and fervent zeal, are eager to introduce candidates early into the Christian ordinances of baptism and the Lord's Supper. Others, again, may have shown an excess of carefulness in admitting to the Church, an extreme of skepticism on the subject of native piety, and the important lack in their intercourse with Hawaiians, of the affable temper of Milton's

> Sociable spirit Raphael, that deigned
> To travel with Tobias, and secured
> His marriage with the seven-times wedded maid.

We have put it down as a maxim that no man can be beloved or popular, as a missionary or a man, in Hawaii-nei, who is not either from natural disposition, or in default of that, from purpose and policy, particularly patient, condescending, and social in his intercourse with the people. Any one that cannot be so, or who will not make up his mind to exercise much self-denial, and spend considerable of his time in talking with the natives, receiving calls, and listening to their *manaos*, (thoughts,) had better not come.

The most beloved and best missionaries are the most easy and gracious in their dealings with the natives. You cannot be cold and reserved, or keep them at a distance, without keeping away their confidence and love. There must be much gentleness, a kind, obliging temper, and a considerable degree of familiarity allowed, or their regard for you will be slight, and your influence over them inconsiderable.

It is much more agreeable to nature to commune in one's study with books, or to be enjoying the society of family and friends, than waiting upon ignorant though well-meaning Kanakas, that can add nothing to one's intellectual stores, patiently unravelling their *hihias*, (moral entanglements,) listening to the tale of their corruptions, or sitting in judgment upon their strifes. But all this must be willingly submitted to if a man will gain influence, and will not quite forego the fruit of his labors. There must be a mutual love and confidence begotten between pastor and people by these offices, or the good that can be done is almost nothing.

There is one part of the pastor's discipline at Waialua that commends itself as wise, and worthy of imitation among more cultivated people than Hawaiians. I mean the way he deals with cases both of gross and minor delinquency, where yet the offenders are not cut off. When church members have confessed to him sin, or it has been found out in any way, and they seem penitent, he confesses it in their stead, and rebukes them publicly before the church on the days of communion, rather than let them confess at length themselves, and lay bare the deep ulcers of their souls, with the horrid kind of delight that some men seem to have in exposing their own depravity.

No careful observer who has been much conversant with men in religious matters, can fail to have taken notice of the secret pleasure which some persons have in detailing their sins, criminating themselves, and minutely relating the circumstances of their guilt. You hear such confessions sometimes in church-meetings, to let brethren and sisters know how wicked they have been; but it is almost always of sins that *were*, and that had better be let alone, except to mourn over them before God; seldom of those to which the man is *now* habituated, and that are a real stumbling-block in his business and family.

The pastor often listens to them with surprise and sorrow in private. Sometimes they are protruded before promiscuous assemblies, with a wanton though concealed pleasure, to be detected by an acute observer, arising from the self-instituted comparison which the confessor makes, and which he supposes his hearers to be making also, between his past wickedness and present goodness, and from the supposed imputation to himself of humility in the minds of others, for being willing to make such disclosures of his sins.

There is not a little of this to be observed in the publicly related experiences of reformed drunkards, of whom he is thought to be the most entertaining, and is made the lion, who can tell the most terrible tale in his own person, (*Quæ-que ipse miserrima vidi, et quorum pars magna fui,*) of the degradation and woe, the bestiality and filth, of intemperance. We shrewdly suspect these public experience-tellers of sometimes adding a thing or two, like the venders of the last words of noted pirates and highwaymen, in order to make out a case, and horrify, and get it to go the better.

And we think there is no small danger of the public taste becoming vitiated by the disgusting exhibitions that are sometimes made. Certain it is that in all such confessions, (those first spoken of,) there is more of pride than of conscious shame, or humble grief, or glory to God. They are alike unedifying to those to whom they are made, and to those by whom they are made, except for the relief they now and then give to a burdened conscience.

True shame and repentance for private sins does not seek the meeting-house, but the closet, to confess in; not the itching ears of men, but the ear of the all-hearing God. It says to him, like David, *Against thee, thee only have I sinned and done evil in thy sight.* If the sin has been public, and an injury to men, then indeed will genuine repentance suggest the reasonableness of making a public confession, and seeking pardon of men as well as of God. But it is, if we mistake not, with heart-felt sorrow for sin as with deep-felt grief for some bereavement: both seek solitude to pray and mourn in, and ask not a stranger's intermeddling therewith.

We always conclude that an affliction is not felt very deeply, that the barbed iron of sorrow has not entered into the soul, when it can be spoken of with every caller or guest, and the wound it has made in the sensibilities handled and shown. It argues a superficial and volatile, rather than a deep-suffering mind, to be able to say much about its sorrow. A heart deeply wounded shuns the sympathy and sight of all but God and a few bosom friends. Its anguish cannot be told and shared with many. The keenly felt trial or bereavement must be touched gently, and will not be talked about as a common theme.

It is only the sentimental and selfish mourner, pierced but skin-deep, yet nursing its grief, fostering its slothful love and dainty sympathy, that can be fluent and frequent upon the subject of it. Hence the language of Cowper, who copied what he wrote from the tablet of his own experience,

> To him that e'er has felt the sting of sorrow,
> Sorrow is a sacred thing.

He would not approach a sufferer rudely and drag him into notice, whether smarting under the sting of sin, or under the rod of God, in some providential bereavement, because experience had taught him that alike, in both cases, the stricken sufferer seeks concealment, and wants but one Physician and one Nurse.

This is true of cultivated and fine minds, both in respect to their sins and sorrows. But it does not hold so certainly of the coarser sort, of uncultivated and gross spirits. Hawaiians, especially, love so well to appear in public, that they are pleased even to be allowed to tell their sins and expose themselves; perhaps glad sometimes of an occasion to be haled before the church that they may make a show.

And they like so well to talk with their religious teacher, and to be talked to, that they will even thank him, and manifest great complacency when he has been giving them a proper dressing for their sins.

Mr. Alexander, of Lahainaluna, had been one day administering a moral bastinado to a man for his wickedness. When he had done, "*Aloha*," said the culprit very complacently, "*Pomaikai au, ua kamailio kaua*" —*Love to you; I am happy, we two have had a talk.* And then he walked off, pocketing his reproof without any sign of malice or displeasure.

When Hawaiians talk in meetings, or among themselves, like Armado in the play, they are apt to draw out the thread of their verbosity finer than the staple of their argument. In words they are never wanting, and almost any Hawaiian can spin a yarn to any length, whether to his Maker or his fellow-men, however pinched he may be for the matter of thought.

Their religious teachers have to conform to their way in this particular; so that they, too, sometimes weave a very large piece of stuff out of a mere pinch or handful of the raw material of thought. But such attenuated fabrics hardly wear better, or bear more using, than the native cloth. Perhaps there is about the same difference between right good sermons in English, and quite common ones in Hawaiian, as between a piece of good American domestics, and an Hawaiian kapa.

Natives now clothe their nakedness quite decently, both in kapas and cloth, wherever foreigners are; and it were a good sign if they were as careful, at such places, to cover up their moral turpitude, and as much ashamed to have it disclosed. But the truth is, when found out, they too often manifest very little or no shame. The blush of virtue, the genuine feeling so well described in the old Roman word *pudor*—Quidam rubor nativus et incalescentia genuina—you seldom see.

They will often hold their heads as high after being

exposed in gross sins as ever before. Such cases, and the fall every now and then of persons who have had much care bestowed on them, and for whom high hopes have been fondly cherished, must make the heart of a faithful missionary very sad. He has need often to say with the Psalmist, *My soul, wait thou only upon God: my expectation is from him.*

One of the deacons at Waialua was convicted not long ago of having promised certain individuals to get them into the church for a consideration of money. The deacon was to tell them beforehand what to say in answer to the examining questions of the pastor.

This *hookamani*, as it is called, or deceitfulness of Hawaiians, stumbles and distresses some of the pastors more than is meet. To me it seems nothing more than should be naturally expected, nor will it, we think, be very wonderful if sin should continue to embarrass missionaries, and unexpected developments of wickedness to give them pain, till the world's end, or the times of millennium! Whoever thinks otherwise, or imagines, at home or abroad, that there is any people or any situation without stumbling-blocks, or any royal way of converting the world, is reckoning without his host. In one shape or another, he will find everywhere the "Peahen."

The present resident missionaries at Waialua, of 1850, are Rev. Messrs. Emerson and Gulick, with their wives. The number of church members in regular standing is six hundred and eighteen. Whole number admitted from the beginning, on profession of faith in Christ, seven hundred and seventy-three. The contributions there, for benevolent purposes, in the two years prior to May, 1848, were nine hundred and two dollars, of which five hundred and fifty-two dollars were in cash. In the nine common schools of the district there are ten teachers, and three hundred scholars.

A few years ago Mr. Locke had charge of a manual labor school at Waialua of twenty-one boys, which he was conducting with the business tact and energy for which he was distinguished, and with efficient aid rendered by a "prudent wife." The pupils had raised their food, and cultivated seven acres of sugar-cane. They ground the crops on the premises, and boiled the juice into syrup, the sale of which more than supported the school.

It was yet an experiment in a nascent state, but at the time of its suspension it had cost the Board nothing, and had a balance of several hundred dollars in its favor. The industry and working habits of the lads, under skilful supervision, were becoming effective, and their proficiency in useful knowledge considerable, through oral instruction given them while at work, and two hours daily study.

It was fairly under way, and giving promise of great usefulness, just as the providence of God, in the death of Mr. Locke, broke it up. By one stroke of disease, the vigorous wife and mother was taken away in the midst of her days and usefulness. By another, the robust husband and father, the youngest of the Mission, was suddenly cut down a year after, only a few days before he was going to embark for America with his three little daughters.

The orphans are providentially cared for and adopted in the family of Mr. Locke's missionary associate, Rev. A. B. Smith, now returned and resettled in the ministry in the United States.

After nearly encompassing the island of Oahu, I have returned to the Metropolis by way of Ewa, the station of Rev. Mr. Bishop. It is not far from mid-way between Waialua and Honolulu, twelve miles from the one, and eighteen from the other. Besides his church, and those at Kaneohe and Waialua, there are two others without a resident pastor, at Hauula and Waianae;* the one having one hundred and eighty members, and the other two hundred and seventy-one; most of whom were set off from the parent churches at Waialua and Ewa.

The church at the latter place, by the minutes of 1848, has in regular standing one thousand five hundred and fifty-eight members. The whole number received on examination is one thousand nine hundred and four, of whom one thousand five hundred and twelve have been dismissed to other churches, one hundred and

* Stephen Waimalu was ordained, Sept. 25th, 1850, pastor of the church and people of Waianae. In giving him a call to settle among them as their pastor, they pledged themselves to raise annually for his support $150. Waimalu is the third native who has been ordained to preach the Gospel at these Islands within ten months.

twenty-nine have died, and two hundred and fifteen remain excommunicated. One thousand dollars were contributed for benevolent purposes in the two years prior to 1848.

For several years before the present experiment of independency by the Hawaiian churches was under way, the station at Ewa was virtually supported by the avails of the mission herd turned to butter-making, under the management of Mrs. Bishop.

At their General Meeting in 1843, the Mission resolved, "That although we consider the salary allowed us by the Board a bona fide salary, still, in our character as missionaries, we are a peculiar people, having wholly consecrated ourselves to the Lord for the spread of the Gospel in the earth; and however it may be proper for other men to engage in speculations, and accumulate property, we cannot consistently with our calling engage in business for the purpose of private gain.

"We therefore deem it inexpedient that members of our body should possess private herds, and resolve that the mission herds be continued, and that those who are destitute be furnished with a reasonable number of cattle out of the herds or the funds of the mission; and that all the cattle, horses, and carts, held by us, be regarded as the property of the American Board, and that the herds be not allowed to increase beyond what is needed for the comfort of the mission."

In May, 1848, we find the sense of the Mission at General Meeting, expressed thus: "That we consider the salary allowed us by the Board, is to be used by us according to our own discretion; accountable only to God, our own conscience, and an enlightened public sentiment; and that all rules of the Mission which may be inconsistent with this principle, be rescinded."

Mr. Bishop, the pastor of Ewa, was one of the first reinforcement, along with Mr. Richards, in 1823. It affords one sincere pleasure to see the two oldest missionaries* now on the ground giving evidence, in their vigorous health and due proportions, of having lived happily and spent well in their good work. After having reared families, founded churches, endured opposition, and borne the burden and heat of the day, they are still the most hearty and hale-looking men of the mission. May God keep them in like prosperous estate for yet many years!

As the Senate and people of Rome used to decree concerning the men who had done their country service, *ut meruissent bene de Republica*, that they had deserved well of the Republic, so may it be declared with like truth of these men and their co-workers, who have continued faithful, that they have deserved well of the American churches, in whose behalf they willingly went on foreign service, when it was a very different undertaking from what it is now.

Mr. Bishop has things to tell of early heathenism, and of the habits of foreigners in those days, to make both the ears of those who hear thereof to tingle. He was one of the deputation that went round Hawaii with Mr.

* Messrs. Bishop and Thurston.

Ellis, in 1824, and his means of becoming acquainted with the traits and abominations of heathenism, and self-made heathen from Christian lands, have been equal to any man's.

It is all the more painful, therefore, to hear him avow the opinion that the licentiousness of young people out of the church is as great now as it ever was, and that early depravity, more than any thing else, is depopulating the nation, by prematurely wasting its productive powers. Out of the whole population of this island of Oahu, twenty-one thousand three hundred and sixty-three, there are only four thousand nine hundred and thirty-one persons under fifteen years of age. There are only four hundred and twenty-eight families that have three or more children, and there is not one child on an average to a family throughout the island.

In what light the Mission generally regard it, may be seen by the report of a committee on moral reform, as follows: That in their opinion the present time calls for very special and efficient measures for the suppression of licentiousness* among this people, and especially

* A very pertinent sermon was preached at the Bethel, in Honolulu, on the evening of the last day of 1843, by the missionary, Rev. Mr. Armstrong. It was on the duty of foreigners to the Hawaiian nation; the text, Jer. xix. 7: *And seek the peace of the city whither I have caused you to be carried away captives, and pray unto the Lord for it; for in the peace thereof shall ye have peace.* It was published by request in "The Friend," and it were well to have it hung up in the shop and office of every man that goes to live at the Sandwich Islands. Among other excellent sentiments and duties aptly enforced, he urges it as obligatory on all residents and visitors to oppose vice, and do all they

among the youth, and they would recommend: 1. That the pastors of the several churches take special pains to instruct the parents belonging to their respective churches and congregations upon this subject, and urge them to provide separate apartments for the different

---

can to deliver the nation from it, and especially intemperance, licentiousness, and gambling. On the middle one of this triad of vices, he speaks forcibly after this wise:

"Would you measure the evils which have come upon this people from this quarter? Look abroad over the length and breadth of the land, and inquire after the multitudes who once inhabited villages now deserted—where are they? Why do you meet so few children in the streets? and why are so many diseased, and sink into premature graves? After long observation and intimate acquaintance with the natives, I am of opinion that the diseases consequent upon the vice of which I now speak, have contributed more than all other causes put together to depopulate these fair Islands, and produce the miseries which the inhabitants now suffer. And what it concerns us particularly to consider is, that these diseases, with all their deadly effects, were introduced here by the licentiousness of men from Christian lands; and for the untold evils which have resulted from them to this unsuspecting people, such men are responsible."

In this opinion the author has the concurrence of all the missionaries, and of every careful inquirer into the causes of the nation's decay, and it is with propriety that he argues at the close—

"If our reasoning in this discourse be correct, what a solemn account will they have to render at the bar of God, who have taken a course directly contrary to that which God requires! I refer to men who have come to these shores from Christian lands, and done evil instead of good; men whose general course of life has been to sink the natives deeper in degradation and misery; to encourage them in their vices, and teach them vices they never knew before, and make heathenism ten-fold more heathenish. For all these things will not God call them into judgment? Are those dark deeds of past years all forgotten? The avenger of blood in Israel did not more resolutely and swiftly pursue the man-slayer, than evil pursues such men. If they are not overtaken in this life, they will be in the next."

sexes in their families, and watch over the children with more than common solicitude in reference to this crying sin of the land; that pastors also use all feasible means to render the institution of marriage honorable and popular among the people.

2. That the teachers of our seminaries and schools form societies among their scholars similar to the plan of "Juvenile Temperance Societies," and make vigorous effort to render the sin of licentiousness, in all its forms, odious and unpopular. 3. That a pledge be adopted which shall be alike in all the Islands, and that the signers of this pledge be furnished with some badge of their membership.

The Hawaiian government does not do so much to suppress the vice of licentiousness at the present time, nor is it so strong to keep good morals by law, as under the energetic administrations of Kaahumanu, at Honolulu, and of Hoapili at Lahaina. With more of liberty, the maxim is now in vogue by importation, that a man's house and premises are his castle, and that a constable has no right to enter them without a warrant. But *then*, on the least suspicion of evil in progress, officers would venture anywhere unresisted, and hale offenders to justice; and so vigilant were they, that vice had to skulk, and was driven out of many a hiding-place.

Once in the time of shipping, Hoapili sent all the women of Lahaina off to the other side of the mountain, and forbade their reappearing on the side where the ships were, under the penalty of imprisonment. Government now is not so despotic, and the Hawaiians of 1850 would not, probably, tolerate a measure that a mere word would have executed in 1824.

With written laws, and more of civil liberty and religion, there is less of personal restraint, and more freedom on the part of the governed, to practise wicked works with them that work iniquity. Houses of infamy are winked at and allowed at Honolulu, on the plea that they have become a necessary evil just as in all other countries, and the arm of government, in which both law and religion have vested the authority to suppress vice, bears the sword in vain as to this species of immorality, provided only it be not caught openly.

This ought not to be, either here or in any other State where there are good laws relative to lewdness. For it is not one of those things of which Milton says, "The law must needs be frivolous which goes to restrain things uncertainly, and yet equally, working to good and evil; and were I the chooser, a dram of well-doing should be preferred before many times as much the forcible hindrance of evil-doing: For God surely esteemeth the growth and perfection of one virtuous person, more than the restraint of ten vicious." But it is a palpable and positive evil, unmixed with good. It is evil only continually. And they, in any community, who, having the administration of law in their hands, do not execute it, but suffer houses that are the way to hell, going down to the chambers of death, to entertain the harlot and the young man void of understanding, they are responsible for the wreck of morals, and the ruin of souls there made. It is THEY who will have to answer for *the many wounded, yea, the strong men slain there, and those guests in the depths of hell!*

The plea of virtue and humanity in respect to what is called a "necessary evil" like this, is, that the prevalence of an acknowledged vice, and the consequent lucrativeness of pandering to it in seaport towns, are no good reason for letting off or lightly punishing one found guilty of it. If a crime were of such a nature that nobody would ever be tempted to repeat it, that circumstance might fairly be urged in bar of any severe or exemplary punishment therefor; but to hold the proneness of depraved humanity to any vice an excuse for those, who deliberately devote their lives to its extension and facilitation, making it a source of affluence, as many do in cities, and living in luxury upon its filthy profits; or to argue gravely that brothels are a necessary consequence of the growth of cities, and cannot therefore be suppressed, this is a perversion of equity and good policy little short of monstrous.

Such reasoning would subvert all morality and virtue whatever, and would excuse any crime, let it be but common, fashionable, and well fortified. Yea, 'twould "sugar o'er the devil himself," and all his devices.

We commend to honorable magistrates at Honolulu and elsewhere the reasonings of the Duke in the moral play called Measure for Measure:

> We have strict statutes, and most biting laws,
> Which for these fourteen years we have let sleep;
> Even, like an overgrown lion in a cave,
> That goes not out to prey. Now, as fond fathers,

Having bound up the threatening twigs of birch,
Only to stick it in their children's sight
For terror, not for use; in time the rod
Becomes more mocked than feared: *So our decrees,*
*Dead to infliction, to themselves are dead,*
*And liberty plucks justice by the nose;*
The baby beats the nurse, and quite athwart
Goes all decorum.
CORRECTION AND INSTRUCTION MUST BOTH WORK,
ERE THIS RUDE BEAST WILL PROFIT.

# CHAPTER XIII.

## RETROSPECTIVE VIEW OF A QUARTER CENTURY IN THE HEART OF THE PACIFIC.

God be with thee, gladsome Ocean!
How gladly greet I thee once more—
Ships and waves, and ceaseless motion,
And men rejoicing on thy shore!
O ye hopes, that stir within me,
Health comes with you from above!
God is with me, God is in me!
I cannot die, if life be love.

S. T. Coleridge.

We join ship and weigh anchor—Life and the world seen from below and from aloft—Differences in the view made by differences in the position and personal estate of the beholder—Light from eternity colored by the stained glass of the mind—Hope for the convalescent—Holding a telescope to the past—The great landmarks—Astonishing statistics of progress—Consecutive review of civilization and Christianity in the Heart of the Pacific—Detail of results and fruits, economic, literary, and religious—Work to be done projected—True relation and uses of the Sandwich Islands to America—Necessary leaning of the one upon the other for years to come—Disastrous effects to be apprehended if the prop should be withdrawn—The true policy of the Christian Church in the missionary enterprise—Purposes of Providence in the Island World—Chain of events—Outlook upon the future—Probable type of society—Transplanted Puritanism—Strict Sabbath-keeping—Anecdote of the governor of Oahu—Facts illustrative of national habits—First law the Decalogue—A change too great to be credited—To whom and what the people ascribe it—Unbounded confidence reposed in their religious teachers—First experiments by the chiefs—Fruits of the trial—Unparalleled instance of a moral ascendency—Illustrative anecdote of the present king—Traducers silenced and put to shame—Position of dignity and eminence—How attained and the ends to be answered by it—Relations of the Hawaiian Islands to China, California, Mexico, and South America—Vista of futurity opened—Conjectures ventured—Ground of their fulfilment—Falsehoods met—Shafts of calumny repelled—Counter testimony—Historians noticed—Volume concluded.

He who has had much experience of suffering and sorrow, who has walked thoughtfully a while in the valley of humiliation and adversity, after treading with eager hope and ambition the heights of prosperity, or the broad table-land of ordinary success, has learned how differently human life and the world look, from the contrasted points of elevation and depression.

The difference is not greater between a wide midsummer landscape, viewed from some commanding eminence, stretching away on one side into the distant mellow haze of noon-tide, and on the other half hidden, but its beauty not marred, by interposing drifts of vapor; and a part of that landscape seen close at hand from some exposed nook in the same, where the clouds are dropping a drizzling rain, where distance, that lent to the view its enchantment, has passed into plain reality, and things appear barren and bare as they are, under all the circumstances of discomfort and disadvantage that invest the place of the beholder.

There are few thinking men who have lived long, that are so happy as not to know what a change is made in the aspect of things outward, by changing spirits, feelings, health, and moods of mind. There are few who have not sojourned a while both in the lights and shades of human life. *Invisibilia non decipiunt;* but the things of time and sense, plans and prospects of life, the aspects and colors of the world, all the dear objects of human pursuit, continually change and delude.

Even the best of men, whose faith in eternal realities is constant, whose hope is steadfast in God, who have learned to put under feet the lying vanities of time, and to walk by a light from eternity, whose eye is cast upward and onward, and their habitual aim is to please God—even they find the hues of feeling tinging the objects of faith, much more giving color to all earthly prospects, like light falling through stained glass; and those hues often changing with variations of bodily health and outward circumstances.

> "The soul hath power, through God's mysterious plan,
> To mould anew and to assimilate
> The outward incidents that wait on man,
> And make them like his hidden, inward state.
> If there's a storm within, then all things round
> The inward storm to clouds and darkness changes;
> But inward light makes outward light abound,
> And o'er external things in beauty ranges.
> If but the soul be right, submissive, pure,
> It stamps whate'er takes place with peace and bliss;
> If fierce, revengeful, and unjust, 'tis sure
> From outward things to draw unhappiness."

I call to mind those remarkable lines of Shelley, worthy of a place with some of the best in Shakspeare or Milton, for the extraordinary combination of delicacy and vastness in this imagination:

> Life, like a dome of many-colored glass,
> Stains the white radiance of eternity.

The difference between my own feelings while leaving Honolulu now, in improved health and spirits, and those with which I approached it more than a year ago, a weary, sea-tossed invalid, is greater than can be told. Depressed and anxious, I was then saying—

> Ah! what avails all other earthly good!
> How tasteless whatsoever can be given,
> When health and drooping spirits go amiss!

God be praised, from whose blessing it comes, that now heart, and hope, and brighter prospects all hanging upon that pregnant old Saxon word HEALTH, give a new face to every thing. Brightening the eye, and investing with its cheerful green even things external, it makes those frowning old craters and barren hill-sides in the vicinity of Honolulu, fairly look verdant, as I gaze on them for the last time, while our anchor is weighing, and recall the propitious providences and friends I have there found.

The gentle readers who may perchance have followed me with pleasure in these wanderings through the Heart of the Pacific, will now take a retrospective glance at facts, through the telescope I hold to them in this chapter, in order that we may see what has been done, and is now doing for the improvement of the Sandwich Island kingdom, and to consider what remains to be done in order to complete the work of Christianizing and civilizing the Hawaiian race.

We have spent some time at all of the nineteen missionary stations but one where there are resident missionaries, except on the island of Kauai. We have surveyed missionary and native life under various aspects, and have become somewhat acquainted with the modes and means of operation upon the native mind, and their results; and with the trials and difficulties which the missionary has to contend with.

We have mingled with the people in the house and by the way, in the field and the school, at their work and their play, in the meeting for religious inquiry and at the public sanctuary. We have seen by observation what they now are, and we have heard from others what they once were. And in instituting our final comparison between the Heart of the Pacific as it was and is, or between times now and times that were, when the first missionaries landed at Kailua, we will take the state of progress found at the lapse of just one quarter of a century, as indicated by a careful survey and comparison of statistics derived on the spot.

In the first place, there labored at the Sandwich Islands from 1820 to 1844, at different times, sixty-one male and sixty-seven female missionaries, who performed in all ten hundred and eighty-eight years of missionary service. By these there were expended $608,865 in their outfit, support, and missionary work. After twenty-five years from the first settling of missionaries among a race of the very lowest savages, there were to be seen erected forty permanent dwelling-houses, two printing-offices and binderies, with which were connected .four printing-presses; four commodious seminary and school buildings, all which, together with large and valuable lands attached to them, were the property of the American Board of Commissioners for Foreign Missions.

Besides these results of Christian industry and perseverance, permanent stone Meeting-houses were found erected at almost every station, by the united skill and resources of missionary and people, giving and laboring voluntarily; and about three hundred and seventy-five school-houses. The Hawaiian tongue had been mastered, we might almost say created, and reduced to writing, and one half the adult population taught to read. There had been established four hundred and three public schools, in which seventeen thousand four hundred and forty children and youth were being instructed.

The entire Bible had been translated from the original tongues, and there had been printed fifty-two thousand copies of the New Testament, and twenty thousand of the Old, besides several editions of one and ten thousand copies of fragmentary portions of the Scriptures, before the entire translation was completed. Up wards of seventy other different works, large and small, had been compiled and issued from the press, and the total number of pages printed at the missionary presses up to 1844, were twenty-two million sixty-one thousand seven hundred and fifty.

There had been organized twenty-five independent native churches, and there had been received to them, on examination, thirty-one thousand four hundred and nine persons, of whom there were then living in regular standing twenty-two thousand six hundred and fifty-two, being more than one-fifth of the entire population of the Islands.

Besides these educational results that can be condensed into statistics, it should be added as a part of their education as a people, that the institutions of the Sabbath and of Christian marriage had been firmly established; government had been rendered comparatively just and stable; a good written constitution and laws had been enacted; life and property were rendered secure; the country's industry and resources were beginning to be developed. The Hawaiian nation's independence had been acknowledged by other nations, and it was admitted into the fraternity of Christian States. The commerce of the Islands, that is, the value of its commercial exchanges, or bills negotiated there for the supply of ships, had grown from little or nothing to two hundred thousand dollars, while the yearly net revenue of the kingdom had reached to seventy thousand dollars, and the annual consumption of foreign goods was one hundred and seventy-five thousand dollars.

For the educational force of the nation there were found employed at the lapse of the first quarter of a century, as religious teachers of the Hawaiian people, or in other missionary service among them, six unmarried and forty married missionaries, having families to the number of one hundred and twenty children. There were five hundred and forty-eight native school-teachers, themselves first taught by the missionary educators. There were four boarding-schools or seminaries, having two hundred and seventy-six pupils. There were two families formerly in the service of the Mission changed to that of the government, but devoted to the improvement of the Hawaiian race.

What then remained to be done before the Sandwich Islands could cease to be missionary ground, and what still remains, in order to complete the education of the Hawaiians, is, more thoroughly to instruct and Christianize the common people; to train up an educated native ministry which the people shall support; to reform the national habits of living; to inculcate upon the sexes modesty and chastity; to efface the dreadful characters of pollution and death, which heathenism has been burning in for ages upon the Hawaiian constitution; to introduce more extensively the improvements and arts of civilization; to develop the country's agricultural resources, and to foster habits and institute new ways of industry.

In order to accomplish all this, there are needed both religious teachers, physicians, artisans, mechanics, and farmers, to lighten the load and do the undone work of worn and weary pastors; to man the institutions of learning, and to afford suitable medical aid to the people, and to the missionary stations remote from each other, and to teach the natives all the arts of peace.

If any man think that where so much has been done little remains to do, in the process of national instruction and elevation, and when he reads that within the last two years the different Hawaiian churches have contributed in cash nine thousand three hundred dollars for building and repairing their churches, supporting preaching and schools, and for other benevolent purposes—if he infer that, therefore, the great American Education Society can soon drop their Hawaiian pupils, we have only to say that a greater mistake could hardly be entertained.

That we may ere long leave the pastors to be supported, after they get there, in great part by the people, is undoubtedly true. But America must continue to supply the men and their outfits, and lend also a helping hand to educational institutions there for at least twenty years longer, and the leading minds in the education of the nation must be from abroad. We do not say that if the American Church should now withdraw its aid, and send to the Heart of the Pacific no more missionaries, that the light of the Gospel would go out along with the lamps of life in the present ministers, and the people all go back to heathenism, or over to the Roman Beast.

Such a result would be impossible; for truth has made too deep an impression, and taken too strong a hold, to be so soon effaced or uprooted. Spiritual life would still linger here and there; and though the leaven of the Gospel might in many cases turn sour and become rank Romanism, yet the salt of Divine truth would have been too widely diffused to let society change in the mass, either into the rottenness of Rome, or the Dead Sea of paganism.

Had missionaries there done nothing (like Schwartz in India) but *preach the Gospel*, this might be. But they have wisely translated and printed the Scriptures, and founded seminaries and schools; and the people would know too much to be befooled into baptized Romish heathenism, or led back blindfold into that sottish form of it which they forsook. They would probably soon fall into practical, lying infidelity, saying to them, what they like, Let us eat and drink, for to-morrow we die.

There would be just enough Christians among them to keep up the form of godliness without its power, and they would retain enough of outward religion to keep them from being feared like barbarians, by foreigners, while they would practise all uncleanness with greediness, and foreigners would join with them in digging the nation's grave with their lusts.

The fact that the Gospel has been fairly offered to a nation of more than one hundred thousand souls within much less than the period of one generation; that multitudes have embraced it with eagerness; that many have died in the faith of Jesus; that many live, the exemplary disciples of Christ, to praise him for having ever put it into the hearts of American Christians to send them the Gospel; and that a nation of besotted, letterless savages has been reformed, by its living educators, into an orderly nation of readers—all this, so far from allowing American philanthropy in the least to relax its efforts, is, as it were, for nothing else in the arrangements of Divine Providence, but to give the Church a standing proof, a visible demonstration, of what would follow from a proportionate outlay of Christian educational agencies upon every barbarous nation on the face of the earth. When it can be said that the Protestant school-master is abroad everywhere, as at the Sandwich Islands; when the teacher, the Christian minister, the editor, and the author—those four leaders in modern civilization—are planted together among all the tribes and families of man, as they now are side by side in the Heart of the Pacific, the education of the world for its golden age will have fairly begun.

The solid, social and religious progress of these heaven-blest Isles of the Pacific is every day becoming more apparent and decided; and soon will shine out clearly the part they are to bear in the Christianization of the great realms that border on the Pacific upon either shore, in the track of whose golden commerce they directly lie. Beyond all doubt, it is for some great end in Providence that they have been so remarkably Christianized, and time will duly develop all the links in the Providential chain of events, that shall yoke this best American missionary experiment with the triumphal chariot of the King of saints.

The Heart of the Pacific shall be one of its noblest trophies, as the conquering car of Emmanuel traverses our globe, in that dear and not distant period when the great voice from heaven is heard, saying, Lo, THE TABERNACLE OF GOD IS AMONG MEN: THE KINGDOMS OF THIS WORLD ARE BECOME THE KINGDOMS OF OUR LORD, AND OF HIS CHRIST; AND HE SHALL REIGN FOREVER AND EVER.

It is natural to remark here upon Sandwich Island life and religion, how the teachings and example of missionary instructors descended from the Puritans, and colonizing like them with their families, for a religious purpose, in the howling wilderness of heathenism, are bringing to pass a state of society that shall prove, we trust, in due time, whatever becomes of the native race, a reprint of Puritanism. There is the more reason to hope for this at the Hawaiian Islands, if the guns of Admiral Tromelin and other French commanders in the Pacific do only instruct *all* the inhabitants so effectively into the nature of Popery, that the influence of the twenty-five Romish priests there shall be neutralized, whose interests the fallen King of the French (Louis Philippe) instructed M. Dillon and the commanders of the French frigates to look after, and whose fidelity in so doing, at the cannon's mouth, Louis Napoleon has rewarded.

True missionary Protestant religion, as it appears in the home education of the family, as it is developed in the children of missionaries, of whom a remarkable proportion* have become Christians at the Sandwich Islands,

* Should the lives of the children of modern missionaries be all written, and compared with the sons and daughters of other Christians, we are persuaded that the preponderance of virtue, and piety, and success in life would be found largely in favor of the former. As prosperous or as happy as the child of a missionary, may yet become a proverb. The children of the Sandwich Island mission, being now upward of one hundred and fifty, have thus far been remarkably favored by Abraham's God. None of them, so far as can be learned, after much inquiry, have turned out poorly. Many of them adorn the Christian Church. Several of the sons have already become themselves foreign missionaries; others are in the process of training. And of the daughters arrived at adult age, there are already valued teachers and wives of ministers, and some delightful exhibitions of youthful piety, that promise much for time to come. Missionary stock will be as honorable to spring from in future times as that of the Puritan is now. May scions worthy of their sires be constantly rising in a long line of future posterity!

Of the whole number of missionary children living at the period when a calculation was made, about twenty years from the first organization of the Sandwich Island mission, eighty-eight were boys, seventy-two girls. Total, one hundred and sixty: whole number of parents, eighty-five; of families, forty-one; so that in about two-thirds of a generation as it is engrafted upon the natives, as it pervades their laws, as it bears upon their morals and upon the observance of the Sabbath, is more like strict old Puritanism than any other national exemplification of religion, which the world at present knows.

The outward keeping of the Sabbath is complained of by foreigners throughout the Islands, as puritanically strict, and it is undeniably much more so than in England or America at the present time. It is called the La Tabu, or the prohibited sacred day. No food is cooked on that day, it being all prepared on the Saturday previous, no fires are kindled, no canoes are paddled. They neither fish nor till the land, and if they are on a journey, they uniformly stop over the Sabbath. I remember to have been at a missionary station when the church in full assembly, and not moved to it immediately by their pastor, adopted this resolution: "That where the Sabbath finds us on a journey, there we will stop and keep the holy day."

Commander Wilkes, of the United States Exploring Squadron, found considerable inconvenience in his ascent of the great mountain of Mauna Loa, the highest volcanic dome in the Pacific, from the natives' unwillingness to travel or work upon the Sabbath. This is owing in part to the fact that when the chiefs, in the process of instruction by their religious educators,

the increase has been one hundred and seventy-five per cent. At the same ratio of increase the descendants of these missionaries in one hundred years would amount to 59,535.

began to feel the necessity of having some written laws, and asked the missionaries very naturally what they should be, they gave them a copy of the Decalogue, then recently translated. This the chiefs said was MAIKAI, i. e. good, and thus the Ten Commandments became the law of the land; and they are in force to this day, along with other written laws; so that a man is fined for unnecessary travel or work on the Sabbath.

The present rulers of the land, as well as the common people, know and acknowledge that it is to their missionary teachers, and the law of their God, that they owe every thing. The confidence they repose in them is, therefore, unbounded, and they sometimes evince a gratitude and love that are truly affecting.

From the outset of the missionary enterprise, the chiefs watched the missionaries with a scrutinizing eye, and agreed to let them stay only for a stipulated time, having their fears awakened by the insinuations and libels of malicious foreigners. The result of the trial was perfectly satisfactory. They became thoroughly convinced that the missionaries were their true friends, having no end but their good; the confidence which they then learned to repose in them has never yet been shaken.

Among the common people, too, there are not a few who would at any time put their own lives in jeopardy, in order to defend their religious teachers. This has been practically put to the proof in several instances, when the safety of missionaries has been endangered by the brutality and malice of licentious foreigners, balked in their hopes of being able to give such full swing to passion as they once could, before the moral influence of missionaries had become so great upon chiefs and people.

The present king, Kamehameha III., was called upon one day a few years ago, by a lawless and rough whaling captain, a lewd man of the baser sort, much oftener met with then than now. He made no concealment of his dislike to the missionaries, and well knowing the king's former fondness for wine and libertinism, he urged him to cut loose from the restraints of the missionaries, and allow himself and people the same indulgences as formerly.

"Stop, (said the king,) did not your shadow fall on me as you came in there at my open door?" "Perhaps it did, and what of that?" "What, but if it had not been for the missionaries, you, or any one else whose shadow should thus fall on the king,* would very likely be a dead man the next hour."

This significant and unexpected turn put the stopper so tightly to the foreign captain's anti-missionary venom, that he had no more fault to find in that presence with the king's religious teachers.

He chose this method of expressing his approbation of the missionaries, and his confidence in them, well aware of the common imputation of their meddling in his politics, an imputation which was never true

* Alluding to one of the ancient tabus in force before the establishment of Christianity.

13*

in any other sense than is both honorable and meet for both. Very happily neither the King, nor his friends the missionaries, see any reason why the latter should avoid being implicated, by advice and recommendation, with government measures that are wise and good.

The present dignified and Christian position among the nations, of the Sandwich Island King and people, has been obtained under missionary guidance and ascendency. It is a position in a sense prophetic, as well as preparatory to the mission, yet to be fulfilled by them in the grand evolutions of Providence along the line of human redemption.

The unprecedentedly rapid and thorough evangelization of these Islands is not an event, which is to stand alone in the history of human progress, and of the Gospel of Christ. It has relations to Japan, to China, to Northeastern Asia, to California, to Mexico, and South America, that are yet to be unfolded, perhaps to the astonishment of the world. Through them may the prophecy yet be fulfilled in reference to Asia—GOD SHALL ENLARGE JAPHETH, AND HE SHALL DWELL IN THE TENTS OF SHEM.

This at least we may rationally conjecture, that it is for some great and wise end, which may soon appear, that the Heart of the Pacific has been so wonderfully prepared by Divine Providence and Grace. As an admitted voluntary member of the American Confederacy, it may soon become the great missionary printing dépôt for Eastern Asia, Japan, and its archipelago of islands, whence the word of God and the living missionary teacher shall make their grand entry into those wide realms of paganism, by a line of trans-Pacific American Steamers.

These lone islands of the Pacific, all unknown as they were to the whole civilized world, until the era of the American Revolution, may soon become such a centre of light, and civilization, and moral power to the vast regions bordering upon the Pacific, as the British Isles have been to the countries bordering upon the Atlantic.

If the men who have been instrumental in establishing Christianity there, do but labor on contentedly with all their might, we believe it will be found ere long that they and their native churches are having a mission to fulfil, in the work of bringing the pagan world to Christ, second to that of no other church in Christendom. The time may be near at hand, when it will be a greater honor and privilege to have preached the Gospel faithfully at the Sandwich Islands, and that, too, in the despised vernacular KANAKA MAOLE, than to have filled ambitiously the best Anglo-Saxon pulpit in England or America.

We say, then, with a slight accommodation to the noble island-band of devoted missionaries who have been laying the foundations in the Heart of the North Pacific for many generations, as it was said by Milton, of the Puritan hero,

Great things, O Islands, we expect of you!
Firm, faithful men of God, who through a cloud
Not of war only, but *detractions rude*,
Guided by faith and matchless fortitude,

To peace and truth your glorious way have ploughed,
And on the ground of pagan temples proud
Have reared God's trophies, and his work pursued!
* * * Yet much remains
To conquer still; peace hath her victories
No less renowned than war: new foes arise,
Threatening to bind our souls with secular chains:
Help us to save free conscience from the paw
Of hireling wolves, whose gospel is their maw.

In concluding this volume, I cannot but express the just sense of indignation, which an honest man should feel, at the meanness of those persons who will belie the labors of Christian missionaries, on the very field of their operations,—a field which mercantile men and officers of government are able to dwell in with safety, only because the patient missionary has been there before them, and, through God's blessing, changed in great part the character and manners of so recently depraved savages.*

* The following is the disinterested testimony of a late U. S. Consul at Honolulu, the Hon. Joel Turrill, formerly a member of Congress from the State of New York: "For several years," he says, "before leaving the United States, I had been disinclined to favor the efforts that were making to send missionaries abroad, believing that such efforts otherwise directed would be productive of much more good; but during my residence in these Islands I have been an attentive observer of the effects produced by those efforts on the Hawaiian race, and I am free to confess that my feelings upon this subject have undergone a material change. I find here as missionaries, individuals who, so far as my observations have extended, are worthy of their high calling; and the result of their labors, so apparent in the vast improvement in the moral and physical condition of its people, forces the conviction on my mind, that they have devoted themselves to their arduous duties with a zeal and singleness of purpose worthy of the great work in which they are

Every effort to traduce their characters and work, or the native churches they have been instrumental of gathering, should be met at once with an irresistible array of opposing evidence and conviction. It were right for the face of Christendom to gather blackness, at such malicious attempts to weaken the faith of the Church in the conduct or results of the glorious missionary enterprise—an enterprise which is yet to attract to itself more true nobility and enthusiasm, than have ever been carried into any enterprise undertaken under the sun. The missionary enthusiasm, which until now has been confined to a few heroic spirits, shall yet pervade the ranks of the Christian Church, disarm opposition, and inspire all hearts.

> The very spirit of the world is tired
> Of its own taunting question, asked so long,
> "Where is the promise of your Lord's approach?"
> The infidel has shot his bolts away,
> Till, his exhausted quiver yielding none,
> He gleans the blunted shafts that have recoiled,
> And aims *them* at the shield of Truth again.

But it is too late in the serious drama of the world's evangelization, for the blunted shafts of slander to retard its course. The testimony of unprejudiced men like the English Rear-admiral Thomas, Sir George Simpson,* Commander Wilkes and other officers of

---

engaged. I do not believe that another instance can be found, where, with the same amount of means, so much good has been done to any people in so limited a period."

* See note B.

the United States Exploring Squadron, saying nothing of the concurrent reports of a host of Christian travellers, is all on file before the world; and in the chancery of public opinion it will outweigh as many anonymous sheets of calumny, as would bridge the Pacific from Panama to Oahu.

If any reader be in quest of authentic Hawaiian annals, he will find his curiosity well gratified in the perusal of the late very full history, by Rev. Hiram Bingham, Hartford; or that by Mr. Jarves, issued in Boston, 1842; or a history by Rev. Sheldon Dibble, printed at the Lahainaluna mission press, Sandwich Islands. While they are each replete with information of substantial interest to the general reader, the last work is to the Christian perhaps the most valuable of the three.

We regard them all as well prepared seed-beds, from which the yet formless garden of Hawaiian history will largely draw. If in this volume there has been contributed one worthy plant, to be set out by the future historian in that fair garden; and if it has helped its readers to a correct view of the Heart of the North Pacific, as it was and is, the end of its author is fulfilled, and on it he inscribes

Χριστῷ Καὶ Εκκλησίᾳ.

# APPENDIX.

# APPENDIX.

WE give below a commercial view of the Heart of the Pacific, as contained in authentic statistics of Exports and Imports at the Sandwich Islands, for the year 1850, a tabular view of their educational and religious progress; also a documentary history of the late controversy with the French at the Hawaiian Islands; and a paper from the London Athenæum, on the comparative history and fortunes of the conquering race, that is so rapidly colonizing and becoming dominant upon the coasts and throughout the Isles of the Pacific, no less than of the Atlantic.

IMPORTS *for the year* 1850, *from the following countries:*

|  |  |
|---|---|
| California | $305,913.28 |
| United States | 283,037.49 |
| Great Britain | 63,987.69 |
| British Colonies | 114,782.11 |
| China | 109,124.19 |
| Chili | 58,097.84 |
| Manilla | 33,187.84 |
| Tahiti | 19,288.29 |
| Vancouver's Island | 15,942.59 |
| France | 7,633.48 |
| Columbia River, Sitka, Bremen, Kamtschatka, Callao, Bonin Isles | 24,063.90 |
| | $1,035,058.70 |

*Statement of Imports, Duties, and Exports claiming Drawback, at the Port of Honolulu, for the year* 1850.

| | Gross invoice value. | Gross Duties. | Value re-exported. | Return Duties. | Net consumption. | Net Duties. |
|---|---|---|---|---|---|---|
| Goods paying 5 per cent. duty, ......... | 920,677.48 | 46,035.58 | 28,233.31 | 1,129.82 | 892,441.17 | 44,905.76 |
| Spirits, wines, &c......................... | 24,451.94 | 112,568.03 | 14,593.41 | 85,557.30 | 9,858.53 | 27,010.73 |
| By Consuls and Missions, free,............ | 24,684.80 | | | | 24,684.80 | |
| Remitted, .......................................... | 49,572.00 | | | | 49,572.00 | |
| By whale-ships under $200 each,....... | 15,672.48 | | | | 15,672.48 | |
| | 1,035,058.70 | 158,603.61 | 42,82[illegible].72 | 86,687.12 | 992,228.98 | 71,916.49 |
| Add amount of spirits and wines in Bond Dec. 31, 1849, estimated at........... | 18,000.00 | 44,000.00 | | | 18,000.00 | 44,000.00 |
| | 1,053,058.70 | 202,603.61 | 42,82[illegible].72 | 86,687.12 | 1,010,228.98 | 115,916.49 |
| Deduct, spirits and wines now in bond which will probably be exported. Estimated at............................... | | | 3,70[illegible].00 | 24,000.00 | 3,700.00 | 24,000.00 |
| | 1,053,058.70 | 202,603.61 | 46,52[illegible].72 | 110,687.12 | 1,006,528.98 | 91,916.49 |

DOMESTIC EXPORTS *from Honolulu and Lahaina for the year* 1850.

HONOLULU and KAUAI.

| | | |
|---|---|---|
| Sugar, | lbs. | 597,831 |
| Molasses, | galls. | 34,900 |
| Syrup, | " | 9,000 |
| Coffee, | lbs. | 194,073 |
| Salt, | bbls. | 5,750 |
| Lime, | " | 100 |
| Beef, | " | 10 |
| Hides, | lbs. | 20,241 |
| Tallow, | " | 3,703 |
| Goatskins, | skins | 24,983 |
| Irish Potatoes, | bbls. | 5,331 |
| Sweet " | " | 4,178 |
| Onions, | " | 252 |
| Yams, | " | 144 |
| Arrow-root, | lbs. | 6,956 |
| Hay, | tons | 28½ |
| Pickles, | bbls. | 90½ |
| Coral, | blocks | 1,628 |
| Mustard-seed, | lbs. | 1,023 |

Cattle 50, Horses 2, Mules 1, Sheep 10, Goats 10, Swine 179, Fowls 49 doz., Turkeys 19 doz., Eggs 2,010 doz., Brooms 410 doz., Pumpkins 4,678, Melons 950, Cocoanuts 2,100, Cocoanut Door-mats 119, Wood 4 cords, Mat-bags 500, Oranges 22,000, Charcoal 69 bags.

Limes, Lime Juice, Peppers, Bananas, Poi, Butter, Rope, Furniture, and Sashes, ........ $603.33

Total value as per Manifests, ........ $139,007.79

LAHAINA.

| | | |
|---|---|---|
| Sugar, | lbs. | 152,407 |
| Molasses, | galls. | 18,955 |
| Syrup, | " | 66,577 |
| Coffee, | lbs. | 14,355 |
| Salt, | sacks | 1,912 |
| Lime, | bbls. | 80 |
| Irish Potatoes, | " | 46,626 |
| Sweet, " | " | 5,453 |
| Onions, | " | 1,606 |
| Yams, | " | 20 |
| Arrow-root, | lbs. | 2,676 |
| Pickles, | bbls. | 627 |
| Coral, | blocks | 1,428 |

Sheep and Goats 182, Swine 444, Fowls 86½ doz., Eggs 504 doz., Pumpkins 62,016, Cocoanuts 22,450, Oranges 117,500, Melons 4,610, Pine-apples 14,300, Cabbages 1,600, Sweetmeats 212 galls., Lime-juice 304 galls., Beans 64 bbls., Corn 5 bbls., Butter 157 lbs., Vinegar 168 galls., Wood 61 cords, Lumber 21,072 feet.

| | |
|---|---|
| Total value as per Manifests, from Lahaina, ........... | $241,314.84 |
| " " " Honolulu .......... | 139,007.79 |
| Value of Domestic Produce exported and furnished to ships at the three ports on the island of Hawaii, (estimated) ...................... | 20,000.00 |
| Domestic supplies furnished to 342 merchant vessels at Honolulu. Average $200 each..... | 68,400.00 |
| Domestic supplies furnished to 106 whale-ships (inside) at Honolulu. Average $250 each.... | 26,500.00 |
| Domestic supplies furnished to 13 ships of war and surveying vessels at Honolulu. Average $500 each ........................................ | 6,500.09 |
| Domestic supplies furnished to 112 whale-ships at Lahaina. Average $220 each................ | 24,640.00 |
| Domestic supplies furnished to 127 merchant ships at Lahaina. Average $80 each......... | 10,160,00 |
| Total value of domestic exports and supplies furnished at Honolulu and Lahaina, for the year 1850 .... ........................................ | $536,522.63 |

MEMORANDUM *of Spirituous Liquors which paid five dollars per gallon duty at the Custom-house in Honolulu, for consumption in the kingdom, during the years* 1847, 1848, 1849, *and* 1850. *And also the amount of each kind consumed during the year* 1850.

| | |
|---|---|
| 1847......3,271 gallons. | 1849......5,717 gallons. |
| 1848......3,443 " | 1850......8,252 " |

1850.

| | | |
|---|---|---|
| Brandy,........................................ | 6,484½ | gallons. |
| Gin, ........................................... | 1,159½ | " |
| Samshoo, (China,)............................. | 112 | " |
| Absinthe,...................................... | 74½ | " |
| Rum, ........................................... | 337¼ | " |
| Scotch Whisky,................................ | 84¼ | " |
| | **8,252** | " |

*Gross receipts at Custom-houses of Oahu, Maui, and Kauai, for* 1850.

HONOLULU.

| | |
|---|---|
| Import duties paid on Goods and on Spirits and Wines actually consumed, | $91,953.11 |
| Transit duties, | 443.42 |
| Harbor dues, | 12,644.54 |
| Stamps, | 2,579.50 |
| Fines and Forfeitures, | 877.46 |
| Interest, | 323.50 |
| Storage, | 3,245.15 |
| | $112,066,68 |
| HARBOR MASTER. | |
| Shipping and discharging Seamen, | 2,711.00 |
| Stamps, | 1,413.00 |
| | $116,190.68 |

LAHAINA.

| | |
|---|---|
| Import duties, | 2,323.48 |
| Transit duties, | 39.92 |
| Harbor dues, | 1,299.60 |
| Stamps, | 1,276.00 |
| Shipping Seamen, | 264.15 |
| | $5,203.15 |
| WAIMEA, KEALAKEAKUA, AND HILO. | |
| Stamps and Harbor dues, | 112.90 |
| | $5,316.05 |
| Add amount from Honolulu, | 116,190.68 |
| Total Receipts, | $121,506.73 |

MEMORANDUM *of Imports and Exports of Houses, House Frames, and Lumber of various descriptions, at Honolulu, during the years* 1848, 1849, *and* 1850.

IMPORTS.

| | 1848. | 1849. | 1850. |
|---|---|---|---|
| Boards, Plank, Joist, &c., | 809,038 ft. | 237,703 | 2,180,448 |
| Large Timber, | | | 145,550 |
| Oak Plank, | 8,230 | | 16,449 |
| Clapboards, | 5,000 | 25,250 | 112,393 |
| Pickets, | 9,500 | | 57,830 |
| Latns, | 44,500 | 155 | 1,687 |
| Palings and Battens, | | | 23,331 |

| | 1848. | 1849. | 1850. |
|---|---|---|---|
| Shingles,............................ | 543,500 | 673 | 2,087,450 |
| Door and window frames, blinds, and sashes. Valued,........... | | $296.63 | $821.90 |
| House frames,...................... | | | 171, No. |
| Houses, (complete, or nearly so,) | | | 169 |
| Total value as per Invoices,....... | $18,856.48 | $7,603.63 | $101,175.19 |

EXPORTS.

| | 1848. | 1849. | 1850. |
|---|---|---|---|
| Boards, Plank, Joist, &c.,............ | None. | 143,111 ft. | None.. |
| Clapboards,........................ | " | 5,000 | " |
| Laths,.............................. | " | 119,000 | " |
| Shingles,............................ | " | 171,000 | " |
| Door Frames and Sashes. Valued, | " | $997.81 | " |
| House frames,...................... | " | 1 | " |
| Bowling Alleys, complete,......... | " | 1 | " |
| Houses,............................. | " | 17 | " |
| Total value as per out'd Manifests, | " | $26,441.11 | " |

*Condition of the Revenue of the Hawaiian Kingdom, for the year ending 31st of March, 1851.*

| | |
|---|---|
| From cash on hand last year....................................... | $46,191.18 |
| The Bureau of Foreign Imposts ................................... | 118,901.38 |
| " Internal Commerce.............................. | 22,514.75 |
| " Internal Taxes.................................... | 52,455.26 |
| " Fees and Perquisites............................ | 15,314.72 |
| " Coasting Trade and Fisheries................. | 4,269.27 |
| " Government Realizations ...................... | 56,495.22 |
| " Fines and Penalties............................. | 14,404.25 |
| | $330,546.03 |

*Table of Disbursements.*

| | |
|---|---|
| For the King and Privy Council ..................................... | $19,966.16 |
| " Department of the Interior.................................. | 140,030.52 |
| " " Foreign Relations.......................... | 4,730.64 |
| " " Finance ........................................ | 15,080.08 |
| " " Public Instruction........................ | 28,825.07 |
| " " Law ............................................ | 10,106.84 |
| For miscellaneous expenses ........................................ | 10,106.84 |
| For amount disbursed on bills payable, less than has accrued on bills receivable.................................................. | 2,126.42 |
| | $250,707.56 |
| Balance.................................................. | $79,838.47 |

*Foreign Merchant Vessels, and Hawaiian Vessels from Foreign Voyages, entered at the Ports of Honolulu and Lahaina during the year* 1850.

| | HONOLULU. | | | | | | LAHAINA. | |
|---|---|---|---|---|---|---|---|---|
| Nation. | Number Inside Harbor. | Number Outside Harbor. | Tonnage Inside. | Tonnage Outside. | Total Number of Vessels. | Total Tonnage. | Number of Vessels. | Amount of Tonnage. |
| United States | 142 | 24 | 43,339 | 11,533 | 166 | 54,872 | 111 | ......... |
| Great Britain and Colonies | 102 | 16 | 19,618 | 4,559 | 118 | 24,177 | 6 | ......... |
| France | 4 | 4 | 929 | 1,371 | 8 | 2,300 | ......... | ......... |
| Tahiti | 7 | ......... | 367 | ......... | 7 | 367 | 1 | ......... |
| Peru | ......... | 2 | ......... | 1,300 | 2 | 1,300 | ......... | ......... |
| Norway | ......... | 2 | ......... | 475 | 2 | 475 | ......... | ......... |
| Hawaii | 14 | ......... | 1,732 | ......... | 14 | 1,732 | 8 | ......... |
| Chili | 8 | ......... | 1,283 | ......... | 8 | 1,283 | ......... | ......... |
| Russia | 3 | ......... | 838 | ......... | 3 | 838 | ......... | ......... |
| Spain | 2 | ......... | 600 | ......... | 2 | 600 | ......... | ......... |
| Mexico | 2 | ......... | 309 | ......... | 2 | 309 | ......... | ......... |
| Hanover | 3 | 1 | 400 | 160 | 4 | 560 | 1 | ......... |
| Belgium | 1 | ......... | 533 | ......... | 1 | 533 | ......... | ......... |
| Denmark | 2 | 1 | 215 | 233 | 3 | 448 | ......... | ......... |
| Bremen | 1 | ......... | 110 | ......... | 1 | 110 | ......... | ......... |
| Sweden | ......... | 1 | ......... | 400 | 1 | 400 | ......... | ......... |
| | 291 | 51 | 70,273 | 20,031 | 342 | 90,304 | 127 | ......... |
| | Number entered in 1849 | | | | 157 | ......... | 18 | ......... |
| | Increase in 1850 | | | | 185 | ......... | 107 | ......... |

## *Vessels of War and Government Surveying Vessels entered at Honolulu,* 1850.

| Date of Arrival. | Name. | Commander. | Nation. | Class. | Guns. | Where from. | Date of Departure. | Where bound. |
|---|---|---|---|---|---|---|---|---|
| Jan. 15, | Ewing, | McArthur, | U. S. Am. | Schooner, | | California *via* Hilo, | | California. |
| Feb. 26, | Wanderer, | Benjamin Boyd, | Gt. Britain, | Yacht, | 10 | Tahiti, | Mar. 10, | San Francisco. |
| May 6, | Herald, | Henry Kellett, | " | Sloop, | 22 | Mazatlan, | May 24, | Arctic Ocean. |
| June 6, | Swift, | Oldham, | " | Brig, | 6 | " | July 5, | Tahiti. |
| " 24, | Enterprise, | Rich. Collinson, C. B. | " | Bark, | | Plymouth, England, | June 30, | Kotzebue Sou. |
| " 29, | Bayonnaise, | Jurien de la Gravier, | France, | Corvette, | 24 | Macao, China, | July 4, | Tahiti. |
| July 1, | Investigator, | McClure, | Gt. Britain, | Bark, | | Plymouth, England, | " 4, | Kotzebue Sou. |
| " 3, | Cockatrice, | Rundle, | " | Schooner, | 6 | Mazatlan, | Aug. 18, | Valparaiso. |
| Oct. 16, | Herald, | Henry Kellett, C. B. | " | Sloop, | 22 | Port Clarence, | Oct. 30, | Hong Kong. |
| " 23, | Dolphin, | Thomas S. Page, | U. S. Am. | Brig, | 10 | Hong Kong, | Nov. 6, | San Francisco. |
| Nov. 10, | Falmouth, | Petigrew, | " | Sloop, | 24 | S. Francisco *via* Hilo | " 21, | South Pacific. |
| Dec. 13, | Serieuse, | Cosnier, | France, | Corvette, | 24 | San Francisco, | In port, | |
| " 25, | Baikaal, | Cousmin, | Russia, | Brig, | 4 | Ochotsk, | " | |

## *Whale-ships entered at the Ports of Honolulu and Lahaina during the year* 1850.

| HONOLULU. | | Tonnage. | Sperm Oil. bbls. | Whale Oil. bbls. | Whalebone. lbs. | LAHAINA. |
|---|---|---|---|---|---|---|
| American, | 106 | | | | | 105 |
| French, | 11 | | | | | 3 |
| Bremen, | 6 | 46,934. | 15,106. | 256,495. | 2,621,000. | 4 |
| British, | 2 | | | | | |

NOTE.—Nineteen of those entered at Honolulu anchored outside the reef, and did not come within the harbor.

A comparative view of the business of the Hawaiian Islands in the years 1849 and 1850, may be obtained from the following estimates and items, as found in the Hawaiian Government Paper of February 8th, 1851, published at Honolulu.

| | |
|---|---|
| Gross receipts at the Custom House, Honolulu, 1849....... | $79,802.75 |
| " " " 1850....... | 116,190.68 |
| Increase in 1850.......................... | 36,387.93 |
| Gross receipts at the Custom House, Lahaina, 1849......... | 3,330.70 |
| " " " 1850......... | 5,203.15 |
| Increase in 1850.......................... | 1,872.45 |
| Gross receipts at Hawaii and Kauai, 1849.................. | 97.87 |
| " " 1850.................. | 112.90 |
| Increase in 1850.......................... | 15.03 |
| Domestic exports from Honolulu and Kauai, 1849.......... | 89,743.74 |
| " " 1850.......... | 139,007.79 |
| Increase in 1850.......................... | 49,264.05 |
| Domestic exports from Lahaina, (estimated,) 1849.......... | 14,000.00 |
| " " 1850.......................... | 241,314.84 |
| Increase in 1850.......................... | 227,314.84 |
| Gross value of imports for 1849................................ | 729,739.44 |
| " " 1850................................ | 1,053,058.70 |
| Increase in 1850.......................... | 323,319.26 |
| Net consumption for 1849........................................ | 622,637.37 |
| " 1850........................................ | 1,006,528.98 |
| Increase for 1850.......................... | 383,891.61 |

*Value of Imports from different countries.*

| | 1849. | | 1850. |
|---|---|---|---|
| United States.................................. | $239,246.42 | ...... | $283,037.49 |
| California .................................... | 131,505.89 | ...... | 305,913.28 |
| Great Britain.................................. | 44,578.11 | ...... | 63,987.69 |
| British Colonies .............................. | 52,821.59 | ...... | 114,782.11 |
| China........................................... | 95,787.27 | ...... | 109,124.19 |
| Chili ............................................ | 87,356.05 | ...... | 58,097.84 |
| France........................................... | 23,455.78 | ...... | 7,633.48 |
| Tahiti ........................................... | 19,340.27 | ...... | 19,288.29 |
| Columbia River, (Vancouver's Island)... | 12,672.38 | .... .. | 15,942.59 |
| Hamburg ........................................ | 9,723.58 | .. .. | none. |
| Miscellaneous ................................. | 13,252.10 | .. .. | 24,063.90 |

The following are the principal items of domestic export for the years 1849 and 1850. The tables for 1849 do not give the exports from Lahaina in a separate list, as is the case for the year 1850. As few vessels loaded at that port, during 1849, direct for California, only 18 merchant vessels are reported as having arrived there; while in 1850, 127 arrived, a large proportion of which took in cargoes, or parts of cargoes, for California.

| | 1849. | | 1850. |
|---|---|---|---|
| Sugar, lbs | 653,820 | ...... | 750,238 |
| Molasses, gallons | 41,235 | ...... | 53,855 |
| Syrup, gallons | none | ...... | 75,577 |
| Coffee, lbs. | 28,231 | ...... | 208,428 |
| Salt, barrels | 2,866 | ...... | 6,000 |
| Lime, barrels | 906 | ...... | 180 |
| Beef, barrels | 158 | ...... | 10 |
| Hides, lbs | 2,512 | ...... | 20,241 |
| Tallow, lbs. | 17,403 | ...... | 3,703 |
| Goat-skins | 31,488 | ...... | 24,983 |
| Irish potatoes, barrels | 858 | ...... | 51,957 |
| Sweet potatoes, barrels | 306 | ...... | 9,631 |
| Onions, barrels ............about | 200 | ...... | 1,858 |
| Yams, barrels | none | ...... | 164 |
| Pumpkins ............about | 1,000 | ...... | 66,694 |
| Cocoanuts | none | ...... | 23,550 |
| Oranges ............about | 10,000 | ...... | 139,500 |
| Melons ............about | 1,000 | ...... | 5,560 |
| Pineapples | none | ...... | 14,300 |
| Fowls | none | ...... | 1,626 |
| Turkeys | 500 | ...... | 228 |
| Swine | none | ...... | 623 |
| Arrow-root, lbs. | none | ...... | 9,632 |
| Eggs, dozen | not stated | ...... | 2,514 |

These are the most important items of export, and it will be seen that the great increase over the previous year has been in what may properly be called the staples of the Islands—sugar, molasses, syrup, salt, Irish and sweet potatoes. Vegetables of less importance and fruits have greatly increased, and arrow-root has again taken its place among the exports from the Islands; and of these articles the production can be almost unlimited. Of syrup none was reported in 1849, and this is an article to which some of the plantations are now directing their whole attention, and which is more profitable than sugar.

Both the increase of the receipts at the Custom-house, and the extraordinary increase of exports, especially from Maui, are gratifying indications of advance in resources and wealth, and they are calculated to add a new stimulant to the coffee-growers and sugar-planters of the Islands. During the first half of the year, the demand for coffee and sugar was so great, that had the quantity on hand been millions of pounds, it would have found a ready sale, at prices highly remunerative. And such, we apprehend, will continue to be the case in future years. At the present moment prices are greatly depressed, and the market at San Francisco is overstocked with these articles; but this very fact will withhold shipments from other countries, and the present stock will be reduced, and command a paying price. When that moment arrives, and it is sure to come, these Islands are the nearest point from whence the demand can be supplied, and, with the speed of steam navigation, Hawaiian staples can be transported thither at the very moment they will pay best. Oregon is fast filling up, and California will, without a doubt, steadily increase in population for many years to come, though not so rapidly as during the past two years. Consumption of the staple products of the Islands will keep pace with the increase of population, and those articles which are peculiar to the tropics will always be in demand to the full extent of the ability to supply. The export of vegetables may not increase, or even come up to that of the year 1850; but fruits, coffee, sugar, syrup, and molasses, there is no doubt, will be required in a constantly increasing ratio, and will command a price that will well remunerate the producers at the Sandwich Islands.

The following comparative view will show how, in another way, the products of the Islands are in increasing demand.

Whole number of vessels that visited the Islands from 1848–'50:—

| | 1848. | 1849. | 1850. |
|---|---|---|---|
| Merchant vessels | 90 | 180 | 469 |
| Whalers | — | 274 | 237 |
| Vessels of war, &c. | — | 13 | 13 |

The supplies furnished to these vessels amounted in 1849 to $81,340.
" " " in 1850 to 140,000.

Almost the whole of these supplies were raised from the soil, and consequently their value was so much added to the ability of the people to purchase the imports of the merchants, and to increase their own comfort.

The increased value of exports and supplies has, however, been more than equalled by the increase of imports. From California and the British colonies they have more than doubled; and the aggregate increase from all countries, for consumption, amounts to $383,891.61.

| | |
|---|---|
| Increase of exports and supplies | 335,238.89. |
| Excess of imports | 58,652.72. |
| The total value of imports for consumption is... | $1,006,528.98. |
| The total value of exports and supplies | 536,522.63. |
| Excess of imports | 470,005.35. |

Of this excess a considerable amount has been in sugar-mills, and agricultural implements for the cultivation of the soil, admitted duty free by government. Another portion was introduced by consuls and missions, for consumption and not for sale. How has the balance (say $400,000) been paid for? In part by the direct introduction of capital invested in plantations, &c.; in part by profits derived from shipments abroad on island account; and in a great degree by money put in circulation by strangers, returned Hawaiians, captains, officers, and crews of ships, which do not come into the calculation of "supplies." There may be a small debt against the Islands on account of imports, but it probably does not exceed the amount of goods still remaining unsold in the hands of importers.

These statistics show progress, and awaken the hope that the Hawaiian Islands have entered upon a course of increasing prosperity, depending almost wholly upon the development of their agricultural resources. To this point the most earnest attention should be given by Government and the people of the Islands. The great desideratum of a ready market now exists at their own doors; and if the demand is not promptly met, it will not be because Providence has not furnished all the means and appliances for so important an object.

From the Reports of Keoni Ana, Minister of the Interior, and of Robert Crichton Wyllie, Minister of Foreign Relations, we learn that the number of foreigners who have taken the oath of allegiance during the year 1850 is 151, citizens of the following countries:—

| | | | |
|---|---|---|---|
| United States | 69 | China | 12 |
| Great Britain | 37 | South America | 2 |
| France | 4 | East Indies | 5 |
| Portugal | 5 | West Indies | 4 |
| Germany | 5 | Polynesia | 4 |
| Denmark | 2 | Africa | 1 |
| Prussia | 1 | | |

The amount of goods sold at auction in the Hawaiian Kingdom during the same year was $1,060,760.38.

The amount received for public licenses is $24,145.

In real estate, the number of royal patents granted during the year is 314.

To aliens............ 25. To subjects............ 319.

By the annexed tables can be seen the number of acres sold on each island, and the gross amount of their price.

| Islands. | Acres. | Amount. |
|---|---|---|
| Oahu | 15,161 | $19,775.20 |
| Maui | 9,338 | 17,927.86 |
| Hawaii | 3,196 | 3,490.68 |
| Kauai | 2,446 | 2,699.58 |
| Molokai | 1,371 | 349.00 |
| Total | 31,518 | $44,352.32 |

The avails to the Treasury of the Interior Department, during the year 1850, have been $84,350.65.

We add to the foregoing exhibition of the commerce and trade of the Sandwich Islands, a tabular view also of educational and religious progress at the Heart of the Pacific.

During the year ending May 1, 1850, 851 members were received on examination into 17 of the churches at these Islands. The number admitted on examination to the churches at Kaanapali, Waiane, and Waimea, and on Molokai, is not reported. The largest number added to any one church is 369, to the first church in Honolulu. This church received, besides, 106 members from other churches.

19 of the churches report a loss by death of 1277 members; while 18 of these churches report the baptism of only 295 children. In connection with 17 of them, there were 1354 marriages.

The following list of contributions to purposes of benevolence shows the amount given by these churches, and the objects to which it was appropriated. The list is not complete, no report having been received from five of the churches.

| | | | |
|---|---|---|---|
| KAUAI.—*Waioli*, | | Monthly concert, for native preacher at Koloa | $15.00 |
| | | Monthly concert, for repairs of church | 46.50 |
| | | For shingling of church | 173.50 |
| OAHU.—*Kaneohe*, | | Objects not stated | 500.00 |
| *Waialua*, | | For French Protestant Mission | 30.86 |
| | | For meeting-houses | 293.00 |
| *Honolulu*, | 2d ch., | Monthly concert | 108.69 |
| | | For support of pastor | 320.00 |
| *Honolulu*, | 1st ch., | Salary of pastor | 500.00 |
| | | Repair of houses for pastor | 500.00 |
| | | To a native preacher | 73.00 |
| | | To Mr. Thurston, to repair loss by fire | 25.00 |
| | | For French Protestant Missions | 37.00 |

| | | |
|---|---|---|
| *Honolulu,* 1st ch., | For American Board | $90.00 |
| | For meeting-house in Kau | 30.00 |
| | For meeting-house in Kohala | 50.00 |
| MAUI.—*Lahaina,* | For support of pastor | 562.00 |
| | French Protestant Missions | 76.00 |
| | American Board | 50.00 |
| | For church communion | 44.75 |
| | For meeting-house on Lanai | 35.00 |
| | For other objects | 120.00 |
| | For seraphina, amount not stated | |
| *Molokai,* | For support of pastor | 420.00 |
| | For Kohala meeting-house | 102.00 |
| | Spread of the Gospel abroad | 501.50 |
| | Relief of the poor | 40.00 |
| *Wailuku,* | For American Board | 426.61 |
| | For French Protestant Missions | 41.85 |
| | For repairing meeting-house | 602.00 |
| *Hana,* | For support of pastor | 125.00 |
| HAWAII.—*Hilo,* | For American Tract Society | 100.00 |
| | For American Board | 607.00 |
| *Waimea,* | Contributions, objects not stated | 200.00 |
| *Kailua,* | For support of pastor and native assistant | 208.00 |
| | For French Protestant Missions | 30.31 |
| | For meeting-house at Kohala | 33.62 |
| *Kau,* | For support of pastor | 93.96 |

The whole amount is $7,213.14, from about 18,000 recent converts from the lowest idolatry.

The entire amount expended on the Sandwich Islands for educational purposes during the year 1850, may be estimated as follows:—

| | |
|---|---|
| On the public schools | $25,891.96 |
| On select schools supported by government | 1,929.52 |
| On select schools supported by voluntary efforts | 11,061.00 |
| Ministers' salary, clerk hire, stationery, &c. | 4,264.11 |
| | $43,146.59 |

Supposing the population on the 1st of January, 1851, to be 85,000, which is not far from the truth, the above amount would be 50 cents for every individual: or supposing the taxable male population to be 15,000, it would amount to $2.08 for each man, were the whole amount raised by taxation. The average annual cost of each school has been $47.68. Average yearly wages of each teacher, $37.99. Average yearly cost of each scholar, $1.69.

*Tabular View of Schools for* 1850,
*Reported by Missionaries.*

| | STATIONS. | Number of Schools. | Scholars. | Readers. | Writers. | Arithmetic. | Geography. | Singing. |
|---|---|---|---|---|---|---|---|---|
| HAWAII,. | Hilo and Puna .... | 48 | 2091 | 1207 | 860 | 1037 | 802 | 91 |
| | Waimea ........... | 21 | 841 | 400 | 285 | 366 | 166 | 31 |
| | Kohala. ........... | 21 | 1116 | 605 | 260 | 759 | 276 | 144 |
| | Kailua.............. | 21 | 972 | 381 | 100 | 374 | 233 | 26 |
| | Kealakekua ....... | 26 | 925 | 404 | 202 | 265 | 141 | 60 |
| | Kau ................. | 13 | 355 | 101 | 45 | 155 | 54 | 19 |
| MAUI, ... | Hana ............... | 27 | 1149 | 579 | 317 | 430 | 411 | 33 |
| | Wailuku ........... | 24 | 837 | 434 | 377 | 174 | 304 | 64 |
| | Lahaina............ | 15 | 899 | 424 | 282 | 341 | 377 | 48 |
| | Kaanapali.......... | 10 | 333 | 117 | 69 | 133 | 101 | 34 |
| | MOLOKAI ........... | 22 | 1016 | 610 | 273 | 685 | 300 | 422 |
| | LANAI............... | 7 | 184 | 162 | 104 | 127 | 103 | 10 |
| OAHU, ... | Honolulu 1st ...... | 23 | 1068 | 407 | 248 | 377 | 292 | 145 |
| | Honolulu 2d....... | 12 | 445 | 203 | 108 | 225 | 102 | 14 |
| | Ewa and Waianae | 27 | 820 | 496 | 312 | 436 | 535 | 97 |
| | Waialua ........... | 26 | 735 | 361 | 247 | 371 | 263 | 122 |
| | Kaneohe ........... | 11 | 529 | 386 | 287 | 356 | 380 | 113 |
| KAUAI, .. | Waioli.............. | 20 | 515 | 331 | 170 | 258 | 179 | |
| | Koloa............... | 15 | 437 | 267 | 135 | 223 | 175 | |
| | Waimea ........... | 15 | 400 | 221 | 68 | 167 | 93 | 21 |
| | NIIHAU.............. | 6 | 141 | 69 | 47 | 29 | 14 | |
| | Total........... | 388 | 11,792 | 7655 | 4523 | 6603 | 5001 | 1494 |

No. of scholars in English, 1850................................ 421

| SEMINARIES, &c. | Now in school. | Received the past year. | Graduated and left the past year. | Expelled the past year. | Died the past. | Sent forth as teachers. |
|---|---|---|---|---|---|---|
| Royal school ............... | 11 | ... | 2 | ... | ... | ... |
| Lahainaluna................ | 64 | ... | 14 | 2 | 1 | 14 |
| Wailuku..................... | 35 | ... | 3 | ... | 5 | ... |
| Hilo.......................... | 62 | 23 | 12 | ... | 1 | 8 |
| Waioli....................... | 48 | 4 | 14 | ... | ... | 7 |
| Total................. | 220 | 27 | 45 | 2 | 7 | 29 |

*Tabular View of Churches for* 1850.

| | STATIONS. | On examination the past year. | Whole number on examination. | Dismissed past year. | Whole number dismissed. | Deceased past year. | Whole number deceased. | Excluded past year. | Remaining excluded. | In regular standing. | Children baptized past year. | Whole number baptized. | Marriages past year. | Average congregations. | Population in the field. | Deaths. | Births. |
|---|---|---|---|---|---|---|---|---|---|---|---|---|---|---|---|---|---|
| HAWAII | Hilo and Puna | 265 | 9647 | 28 | 453 | 703 | 3301 | 25 | 387 | 5906 | 108 | 3191 | 91 | ... | 9031 | 934 | 173 |
| | Waimea | 96 | 5955 | 12 | 812 | 264 | 1464 | 51 | 800 | 2292 | 39 | 1226 | 62 | 200 | 4114 | 550 | 100 |
| | Kohala | 26 | 1791 | 19 | 188 | 130 | 500 | 23 | 80 | 1264 | 27 | 793 | 80 | 900 | 4712 | 415 | 189 |
| | Kailua | ... | 2339 | 67 | 466 | 139 | 575 | 33 | 95 | 1465 | 12 | 1692 | 22 | 450 | 3544 | 273 | 51 |
| | Kealakekua | ... | 2694 | 16 | 841 | 59 | 574 | 14 | ... | 1265 | 23 | ...... | 46 | ... | 3522 | 283 | 32 |
| | Kau | 97 | 1294 | 26 | 236 | 130 | 377 | 2 | 51 | 924 | 25 | 395 | 40 | ... | 2281 | 271 | 40 |
| MAUI | Hana | ... | 626 | 2 | 20 | 58 | 98 | 10 | 51 | 566 | ... | 276 | 78 | ... | 5583 | 450 | 97 |
| | Wailuku | 55 | 1573 | 9 | 319 | 58 | 212 | 18 | ... | 1262 | 17 | 979 | 73 | ... | 4226 | 361 | 67 |
| | Lahaina | 90 | 1119 | 48 | 222 | 126 | 363 | 5 | 20 | 762 | 53 | 1105 | 55 | ... | 5646 | 524 | 67 |
| | Lahainaluna | ... | ...... | ... | ... | ... | ... | ... | ... | ...... | ... | ...... | ... | ... | | ... | ... |
| | Kaanapali | ... | ...... | ... | ... | ... | ... | ... | ... | ...... | ... | ...... | ... | ... | ...... | ... | ... |
| | MOLOKAI | 276 | 1401 | 8 | 45 | 85 | 235 | 40 | 16 | 1129 | ... | ...... | 52 | ... | 3429 | 412 | 52 |
| OAHU | Honolulu 1st | 306 | 2280 | 16 | 184 | 164 | 486 | 14 | ... | 1595 | 34 | 636 | 134 | 1200 | 7389 | 627 | 132 |
| | Honolulu 2d | 126 | 2121 | 26 | 273 | 134 | 624 | 14 | 458 | 1131 | 24 | 626 | 137 | 1000 | 6375 | 793 | 122 |
| | Ewa | 10 | 1914 | 18 | 290 | 111 | 356 | 8 | 167 | 1430 | 35 | 559 | 44 | 900 | 3308 | 323 | 37 |
| | Waianae | 5 | 256 | 8 | 21 | 49 | 79 | 6 | 13 | 334 | 4 | ...... | ... | ... | ...... | ... | ... |
| | Waialua | 151 | 924 | 5 | 70 | 52 | 155 | 8 | ... | 610 | 36 | 654 | 35 | ... | 3241 | 298 | 54 |
| | Kaneohe | 36 | 326 | 3 | 22 | 21 | 90 | 1 | 22 | 203 | 2 | 151 | 37 | 450 | 2832 | 368 | 51 |
| KAUAI | Waioli | 40 | 292 | 1 | 29 | 20 | 78 | 4 | 17 | 259 | 12 | 102 | 40 | ... | 2340 | 216 | 57 |
| | Koloa | 8 | 269 | 1 | 79 | 11 | 56 | ... | ... | 201 | 3 | 160 | ... | ... | 2732 | 259 | 68 |
| | Waimea | 7 | 403 | 2 | 82 | 32 | 134 | 2 | 29 | 233 | 8 | 179 | 58 | 350 | 1869 | 211 | 29 |
| | Total | 1594 | 37,224 | 315 | 4652 | 2352 | 9754 | 278 | 2206 | 22,831 | 462 | 12,724 | 1084 | | | | |

*Late Census of the Hawaiian Islands, from Official Documents,* 1850.

| Islands. | Population. |
|---|---|
| Hawaii | 27,204 |
| Oahu | 23,145 |
| Mauai | 18,671 |
| Kauai | 6,941 |
| Molokai | 3,429 |
| Niihau | 723 |
| Lanai | 528 |
| Total aggregate | 80,641 |
| **Foreigners.** | |
| Unmarried | 409 |
| Living with foreign wives | 133=266 |
| Children | 239 |
| Living with native wives | 343 |
| Half castes | 471 |
| Foreigners in Hilo | 59 |
| Total foreigners | 1,787 |
| Natives | 78,854 |
| Grand total | 80,641 |

Aggregate amount of each description of persons included opposite.

| Males. | | Females. | |
|---|---|---|---|
| Under 17 years of age | 10,773 | Under 17 years of age | 9,593 |
| Of 17 and under 30, | 6,327 | Of 17 and under 30, | 5,719 |
| Of 30 and under 50, | 10,819 | Of 30 and under 50, | 9,696 |
| Of 50 and upward, | 8,353 | Of 50 and upward, | 8,121 |
| Total males | 36,272 | Total females | 33,128 |

Excess of males.........3,143.

| | |
|---|---|
| Blind | 337 |
| Deaf | 144 |
| Hilo (not included) | 8,972 |
| Native population | 78,854 |

Schools, &c.

| | |
|---|---|
| Number of English schools | 9 |
| " English scholars | 421 |
| " high schools | 6 |
| " high scholars | 256 |
| " primary and common schools | 505 |
| " primary and common scholars | 18,022 |

## HONOLULU A COMMERCIAL DEPOT.

THE peculiar advantages of Honolulu, as a depot for the commerce of the Northern Pacific, have not received that attention from commercial men which they deserve, and to which their intrinsic merits entitle them. To some of these we will now allude, in the hope that they may arrest the attention of those interested in the prosperity of this kingdom, and engaged in its rapidly extending commerce.

In the first place, we have a safe and convenient harbor, into which any number of vessels, ever likely to require accommodation, can enter, and be perfectly safe from all casualties of wind and tempest. This is a point of great importance to be known, as thereby the rate of insurance would be reduced, and the anxieties of shippers diminished. Our harbor is also of easy access, and vessels are subjected to but little delay in entering. Whenever delays occur on account of strong winds, those winds blow off shore, and ships can safely ride at their anchors, outside, until they can come in. But with a small steam-tug to tow ships in, no delay whatever need occur. They could be brought in in any weather. The southerly gales that bring ships at anchor outside upon a lee shore, blow directly in, and vessels can always slip and run in, even if they cannot stay to get their anchors. Almost every wreck upon our coast, for many years past, has been of ships bound off, and which did not wish to come inside. Our harbor, therefore, may be considered as safe as any other in the Pacific, and furnishes sufficient accommodation for a large fleet. At one time during the last shipping season, a hundred vessels were counted, and there was room for more.

Another indispensable requisite, in connection with the commercial advantages of Honolulu, is good and sufficient wharfage, where ships of the largest class can come alongside and discharge, without the expense and delay of lighters. This, we are happy to say, is now being provided by the government, and will soon furnish all that will be required for many years, even should the business of the port increase in a large ratio. The new wharves are being constructed in a firm and durable manner, and are run out into from ten to eighteen feet water, thus affording vessels of a large class all the advantages they need for rapidly discharging their cargoes. When these are completed—which they will be in a few weeks—no delay need occur, as has formerly been the case, from a want of accommodation at the wharves.

Secure and convenient storage is another advantage possessed here, of great value to the port as a general depot for goods awaiting a market. There are several large and commodious warehouses, owned by the government and by individuals, of easy access, and convenient to the wharves, where a large amount of goods can be safely stored. Some of these buildings are fire-proof, and others so nearly so as to render them quite safe from the casualties of fire. Should those now built be found inadequate to the demand, there is abundant room for the erection of more, in the near vicinity of the wharves; and such structures would be multiplied as rapidly as the demand increased. At present there is a large amount of storage room unoccupied—sufficient for the cargoes of many ships, and at rates far below those of San Francisco, or any other port in the Northern Pacific. Goods can also be landed and stored at this port at a cheap rate, compared with the ports on the coast, where labor is so excessively high. We have this fact from a gentleman, now here in commercial pursuits, and who is thoroughly versed in the details of expenses of this kind on the coast.

In view of these facts, and with the knowledge that goods can be entered here for re-shipment, subject only to a transit duty of one per cent., the advantages of this port, as a depot for goods awaiting a market, must appear quite apparent. If the late decision of the Collector of San Francisco is carried into execution, we submit to consignees there, having cargoes upon their hands, whether it would not be a material saving of expense to send their ships here to discharge and store their goods, until a favorable moment arrives for effecting sales.

We shall, without doubt, have a line of steamers running between the Islands and the coast within a few months. By this expeditious mode of intercourse goods could be thrown into that market within a month or six weeks, and merchants there would always know the state of the demand, and the proper time to have them forwarded.

In addition to the above facilities, vessels can get stone ballast, wood, and water, of the very best description, in any quantity, and so convenient, that casks can be filled in a lighter or ship's boat from the hose, as it comes from the iron pipes. This water is perfectly soft, being brought from a spring some hundreds of feet above the sea, without coming in contact with the ground.

We are confident in the belief that Honolulu possesses all the advantages for a large commercial depot for the North Pacific, especially for California and Oregon, which will, ere long, be appreciated and employed, in preference to Valparaiso or any other port in this ocean; and where assorted cargoes for those points, and for the more northern possessions of the Russians, can be made up at the very shortest notice. —*Polynesian.*

## FRENCH DIFFICULTIES AT THE SANDWICH ISLANDS.

The principal demands of France were, 1. That a portion of the money raised by the government for the support of schools shall be placed in the hands of a few Catholic priests who reside there. This money is now collected and expended by an officer of the government, called the Minister of Public Instruction, and schools are thus provided for nearly or quite all the children on the Islands. 2. That the price of licenses for retailing French brandy shall be regulated by France. The object is to take away all power of the government from restraining those habits of intoxication among the people, which were once almost universal, but are now very extensively abandoned, and thus make an increased sale for brandy.

It will be recollected that Dillon with his frigate did not succeed in enforcing these demands. After failing to persuade the government to yield to them, he went on shore with a body of armed troops, paraded through the streets of Honolulu, went to the fort, hoisted the French flag, sent for the Governor and demanded the surrender of his soldiers. The noble Islander, in a calm and dignified manner, replied, "I HAVE NO SOLDIERS." Dillon's troops then went to work to do what injury they could to the public property, by turning over the small out-buildings, cutting down trees, and making obscene pictures, and writing obscene words on the walls of the fort; and, after other proceedings of a similar character, and destroying property to the amount of $100,000, retired on board their vessel. They soon left for California, and, upon their own account of their proceeding, the California papers spoke of them as pirates; and their proceedings were undoubtedly nothing better than piratical.

The Grand Nation has now sent out Perrin to reassert their claims; and, as the government has no military force, he gave them a limited time to save the town from destruction by compliance. In this extremity, the government has proposed to Mr. Severance, the American Commissioner, as it is understood, to yield the sovereignty of the Islands to the United States, and place themselves under the protection of the *Stars and Stripes*. It is also understood that he has accepted the offer provisionally, to await the action of our government. The Vandalia, one of our ships of war, is there. It is said, that not only Mr. Severance and Mr. Allen, our Consul, and the commanding officer of the Vandalia, but Gen. Miller, the British Consul, and all the respectable foreign residents, justify the position of the Hawaiian government, and condemn the proceedings of Perrin. And this brutal exercise of power over a defenceless people just emerged from barbarism, is disgracing France in the eyes of the civilized world. It is really a dastardly business.

France has no important interests at the Island. There are scarcely a dozen French residents there. The American interests, on the contrary, are of very great and growing importance. Several thousand Americans reside on the Islands, many of whom are owners of large tracts of land, and are engaged in agriculture. There is always a great amount of American shipping in their ports. It often amounts to millions of dollars in value. Eighty ships are no uncommon sight in the harbor of Honolulu, mostly of a very large class. The connection with Oregon and California is constant, and there is a regular mail between Honolulu and the United States. At the present rate of increase, a large proportion of the inhabitants will soon be Americans. It is to be hoped that our government will protect these interests of our citizens against France, and assume a decided tone against any attempts on the part of the French government to interfere with the independence of the Island. If the Islands must be annexed to this country to protect them against French piracy, it will be a righteous annexation. The people of Honolulu, both foreign and native, are extremely desirous of living under a flag which the French will not dare to insult.

It is understood that an Agent of the Government of the Sandwich Islands is now at Washington, with full power to negotiate important changes in the relations between the Islands and the United States. He is the bearer of two propositions: one, for the establishment of an American Protectorate over the Islands, their government and internal organization remaining as now; the other, for the abdication of the king, the complete resignation of the authority into the hands of the people under suitable republican forms, and the definite annexation of the Islands to this Republic. These propositions are submitted to our Government for its choice and acceptance, with an earnest request from the king and all his ministers that one or the other of them may be promptly embraced and acted upon. This step, we have reason to believe, has not been taken without deliberation and perfect conviction that it is both necessary and timely.

To take the Islands under the protection of the United States would be of little, if any, advantage to either of the two parties. Our protection could hardly be rendered efficacious in a country where our right to exercise it might be denied, while it might entangle us in unpleasant difficulties with other nations.

In our view, the only question to be entertained is that of annexation. As a territory of the United States, the Islands would be exempt from foreign interference, and the authority of our flag and the force of our laws would not be disputed. To the inhabitants and future settlers, annexation would be a blessing. It would insure tranquillity, order, and a more active development of the rich natural resources of the country. Of its present white population, by far the greater and predominantly influential part are Americans, who long once more to live under the stars and stripes. Its civilization and its commerce are American; its laws and government are, already, to a great extent, modelled upon ours. And as the trade of the Pacific is developed, the value of the Islands will increase, not only to ourselves, but to other nations.—*American newspaper.*

"THE following is a copy of the Rules of Conference finally agreed upon between the Commissioner of the French Republic and the Minister of Foreign Affairs of the Hawaiian Kingdom, at Honolulu, the 10th of January, 1851. Appended are the most important Diplomatic Notes and Protocols that passed between the parties while negotiations were pending, and the final Declaration to which they arrived.

## RULES OF DIPLOMATIC CONFERENCES.

THE undersigned Negotiators of the Treaty, concluded on the 26th of March, 1846, between France and the Hawaiian Islands, chosen by the President of the French Republic and the King of the Sandwich Islands, to put an end to the much regretted differences that have supervened between the two countries, and to arrest in their source all causes of ulterior difficulties; after having each—in four dispatches, which have recently been exchanged—restored to the political relations of the two countries the character of mutual confidence and honorable loyalty which they had sought to establish, have agreed to subject themselves to the following preliminary articles, in the conduct of the Diplomatic Conferences, rendered necessary by the negotiation with which they are charged:—

### ARTICLE I.

With the view of recording the results obtained during the course of the negotiations, it is agreed that Protocols of each sitting shall be prepared, successively, during the discussions, to be read and signed by the two Commissioners, at the opening of the following sitting.

The order of signatures shall be the same as that adopted by the undersigned, at the conclusion of the Treaty of 26th March, 1846.

### ARTICLE II.

For the success of the negotiation itself, and in order that each Commissioner may be able to perform his other important duties, each Conference shall last only from eleven in the morning to two in the afternoon; to be resumed at the same hour, on such other day as it may please the two negotiators to fix, before they separate.

### ARTICLE III.

The Hawaiian language not being understood by either of the two undersigned, it is agreed that, for the drawing up of the Protocols, only, the English and French languages shall be used, exclusively.

ARTICLE IV.

The two Commissioners shall only propose to themselves to seek for the true interests of their respective nations; observing all the respect due to nations very unequal in force, though perfectly equal in regard to sovereignty and independence; it has been agreed that, with this object, the two negotiators shall judge of the facts, in themselves, with calm loyalty and impartiality, and that they shall, reciprocally, demand nothing which they would not be ready to grant, in turn, in analogous circumstances.

ARTICLE V.

To secure this desirable result, which is altogether indispensable to the dignity and honor of the two States, the two negotiators, in their conferences, shall divest themselves of all prejudices and passion, and will carry their investigations back to the visit to this Archipelago, made in 1837, by Vice-admiral Du Petit Thouars.

ARTICLE VI.

The undersigned shall endeavor to guard themselves against every source of error, and, so far as their personal influence may permit, to dispose their respective governments to renounce every idea, or every demand which shall appear to them not sufficiently established.

ARTICLE VII.

With the view of preventing all surprise, and for the sake of a political liberty of great propriety, it has been decided that the points, successively agreed upon in the discussion, shall not be definitively obtained, till after the whole discussion has been closed.

ARTICLE VIII.

To do homage to truth, and record an historical fact, the two negotiators have solemnly recognized that, in the eyes of the two contracting parties, the Treaty of the 26th of March, 1846, has been, hitherto, maintained in its integrity.

ARTICLE IX.

All the documents that may be examined shall be numbered and marked by the initials of the two Commissioners.

ARTICLE X.

The discussion shall be pursued and terminated in conformity with the general principles of the laws of nations, and the diplomatic usages of the great powers.

ARTICLE XI.

It has also been agreed that if—impossible though it seem to be—the government of the French Republic should admit the mediation of a third power, for the adjustment of the difficulties confided to the undersigned, before the latter have completed their task, the two negotiators, undersigned, shall each conform to the decision which shall have been agreed upon, between France and the mediating Power, in such an event.

ARTICLE XII.

The result of the negotiations, recorded in the Protocols, shall be embodied in a Declaration, signed by the two Commissioners in the name of their respective governments, in a place which shall be hereafter agreed upon: That signature shall be followed by a salute exchanged between the shore and the Serieuse: That final Act shall be drawn up in French and Hawaiian, with a translation in the English language; and as it shall not be considered in the light of a new Convention, but simply an Act interpreting the existing Convention, and designed to insure its execution, there will be no occasion for ratification on the part of any of the governments of the two contracting parties.

Done in duplicate, in Honolulu, this 10th day of January, 1851.

R. C. WYLLIE,
Minister of Foreign Relations.

Le Commissaire de la République Française,
EM. PERRIN.

PROTOCOL.

SATURDAY, *15th March*, 1851.

Mr. Wyllie alleging reasons of State, asked M. Perrin's permission to give him a perusal of the instructions framed in April and September 1849, for Mr. Jarves and Mr. Judd, during their mission to the governments of France, Great Britain, and the United States, and accordingly gave a reading of each of these documents.

M. Perrin, in his turn, read a "*verbal note*," dated this day, serving as a reply to his memorandum on Schools, to the notes and historical memorandum latterly addressed by the Minister, Mr. Wyllie, after having denied some of the consequences deduced by M. Perrin, as contrary both to the object of these writings and to his own intentions, asked a copy of the note to reply to it, if it was to have any official force against the Hawaiian government; M. Perrin answered that his desire was not to delay too much the entering upon the draft of the final note; he did not think it proper at present to leave a copy of that which he had read.

Mr. Wyllie then communicated to M. Perrin the explanation furnished in the name of the Hawaiian government, upon all the demands of France presented by her special Commissioner.

R. C. WYLLIE,
Minister of Foreign Relations.

Le Commissaire de la République Française,
EM. PERRIN.

The following are the explanations referred to, and the Demands of the French Republic to which they apply, presented by M. Perrin, at the conference of 1st February, 1851.

*Demands* to which the Government of the French Republic thinks that satisfaction ought to be made, before the re-establishment of Diplomatic Relations can take place with that of the Hawaiian Islands.

1. The adoption complete, entire, and loyal, of the Treaty of the 26th March, 1846, as it was drafted in the French Text.

2. The establishment of a duty from 1 to 2 dollars a gallon, of 5 bottles on spirits, containing less than 55 per cent. of alcohol.

3. A treatment rigorously equal, granted to the two worships, Catholic and Protestant.

The direction of instruction confided to two Superior Committees formed in each of the two religions.

The submission of the Catholic Schools to Catholic Inspectors.

The proportional division between the two religions of the Tax raised by the Hawaiian Government for the support of Schools.

4. The adoption of the French language, in the relations between French Citizens and the Hawaiian Administration.

5. The withdrawal of the exception imposed upon French whalers, importing wines and spirits, and the abrogation of the regulation which obliges ships laden with liquors to pay, and support the Custom-house guard, put on board to watch over their shipment or discharge.

Large facilities of deposit, of transit, and of transhipment granted to the trade in spirits.

6. The reimbursement of all the duties received in virtue of the disposition, the withdrawal of which is demanded by the paragraph above mentioned; or a proportional indemnity given for the damage occasioned to French commerce, by the restriction which has suspended its relations.

7. The reimbursement of the fine of 25 dollars, paid by the French ship General Teste, and besides an indemnity of 60 dollars for the time during which she was unjustly detained here.

8. The insertion in the official journal of the Hawaiian Government, of the punishment inflicted upon the scholars of the high-school, whose impious conduct occasioned the complaints of the Abbé Coulon.

9. The removal of the governor, who caused or allowed to be violated on Hawaii, the domicil of the Abbé Marechal, or the order to that governor to make reparation to that missionary, the one or the other decision to be inserted in the official journal.

10. The payment to a French citizen, proprietor of the Hotel of France, of the damages committed in his house by foreign sailors, against whom the Hawaiian Government took no process.

The Commissioner of the French Republic,

(Signed,) EM. PERRIN.

Honolulu, 1st February, 1851.

## REPLIES BY MR. WYLLIE.

On behalf of the Hawaiian Government, to the demands of the French, presented by M. Perrin, on the 1st February, 1851, to enable him to satisfy himself and the French government, upon all points.

1. The adoption complete, entire, and loyal, of the Treaty of the 26th March, 1846, as it was drafted in the French Text, and signed in the Hawaiian and French languages, and in all cases before the foreign judges who do not understand French, the text of the British Treaty declared by M. Guizot, to have been drawn up, in the same terms with the French, and so declared by M. Perrin himself at the conference of the 26th March, 1846, to be held as a translation of the French Text, the correctness of which is not to be disputed.

2. The Hawaiian Government do not admit that in the duty of $5 per gallon, on spirits, they have gone beyond the power conveyed to them exclusively by France herself in the words used by her in the VI. article of the said Treaty; they have shown that the effect of that duty has been beneficial to France, in an eminent degree, while it has been injurious to the trade in British and American spirits; but they are willing to submit the question of a reduction to $2 per gallon to the approaching Legislature, as a measure of political economy, and upon moral grounds recommended by the Chamber of Commerce.

3. The King's Government cannot admit the right of any foreign nation to dictate to them, or prescribe laws on matters affecting only the religious belief and secular education of the King's native subjects. But they are willing to receive the demands of M. Perrin, under the 3d article, in the light of friendly suggestions for the consideration of the Legislature, so far as the already perfect equality of Catholics and Protestants, under the Constitution and Laws, of which abundant proof has already been given, may leave any thing to be provided for.

4. Documents presented by French citizens in their own language shall be received in all cases where documents in English are received, but in cases where the officer whose duty it is to act upon them does not understand the French, it shall be the duty of the applicant to furnish a translation of his document, which, to prevent dispute or error of judgment, shall be by him authenticated, under the signature and seal of the Consul of France.

5. The King's Government would gladly withdraw any exception to French whalers, if any such existed, but it has been already shown that no such exception ever existed. French whalers are entirely upon the same footing in all respects as the whalers of any other foreign nation. France cannot claim more, in accordance with the Treaty of 26th March, 1846, and the King cannot grant more to France, in conformity with his

treaties with other powers. The same remark applies to the Custom-house regulations respecting the payment of a guard on board, deposit, transit, and transhipment of spirits.

6. No reimbursement or indemnity can be given where no wrong has been done. To admit the contrary would imply a violation of the Treaty, which the King's Government are justified by all concurrent opinion, and by the clear and natural wording of the Treaty, in denying. France cannot insist that this government should affix upon itself a stain, which in its own opinion and that of the world it does not deserve.

7. The King's Government would annihilate their right to claim of foreign ships the observance of their Port Regulations, if they were to return the fine of $25 imposed on the ship General Teste; or allow $60 for a delay in port, for which the captain alone was to blame. All that was shown clearly to M. Dillon, in Mr. Wyllie's dispatch No. 53, of 25th November, 1848, published at page 41 of the published correspondence with that gentleman. The King's Government always considered, and consider still, that they deserve thanks for having reduced the fine, legally incurred by the General Teste, from $500 to $25. The law which the captain of the General Teste had violated is quoted at page 44 of that correspondence.

8. All that M. Dillon asked for on the 16th April, 1849, with reference to the complaint of the Abbé Coulon, was to be informed what measures would be taken to prevent such acts as he had complained of. That was all that the Rev. Abbé, who, with a moderation worthy of his clerical character, had declined appearing before the native judge, had required him to do. Mr. Wyllie courteously received M. Dillon's dispatch, and referred the complaint to the King's Minister of Public Instruction, as will be seen by referring to Mr. Wyllie's note No. 34, of 19th April, 1849, page 317, of the same correspondence, and that Minister, after explaining the case, replied, as will be seen at page 360, that should like cases occur in future, on being duly informed it will be his duty to give notice to the proper officer, that he might proceed against the offenders according to law. It is understood the native judge before whom the boys were carried dismissed the case, on the ground of want of proof. If the Rev. Abbé had made his complaint to the Minister of Public Instruction, either directly or through his bishop, (which would have been preferable,) on proof of their delinquency, the boys would have been punished severely, under the law, section VI., chapter VI., part IV., second Act of Kamehameha III.; and if the judge had neglected his duty, he would have been liable to the punishment provided for in the law of 31st May, 1841, page 89 of the old laws. The King's Government do not encourage sacrilege of any kind; the law amply provides for its punishment, and if the Bishop will instruct his clergy in all such cases to prefer a written complaint to the Minister of Public Instruction, it will be his duty to see the law rigidly enforced against proved delin-

quents. It is not believed that the offence complained of has since been repeated anywhere on the Islands.

9. The facts stated by his Excellency, the Governor of Hawaii, published at page 59 of the official correspondence with Admiral de Tromelin, make it appear that the Abbé Marechal either screened or caused to be screened, in his domicil, a fugitive from justice. By referring to Mr. Wyllie's dispatch of the 24th August, 1849, published at page 67 of the same correspondence, it will be seen that the King's Government had no intelligence of such a complaint till it had been magnified very irregularly with a formal international demand. It will not be contended that on the mere complaint of a Catholic priest to a French Consul (in itself a contempt of the magistracy of the country) there should be a just cause why the Governor of the largest island of the kingdom should be dismissed without a hearing. That would indeed be a strange doctrine under the laws of nations, and a singular interpretation of the 2d article of the Treaty of the 26th March, 1846. Process at law against the Governor, before the King's chief-justice, was offered to M. Dillon, and even a free passage to Hawaii in the King's yacht, that he might witness the fairness of the proceedings. M. Dillon did not accept the offer, but the courts of the country are still open to the Rev. Abbé if he wish to prosecute.

10. The receipt of Victor Chancerel for $93.50, is in the archives of the Foreign Office. It rests upon the authority of British officers that Victor's original bill for damages was only for $8, (see page 53 of the same correspondence,) so that the claim of Chancerel was paid more than ten times over, on the 30th of August, 1849, a fact with many others, which General Lahitte could not possibly have known when he placed the ten demands of France in the hands of M. Perrin.

The King's Government invite the Government of France to adopt the same Treaty, *mutatis mutandis*, as that lately formed with the United States, or to consider the present Treaty at an end in 12 months from this date, and in the mean while to form a new Treaty free from the objections and ambiguities of the old.

The King's Government consider that France is specially bound to remove all the restrictions imposed on the King, in the 3d and 6th articles of the Treaty of 26th March 1846, both because he was deprived of his rightful prerogatives of sovereignty by a French officer, under a threat of instant war, and because the Government consented to the reduction of the duties on wines, on the condition of the removal of those restrictions to which M. Dillon repeatedly pledged himself with emphatic promises of his best endeavors.

The King's Government desire a mutual accord between France, Great Britain, and the United States, so as to render their treaties uniform on these Islands, to provide for a settlement of all disputes arising under them by amicable reference, to respect the King's neutrality in all wars one with another, and to adopt one common rule, in regard to the duties and conduct of their political agents, towards the King's Administration, so as to relieve it from an oppressive and vexatious interference, depriving the King's officers of all time to attend to the internal interests of the country. If things are to continue as they have been, the Government of the country as an independent state is an *impracticability*.

R. C. WYLLIE.

Foreign Office, 15th March, 1851.

PROTOCOL *of Tuesday*, 18*th March*, 1851.

The undersigned met at the usual hour; the Commissioner of the French Republic returned the draft of explanations on each of his ten demands, which he had received from Mr. Wyllie, and at the same time delivered to him a draft of the final note drawn up by him and containing the whole of the solutions given to the demands above mentioned. After having read that document, Mr. Wyllie declared that he refused to admit its tenor, because it exacted of the King what, in his eyes, could not be demanded of him, either by right of the laws of nations, or in virtue of the existing treaty with France; adding, however, that he would translate the draft as received, and would try its lawfulness by comparisons with the text of the Laws of Nations, and would produce, in the name of the Hawaiian Government, a commentary on each of the articles of the treaty, showing that that Convention had been faithfully executed, in every part, to this very day.

M. Perrin refused to enter upon such a course, asserting that at the point to which the negotiation had arrived, such a proposal was inadmissible.

Mr. Wyllie then said that he could not think the desire of M. Perrin was to render the Government of the King impracticable, and to provoke a crisis disastrous to his independence and for the future interests of the commerce and shipping of France in the Northern Pacific Ocean. He suggested, in consequence, a solution of all the questions, honorable in his view for France, acceptable and beneficial to the King.

M. Perrin declared that he would consider all these projects, in view of the graveness of circumstances.

Mr. Wyllie asked permission to add, on the subject of a suggestion contained in the project of M. Perrin, and relative to a national salute to be given by the Hawaiian Fort to France, at the moment when the French Consular Flag should be again raised, that M. Dillon had voluntarily hauled down his flag, in spite of the protest of the Hawaiian Government, and that he could notify to M. Perrin, officially, with the full authority of the King, as he now did, that the Government of Kamehameha III. would never accept one dollar of indemnity from France, for the damages occasioned, and for the royal yacht taken away, unless a clear expression of regret for such injuries, and a salute in honor of the

King as sovereign, whose authority had been usurped in his own dominions, should first be granted.

M. Perrin expressed his regret on being so late informed of an opinion entirely contrary to the views of the French Government; he brought to mind that often already he had officially and verbally announced that the object of his mission was not to come and give satisfaction to a Government, although he came, on the contrary, to demand it with all the moderation which became the power of the French Republic, adding that that declaration had never provoked the least observation on the part of Mr. Wyllie. The Minister then said that that Resolution had only recently been taken in Council.

Mr. Wyllie besides declared that if this point of etiquette, in the opinion of M. Perrin, should prevent the re-establishment of diplomatic relations with France, she would lose nothing by it; that her interests in this Archipelago would not suffer, because he believed that the King would not the less continue to treat the French and their interests on the footing of the most favored nation.

The undersigned adjourned until to-morrow at 11 A. M.

R. C. WYLLIE,
Minister of Foreign Relations.

Le Commissaire de la République Française,
EM. PERRIN.

PROTOCOL *of Wednesday*, 19*th March*, 1851.

The undersigned met at the usual hour.

After having compared together the two drafts of declaration proposed by Mr. Wyllie, and that which he himself had brought the day before, the Commissioner of the French Republic offered to Mr. Wyllie to accept, in the name of France, four of the solutions which the Minister had indicated in his draft of the 15th instant, reserving to himself to ask new instructions from his Government in regard to the solutions offered on the other points of his note of the 1st February last, before proceeding further.

This proposal having been agreed to, the Minister said that he would submit the drafts of Declaration to the King in Cabinet, and then in Privy Council; and to allow time for that consultation and deliberation, the undersigned agreed to postpone their next meeting until Saturday the 22d instant.

M. Perrin added that in a note to be dated this day he would define the character in which he would remain, until his new instructions should arrive from France.

R. C. WYLLIE,
Minister of Foreign Relations.

Le Commissaire de la République Française,
EM. PERRIN.

PROTOCOL *of Saturday, 22d March*, 1851.

The two negotiators, undersigned, met at mid-day, as had been agreed upon.

Mr. Wyllie presented to M. Perrin a translation in the English language of the Declaration agreed upon, in which the *Alternat* was clearly preserved in favor of the King of the Sandwich Islands.

M. Perrin remarked that before all he had to sign the French and Hawaiian Texts, which were not prepared; that in these original documents he could not grant the *Alternat* to the King of the Hawaiian Islands, in conformity with the usage of France, Great Britain, and the United States; that from the 15th of January he had announced to the Minister that it would be only after the adjustment of the difficulties actually pending, that he could examine this question of etiquette, referring it to Paris, and then conforming to the orders which he should receive; that until then he could only maintain the *statu quo;* that this measure adopted for the originals ought necessarily to be in their translation. Mr. Wyllie having replied that he understood the Alternat as allowed to the King both by Great Britain and the United States, and that it was generally granted between the great powers, and even the middling, M. Perrin answered that he did not consider that the Hawaiian Kingdom had attained either of these two ranks.

Mr. Wyllie then produced one original of the English treaty of the 26th March, 1846, in which the signature of the Minister was before that of the Consul-general of England. M. Perrin observed that the only original published by the Hawaiian Government placed the signature of the agent of Great Britain on the same line as that of the Minister. To cut this discussion short, the undersigned have agreed from this time to follow the precedent of England, under all the reserves of the rights of both Governments.

It was agreed that the resolution of the King of the Sandwich Islands, containing the promise to refer to the decision of the President of the French Republic the question of indemnities reclaimed by the Hawaiian Government in consequence of the events of the month of August, 1849, shall be (subject to the King's pleasure) transmitted in an official note, to which the Commissioner of the French Republic will reply, accepting that offer, in the name of the Prince President.

The undersigned, at their separation, agreed to meet again on Tuesday next at mid-day.

R. C. WYLLIE,
Minister of Foreign Relations.

Le Commissaire de la République Française,
EM. PERRIN.

PROTOCOL *of Tuesday, 25th March*, 1851.

The undersigned negotiators met this day, as had been agreed upon at their last conference of the 22d instant.

Before proceeding to the exchange of their respective powers, the undersigned employed themselves in comparing the French and English texts of the PROTOCOLS of the 15th, 18th, 19th, and 22d instant, and afterwards affixed thereto their signatures.

Mr. Wyllie remarked that after having hastily finished translations of M. Perrin's dispatch No. 18, of the 22d of this month, and of his "VERBAL NOTE" accompanying it, he desired to revise them with the French Commissioner, so as that when rendering an account thereof to the King and Council, he might be sure to convey the true meaning of M. Perrin. This verification was immediately made.

Mr. Wyllie then begged permission of the French Commissioner to read to him the notes No. 22, 23, 24, and 25, dated this day, all drafted in haste by him, but which it had been impossible for his Secretary to copy.

After reading them, the Minister expressed his strong hope that the French Government would consider all the points upon which a solution was deferred till after their Commissioner had referred them, as insignificant compared with those which had been settled; the Commissioner of the French Republic manifested a different opinion, and the two negotiators then agreed to give a new proof of their sincere desire to arrive, as soon as possible, at the re-establishment of relations between the two countries, by continuing to discuss, officially, and in a conciliatory spirit, in a series of new conferences, the divers points remaining to be settled, but that no new *Declaration* shall be made, till after the arrival of the instructions asked for of the French Government, by their Special Commissioner.

Mr. Wyllie asked M. Perrin's leave to call his attention to a claim which he had completely forgotten, at the moment of making out the *Schedule* of indemnities.

The undersigned then exchanged their respective powers, signed and sealed three originals of the Declaration agreed upon in French and Hawaiian, at 5 o'clock P. M., making mutual reserves in regard to the right of "*Alternat.*"

The undersigned then adjourned their sitting, *sine die.*

R. C. WYLLIE,
Minister of Foreign Relations.

Le Commissaire de la République Française,
EM. PERRIN.

## DECLARATION.

THE President of the French Republic, and the King of the Hawaiian Islands, animated by an equal desire to terminate the adjustment o pending difficulties between the two countries, and to prevent their return for the future, by assuring the just and complete execution of the convention of the 26th of March, 1846, in regard to the points in controversy, through a new official act, destined to interpret it, have chosen, for this purpose, the undersigned Commissioner of the French Republic, and Minister of Foreign Affairs of the Hawaiian Kingdom, the signers of the Treaty above mentioned, who, after having exchanged their full powers, found in good form, have agreed to the terms of the following declaration:

1. The Treaty of the 26th of March, 1846, will be faithfully adopted and interpreted in the two texts, French and Hawaiian, the only ones officially signed. It remains agreed in all the cases where the foreign judges not understanding French have to decide, the texts of the English treaty, officially declared identical, under reserve of the III. article, shall be considered as an exact translation.

2. Without admitting that by the establishment of a Custom-house duty of $5 per gallon upon spirits, the Hawaiian Government have gone beyond the exclusive power which France herself had granted to them, through the means of the wording of the VI. article of the Treaty above mentioned—an assertion, in regard to which, the undersigned French Commissioner makes all reserves—and after having proved that the effects of that duty have been profitable to France, and hurtful to the English and American trade in spirits—the King of the Sandwich Islands declares himself disposed to submit the question of the reduction of duty to $2.50 cents per gallon, as a *maximum*, to the legislature, which is to assemble next month, as a measure of political economy, which the Chamber of Commerce of Honolulu have recommended on strong grounds.

3. The government of the king cannot recognize, on the part of any foreign nation, the right of dictating or prescribing laws to them, on matters which affect only the religious belief or secular education of the native subjects of the king; nevertheless, disposed to admit the third of the demands presented by M. Perrin, on the 1st of February last, as a friendly suggestion, destined for the examination of the legislature which is to assemble this year, the Hawaiian Government will place these assemblies in a position to decide, if the equality between the Catholics and the Protestants, under the protection of the Constitution and the Laws, of which numerous proofs have been furnished, do not yet require something for its perfect application.

4. Documents presented by French citizens, in their own language,

will be received in all the cases in which documents in the English language are received; but, in the cases where the employees whose duty it is to make use of these documents do not understand French, it shall be incumbent, provisionally, on the party interested, to furnish a translation of the document produced, which, to prevent all error and discussion, shall be certified by him as true.

*Honolulu, 25th March,* 1851.

R. C. WYLLIE,
Minister of Foreign Relations.

Le Commissaire de la République Française,
EM. PERRIN.

From the foregoing papers it will be seen that the controversy of the Hawaiian government with the French is in the way of adjustment. "All that is wanting is for France to restore harmony; for, on behalf of the king's government, they have never for one moment deviated from their policy of treating France, her citizens, and all their interests, on the footing of the most favored nation. That this wise and unresenting policy will be duly appreciated by the French government, is not to be doubted. But, to crown all, King Kamehameha III., with a magnanimity worthy of a sovereign, refers his claims for indemnity for severe losses sustained, without requiring the punishment of the authors, to the President of France himself; thus proving to the world alike his confidence in the justice of his own cause, and in the justice of Prince Louis Napoleon Bonaparte, in whose hands he places it."

In his speech at the opening of the Hawaiian Parliament, on the 10th of May, 1851, the king uses the following language: "Diplomatic Relations have not been fully restored with France, but having, on my part, referred certain claims for indemnity to the President of the French Republic, I hope that he, meeting me in a corresponding spirit, will issue such instructions as to put an end to an attitude of hostility towards my kingdom, taken by France, which I have ever regretted, and have never sought, in any way, to retaliate. *I am not conscious of any act of my government, of which France has any reason to complain.*"

The simple utterance of the above sentence by His Majesty, says the Polynesian, felt, as it is, to be the simple truth, has more force than a thousand volumes of subtle reasoning, in convincing the judgment, and in nerving the heart. And the sentiment is not confined to the breast of His Majesty; it is entertained by every member of his government, and is the universal sentiment of the world. Its truth calls forth the sympathies of all his subjects, and unites the opinions of all classes upon his shores.

It is understood that negotiations are in progress with the United States, at Washington, through an authorized agent of the Hawaiian kingdom, which have for their end either the establishment of an American Protectorate at the Sandwich Islands, or their annexation to the American Union, in the event of the non-establishment of permanent friendly relations with France on a satisfactory and independent basis. Certain significant events of Providence, and the fact that the Hawaiian Islands are already a virtual colony of the United States, a missionary offshoot from the stock of New England, together with the "manifest destiny" view of the extension of American institutions, give a strong probability to what might otherwise seem but a presumption, namely, that the lapse of a few years will find the Heart of the Pacific a twin heart with the great American Republic, organized under the same laws, and beating with the same Anglo-Saxon blood that shall animate the united millions of all North America between the Atlantic and Pacific. The law of progress and of conquest by arts and emigration is so clearly impressed upon the American division of the Anglo-Saxon family, that it is like a denial of Providence and Destiny to doubt its great and glorious issues, or the triumphs it is yet to achieve on the field of social progress and humanity. We quote, as in place here, the following paper on

## THE PROGRESS OF THE ANGLO-SAXON RACE.

By a fortunate coincidence, the general total of the American census taken last year has just been received, and we are enabled, in conjunction with the returns made on the 31st of March for this country, to measure the absolute progress of the Anglo-Saxon race in its two grand divisions, and to compare the laws of their respective growths in relation to each other and to the rest of the world. It is estimated, including Ireland and the colonies, that there is a grand total of men speaking the same language and manifesting the same general tendencies of civilization, of fifty-six millions, from which is to be deducted the three millions of negro slaves in the United States, leaving a remainder of fifty-three millions, chiefly of Anglo-Saxon descent, and deeply impregnated with its sturdy qualities of heart and brain, as the representative of this advancing stock.

Two centuries ago there were not quite three millions of this race on the face of the earth. There are a million more persons of Magyar descent, speaking the Magyar language, at the present moment in Europe than there were in Europe and America of this conquering and colonizing people in the time of Cromwell. How vain, then, for men to talk of the political necessity for absorbing small races! Sixty years ago, the Anglo-Saxon race did not exceed seventeen millions in Europe and America. At that time it was not numerically stronger than the

Poles. Thirty years ago it counted only thirty-four millions; being altogether only three millions and a fraction more than the population of France at that time, and considerably less than the Teutonic population of Central Europe. In 1851 it is ahead of every civilized race in the world. Of races lying within the zones of civilization, the Sclaves alone are more numerous, counted by heads; but comparatively few of this plastic and submissive stock have yet escaped from the barbarism of the dark ages. In wealth, energy, and cultivation, they are not to be compared with the Frank, the Teuton, and the Anglo-Saxon. Number is almost their only element of strength.

Of all the races which are now striving for the mastery of the world, to impress on the future of society and civilization the stamp of its own character and genius, to make its law, idiom, religion, manners, government, and opinion prevail, the Anglo-Saxon is now unquestionably the most numerous, powerful, and active. The day when it might possibly have been crushed, absorbed, or trampled out, like Hungary and Poland, by stronger hordes, is gone by forever. That it was possible at one time for this people to be subdued by violence, or to fall a prey to the slower agonies of decline, there can be little doubt. In 1650 the United Provinces seemed more likely to make a grand figure in the world's future history than England. Their wealth, activity, and maritime power were the most imposing in Europe. They had all the carrying trade of the west in their hands. Their language was spoken in every port. In the great Orient their empire was fixed and their influence paramount. England was then hardly known abroad. Her difficult idiom grated on foreign ears, and her stormy coasts repelled the curiosity of more cultivated travellers. And if the thought of a day arriving when any single European language would be spoken by millions of persons, scattered over the great continents of the earth from New Zealand to the Hebrides, and from the Cape of Storms to the Arctic Ocean, occurred to any speculative mind, Dutch, not English, would probably have been the tongue to which he would have assigned the marvellous mission.

Yet Holland has fallen nearly as much as the Saxon has risen in the scale of nations. Her idiom is now acquired by few. Her merchants conduct their correspondence and transact their business in French or in English. Even her writers have many of them clothed their genius in a foreign garb. On the other hand, our literature and language have passed entirely out of this phase of danger. Dutch, like Welsh, Flemish, Erse, Basque, and other idioms, is doomed to perish as an intellectual medium; but whatever may be the future changes of the world, the tongue of Shakspeare and of Bacon is now too firmly rooted ever to be torn away. No longer content with mere preservation, it aims at universal mastery. Gradually it is taking possession of all the ports and coasts of the world; isolating all rival idioms, shutting them up from intercourse with each other, making itself the channel of every commu nication. At a hundred points at once it plays the aggressor. It contends with Spanish on the frontiers of Mexico; drives French and Russian before it in Canada and in the Northern Archipelago; supersedes Dutch at the Cape and Natal; elbows Greek and Italian at Malta and in the Ionian Islands; usurps the right of Arabic at Suez and Alexandria; maintains itself supreme at Liberia, Hongkong, Jamaica, and St. Helena; fights its way against multitudinous and various dialects in the Rocky Mountains, in Central America, on the Gold Coast, in the interior of Australia, and among the countless islands in the Eastern Seas. No other language is spreading in this way. French and German find students among cultivated men; but English permanently destroys and supersedes the idioms with which it comes in contact.

The relative growth of the two great Anglo-Saxon States is noteworthy. In 1801 the population of Great Britain was 10,942,646; in 1800 that of the United States was 5,319,762, or not quite half. In 1850 the population of the United States was two millions and a third more than that of Great Britain in 1851; at this moment it probably exceeds it by three millions. The rate of decennial increase in this country is less than 15 per cent., while in America it is about 35 per cent. In the great Continental States the rate is considerably lower than in England. According to the progress of the last fifty years in France and in America, the United States will have the larger population in 1870; in 1900 they will exceed those of England, France, Spain, Portugal, Denmark, Sweden, and Switzerland combined. Prudent statesmen should bear these facts in mind. Many persons now alive may see the time when America will be of more importance to us, socially, commercially, and politically, than all Europe put together. Old diplomatic traditions will go for little in face of a transatlantic power numbering one hundred millions of free and energetic men of our own race and blood.—*Athenæum.*

---

## COPY OF THE LATE TREATY BETWEEN THE UNITED STATES AND SANDWICH ISLANDS.

THE UNITED STATES OF AMERICA AND HIS MAJESTY THE KING OF THE HAWAIIAN ISLANDS, equally animated with the desire of maintaining the relations of good understanding which have hitherto so happily subsisted between their respective States, and consolidating the commercial intercourse between them, have agreed to enter into negotiations for the conclusion of a treaty of Friendship, Commerce, and Navigation, for which purpose they have appointed Plenipotentiaries, that is to say:

The President of the United States of America, John M. Clayton, Secretary of State of the United States; and His Majesty the King of the Hawaiian Islands, James Jackson Jarves, accredited as his Special

Commissioner to the Government of the United States; who, after having exchanged their full powers, found in good and due form, have concluded and signed the following articles:

ARTICLE 1.—There shall be perpetual peace and amity between the United States and the King of the Hawaiian Islands, his heirs, and his successors.

ARTICLE 2.—There shall be reciprocal liberty of commerce and navigation between the United States of America and the Hawaiian Islands.

No duty of customs or other impost shall be charged upon any goods, the produce or manufacture of one country, upon importation from such country into the other, other or higher than the duty or impost charged upon goods of the same kind, the produce or manufacture of, or imported from any other country; and the United States of America, and His Majesty the King of the Hawaiian Islands do hereby engage, that the subjects or citizens of any other State shall not enjoy any favor, privilege, or immunity whatever, in matters of commerce and navigation, which shall not also, at the same time, be extended to the subjects or citizens of the other contracting parties gratuitously, if the concession in favor of that other State shall have been gratuitous, and in return for a compensation, as nearly as possible, of proportionate value and effect, to be adjusted by mutual agreement, if the concession shall have been conditional.

ARTICLE 3.—All articles, the produce and manufacture of either country which can legally be imported into either country from the other, in ships of that other country, and thence coming, shall, when so imported, be subject to the same duties, and enjoy the same privileges, whether imported in ships of the one country, or in ships of the other; and in like manner, all goods which can legally be exported or re-exported from either country to the other, in ships of that other country, shall, when so exported or re-exported, be subject to the same duties, and be entitled to the same privileges, drawbacks, bounties, and allowances, whether exported in ships of the one country or in ships of the other; and all goods and articles, of whatever description, not being of the produce or manufacture of the United States, which can be legally imported into the Sandwich Islands, shall, when so imported in vessels of the United States, pay no other or higher duties, imposts, or charges, than shall be payable upon the like goods and articles, when imported in the vessels of the most favored foreign nation other than the nation of which the said goods and articles are the produce or manufacture.

ARTICLE 4.—No duties of tonnage, harbor, light-houses, pilotage, quarantine, or other similar duties, of whatever nature, or under whatever denomination, shall be imposed in either country upon the vessels of the other, in respect of voyages between the United States of America and the Hawaiian Islands, if laden, or in respect of any voyage, if in ballast, which shall not be equally imposed in the like cases on national vessels.

Article 5.—It is hereby declared, that the stipulations of the present treaty are not to be understood as applying to the navigation and carrying trade between one port and another situated in the States of either contracting party, such navigation and trade being reserved exclusively to national vessels.

Article 6.—Steam-vessels of the United States which may be employed by the government of the said States, in the carrying of their public mails across the Pacific Ocean, or from one port in that ocean to another, shall have free access to the ports of the Sandwich Islands, with the privilege of stopping therein to refit, to refresh, to land passengers and their baggage, and for the transaction of any business pertaining to the public mail service of the United States, and shall be subject in such ports to no duties of tonnage, harbor, light-houses, quarantine, or other similar duties, of whatever nature or under whatever denomination.

Article 7.—The whale-ships of the United States shall have access to the ports of Hilo, Kealakekua, and Hanalei, in the Sandwich Islands, for the purposes of refitment and refreshment, as well as to the ports of Honolulu and Lahaina, which only are ports of entry for all merchant vessels, and in all the above-named ports, they shall be permitted to trade or barter their supplies or goods, excepting spirituous liquors, to the amount of two hundred dollars, *ad valorem*, for each vessel, without paying any charge for tonnage or harbor dues of any description, or any duties or imposts whatever upon the goods or articles so traded or bartered. They shall also be permitted, with the like exemption from all charges for tonnage and harbor dues, further to trade or barter, with the same exemption as to spirituous liquors, to the additional amount of one thousand dollars, *ad valorem*, for each vessel, paying upon the additional goods and articles so traded and bartered, no other or higher duties than are payable on like goods and articles, when imported in the vessels and by the citizens or subjects of the most favored foreign nation. They shall also be permitted to pass from port to port of the Sandwich Islands for the purpose of procuring refreshments, but they shall not discharge their seamen or land their passengers in the said Islands, except at Lahaina and Honolulu; and in all the ports named in this article, the whale-ships of the United States shall enjoy in all respects whatsoever, all the rights, privileges, and immunities, which are enjoyed by, or shall be granted to, the whale-ships of the most favored foreign nation. The like privilege of frequenting the three ports of the Sandwich Islands above-named in this article, not being ports of entry for merchant vessels, is also guarantied to all the public armed vessels of the United States. But nothing in this article shall be construed as authorizing any vessel of the United States, having on board any disease usually regarded as requiring quarantine, to enter, during the continuance of such disease on board, any port of the Sandwich Islands, other than Lahaina or Honolulu.

ARTICLE 8.—The contracting parties engage, in regard to the personal privileges, that the citizens of the United States of America shall enjoy in the dominions of His Majesty the King of the Hawaiian Islands, and the subjects of his said Majesty in the United States of America, that they shall have free and undoubted right to travel and to reside in the States of the two high contracting parties, subject to the same precautions of police which are practised towards the subjects or citizens of the most favored nations. They shall be entitled to occupy dwellings and warehouses, and to dispose of their personal property of every kind and description, by sale, gift, exchange, will, or in any other way whatever, without the smallest hindrance or obstacle; and their heirs or representatives, being subjects or citizens of the other contracting party, shall succeed to their personal goods, whether by testament or ab intestato; and may take possession thereof, either by themselves, or by others acting for them, and dispose of the same at will, paying to the profit of the respective governments such dues only as the inhabitants of the country wherein the said goods are, shall be subject to pay in like cases. And in case of the absence of the heirs and representative, such care shall be taken of the said goods as would be taken of the goods of a native of the same country in like case, until the lawful owner may take measures for receiving them. And if a question should arise among several claimants as to which of them said goods belong, the same shall be decided finally by the laws and judges of the land wherein the said goods are. Where, on the decease of any person holding real estate within the territories of one party, such real estate would, by the laws of the land, descend on a citizen or subject of the other, were he not disqualified by alienage, such citizen or subject shall be allowed a reasonable time to sell the same, and to withdraw the proceeds without molestation, and exempt from all duties of detraction on the part of the government of the respective States. The citizens or subjects of the contracting parties shall not be obliged to pay, under any pretence whatever, any taxes or impositions, other or greater than those which are paid, or may hereafter be paid, by the subjects or citizens of the most favored nations in the respective States of the high contracting parties. They shall be exempt from all military service, whether by land or by sea; from forced loans, and from every extraordinary contribution not general and by law established. Their dwellings, warehouses, and all premises appertaining thereto, destined for the purposes of commerce or residence, shall be respected. No arbitrary search of, or visit to their houses, and no arbitrary examination or inspection whatever of the books, papers, or accounts of their trade, shall be made; but such measures shall be executed only in conformity with the legal sentence of a competent tribunal; and each of the two contracting parties engages that the citizens or subjects of the other residing in their respective States, shall enjoy their property and personal security, in as full and ample manner as their own citizens or subjects, or the subjects or citizens of the most favored nation, but subject always to the laws and statutes of the two countries respectively.

ARTICLE 9.—The citizens and subjects of each of the two contracting parties shall be free in the States of the other to manage their own affairs themselves, or to commit those affairs to the management of any persons whom they may appoint as their broker, factor, or agent; nor shall the citizens and subjects of the two contracting parties be restrained in their choice of persons to act in such capacities, nor shall they be called upon to pay any salary or remuneration to any person whom they shall not choose to employ. Absolute freedom shall be given in all cases to the buyer and seller to bargain together, and to fix the price of any goods or merchandise imported into, or to be exported from, the States and dominions of the two contracting parties; save and except generally such cases wherein the laws and usages of the country may require the intervention of any special agents in the States and dominions of the contracting parties. But nothing contained in this or any other article of the present treaty shall be construed to authorize the sale of spirituous liquors to the natives of the Sandwich Islands further than such sale may be allowed by the Hawaiian laws.

ARTICLE 10.—Each of the two contracting parties may have, in the ports of the other, consuls, vice-consuls, and commercial agents, of their own appointment, who shall enjoy the same privileges and powers with those of the most favored nation; but if any such consuls shall exercise commerce, they shall be subject to the same laws and usages to which the private individuals of their nation are subject in the same place. The said consuls, vice-consuls, and commercial agents, are authorized to require the assistance of the local authorities for the search, arrest, detention, and imprisonment of the deserters from the ships of war and merchant vessels of their country. For this purpose they shall apply to the competent tribunals, judges, and officers, and shall in writing demand the said deserters, proving, by the exhibition of registers of the vessels, the rolls of the crews, or by other official documents, that such individuals formed part of the crews; and this reclamation being thus substantiated, the surrender shall not be refused. Such deserters when arrested shall be placed at the disposal of the said consuls, vice-consuls, or commercial agents, and may be confined in the public prisons at the request and cost of those who shall claim them, in order to be detained until the time when they shall be restored to the vessel to which they belonged, or sent back to their own country by a vessel of the same nation or any other vessel whatsoever. The agents, owners, or masters of vessels, on account of whom the deserters have been apprehended, upon requisition of the local authorities, shall be required to take or send away such deserters from the States and dominions of the contracting parties, or give such security for their good conduct as the law may require. But if not sent back nor reclaimed within six months from the day of their arrest, or if all the expenses of such imprisonment are not defrayed by the party causing such arrest and imprisonment, they shall be set at liberty, and shall not be again arrested for the same cause. However, if the deserters should be found to have committed any crime or offence, their surrender may be delayed until the tribunal before whom their case shall be depending shall have pronounced its sentence and such sentence shall have been carried into effect.

ARTICLE 11.—It is agreed that perfect and entire liberty of conscience shall be enjoyed by the citizens and subjects of both the contracting parties, in the countries of the one and the other, without their being liable to be disturbed or molested on account of their religious belief. But nothing contained in this article shall be construed to interfere with the exclusive right of the Hawaiian Government to regulate for itself the schools which it may establish or support within its jurisdiction.

ARTICLE 12.—If any ships of war or other vessels be wrecked on the coasts of the States or territories of either of the contracting parties, such ships or vessels, or any parts thereof, and all furniture and appurtenances belonging thereunto, and all goods and merchandise which shall be saved therefrom, or the produce thereof if sold, shall be faithfully restored with the least possible delay to the proprietors, upon being claimed by them, or by their duly authorized factors; and if there are no such proprietors or factors on the spot, then the said goods and merchandise, or the proceeds thereof, as well as all the papers found on board such wrecked ships or vessels, shall be delivered to the American or Hawaiian consul or vice-consul in whose district the wreck may have taken place; and such consul, vice-consul, proprietors, or factors, shall pay only the expenses incurred in the preservation of the property, together with the rate of salvage and expenses of quarantine which would have been payable in the like case of a wreck of a national vessel; and the goods and merchandise saved from the wreck shall not be subject to duties unless entered for consumption; it being understood that in case of any legal claim upon such wreck, goods, or merchandise, the same shall be referred for decision to the competent tribunals of the country.

ARTICLE 13.—The vessels of either of the two contracting parties which may be forced by stress of weather or other cause into one of the ports of the other, shall be exempt from all duties of port or navigation, paid for the benefit of the State, if the motives which led to their seeking refuge be real and evident, and if no cargo be discharged or taken on board, save such as may relate to the subsistence of the crew, or be necessary for the repair of the vessels, and if they do not stay in port beyond the time necessary, keeping in view the cause which led to their seeking refuge.

ARTICLE 14.—The contracting parties mutually agree to surrender, upon official requisition, to the authorities of each, all persons who, being charged with the crimes of murder, piracy, arson, robbery, forgery, or the utterance of forged paper, committed within the jurisdiction of either, shall be found within the territories of the other; provided that this shall only be done upon such evidence of criminality as, according to the laws of the place where the person so charged shall be found, would justify his apprehension and commitment for trial if the crime had there been committed; and the respective judges and other magistrates of the two governments shall have authority, upon complaint made under oath, to issue a warrant for the apprehension of the person so charged, that he may be brought before such judges or other magistrates respectively, to the end that the evidence of criminality may be heard and considered; and if on such hearing the evidence be deemed sufficient to sustain the charge, it shall be the duty of the examining judge or magistrate to certify the same to the proper executive authority, that a warrant may issue for the surrender of such fugitive. The expense of such apprehension and delivery shall be borne and defrayed by the party who makes the requisition and receives the fugitive.

ARTICLE 15.—So soon as steam or other mail packets under the flag of either of the contracting parties shall have commenced running between their respective ports of entry, the contracting parties agree to receive at the post-offices of those ports all mailable matter, and to forward it as directed, the destination being to some regular post-office of either country; charging thereupon the regular postal rates as established by law in the territories of either party receiving said mailable matter, in addition to the original postage of the office whence the mail was sent. Mails for the United States shall be made up at regular intervals at the Hawaiian post-office, and dispatched to ports of the United States, the postmasters at which ports shall open the same, and forward the inclosed matter as directed, crediting the Hawaiian Government with their postages as established by law and stamped upon each manuscript or printed sheet.

All mailable matter destined for the Hawaiian Islands shall be received at the several post-offices in the United States, and forwarded to San Francisco or other ports on the Pacific coast of the United States, whence the postmasters shall dispatch it by the regular mail-packets to Honolulu, the Hawaiian Government agreeing on their part to receive and collect for, and credit the post-office department of the United States with, the United States rates charged thereupon. It shall be optional to prepay postage on letters in either country, but postage on printed sheets and newspapers shall in all cases be prepaid. The respective post-office departments of the contracting parties shall, in their accounts, which are to be adjusted annually, be credited with all dead letters returned.

ARTICLE 16.—The present treaty shall be in force from the date of the exchange of the ratifications for the term of ten years, and further, until the end of twelve months after either of the contracting parties shall have given notice to the other of its intention to terminate the same, each of the said contracting parties reserving to itself the right of giving such notice at the end of the said term of ten years, or at any subsequent term.

Any citizen or subject of either party infringing the articles of this treaty shall be held responsible for the same, and the harmony and good correspondence between the two governments shall not be interrupted thereby, each party engaging in no way to protect the offender or sanction such violation.

ARTICLE 17.—The present treaty shall be ratified by the President of the United States of America, by and with the advice and consent of the Senate of the said States, and by His Majesty the King of the Hawaiian Islands, by and with the advice of his Privy Council of State, and the ratifications shall be exchanged at Honolulu within eighteen months from the date of its signature, or sooner if possible.

In witness whereof, the respective plenipotentiaries have signed the same in triplicate, and have thereto affixed their seals. Done at Washington, in the English language, the twentieth day of December, in the year one thousand eight hundred and forty-nine.

JOHN M. CLAYTON,
JAMES JACKSON JARVES.

And whereas we have carefully examined all the points and articles thereof, by and with the advice of our Privy Council of State, we have confirmed and ratified the foregoing treaty, and we do confirm and ratify the same in the most effectual manner, promising on our faith and word as King, for us and our successors, to fulfil and observe it faithfully and scrupulously in all its clauses.

In faith of which we have signed this ratification with our own hand, and have affixed thereto the great seal of our kingdom.

Given at our palace of Honolulu, this nineteenth day of August, in the year of our Lord one thousand eight hundred and fifty, and in the twenty-fifth of our reign.

KAMEHAMEHA.

KEONI ANA.

By the King and the Premier.

R. C. WYLLIE,
Minister of Foreign Relations.

EXCHANGE OF RATIFICATIONS.

We the undersigned, Robert Crichton Wyllie, Minister of Foreign Relations of his Majesty the King of the Hawaiian Islands, and Charles Bunker, Consul of the United States for Lahaina, having been authorized by our respective governments to exchange the ratifications of the treaty of friendship, commerce, and navigation between his Hawaiian Majesty and the United States, concluded and signed at Washington, on the twentieth day of December, one thousand eight hundred and forty-nine, certify,

That we have this day met for that purpose, and after comparing the said ratifications each with the other, and both with the original of said treaty, have effected the exchange accordingly.

In witness whereof, we have signed this certificate, at Honolulu, this twenty-fourth day of August, one thousand eight hundred and fifty, and have thereunto affixed our respective seals.

R. C. WYLLIE,
CHARLES BUNKER.

---

NOTE A, p. 196.

THE late researches of Professor Agassiz into the world of corals naturally suggest the inquiry whether the coral insect may not yet be employed by man for the construction of sea-walls and reefs, in places within or near the tropics, where they are needed. He has succeeded in obtaining living specimens of the coral zoophyte, and carefully preserving them so as to study at his leisure their habits and motions. Why, then, as we employ the silkworm and furnish it with food and material to spin for us our silks, and as we plant and form beds of oysters in favorable locations, where we please, why may we not also employ the agency of the coral lithophyte to lay the foundations, for instance, of a light-house, or to form a breakwater where one is needed? Such a practical result is by no means improbable from the minute and scientific observations now making upon the busy little builders of the deep.

The coral reefs of Florida have been carefully examined by Professor Agassiz, and he finds them to be barrier reefs, extending from the Tortugas to the mainland, conforming generally to the outline of the shore. Lagoon or circular reefs also occur, but there is no evidence there of the subsidence or elevation observed in the Pacific Ocean; these are only 12 or 13 feet above the level of the sea. The Florida reefs consist of the Astrea and Porites at the bottom, in a depth of from 60 to 100 feet. They are large hemispherical masses, some of them 12 feet in diameter, and containing 4,000,000 of individual polyps. Next succeeds the Meandrina, which is also hemispherical in form, and sometimes 13 feet in diameter. At the top is found the Madrepore, of much harder texture than the preceding. It can exist only where the water is in constant motion, and thoroughly commingled with air—*i. e.* in a breaker or surf—they die in quiet waters.

Throughout the whole extent of the Florida reef, openings occur, and produce islands called *Keys*, from one to fifteen miles long, and covered with a tropical vegetation. The reefs suffer abrasion by the action of the sea, and are broken up on a large scale by the perforations of shell-fish and marine worms. The coral sand which results from the attrition of the reefs is cemented by the carbonate of lime dissolved in the water, and a firm limestone is formed exhibiting indications of stratification, but little or no trace of original organic structure. Professor Agassiz has formerly spent much time in the careful study of the remarkable geological formation of the Oolitic—Jura limestone. He found that the resemblances presented by these Florida reefs were so strong that he could not doubt that the Jura limestone had such an origin. The southern portion of the peninsula consists of ancient reefs, (hummocks,) and intervening levels, low and marshy, (everglades,) the whole having been won from the ocean by the coral polyps.

These reefs are regarded with terror by the navigators, but behind them lie the wreckers, in quiet waters, while the storm rages without. With light-houses and appropriate beacons the openings through the reefs might furnish safe harbors. In answer to a question whether this process of reef-building would continue, obliterating the channel and joining the West Indies to the mainland, Professor Agassiz gave it as his conviction that the limit is already attained; that the depth of water outside the present reefs is such as to prevent any more rising, but the present reefs may expand somewhat laterally.

The island of Molokai were as well worth the visit of an Agassiz, for the study of its corals, as of the Christian traveller for its institutions of religion. We commend it as a field of study both to Agassiz and Guyot, which they will find equal facilities for investigating, either as annexed to, or under the protectorate of the United States. The following is the latest view of it as a missionary field, contained in the August number of the Journal of Missions for 1851.

Seventeen years ago the inhabitants of Molokai, one of the Sandwich Islands, were living in a state of heathenism, which the officers of the United States Exploring Expedition represent as one of the most sunken in which any portion of the human race has ever been found. They had no civilization or letters; they scarcely had clothing or property of the lowest kind; they lived in miserable huts, so fashioned that Modesty could not find entrance to them; but in their deep degradation they had passions as evil and as strong as any other people.

The following year, 1835, their present missionary, Mr. Hitchcock, took up his abode among them. God has greatly blessed his labors. Through his instrumentality chiefly, a change has been effected, which it does not often fall to the lot of man to witness. There are many aspects in which this change might be exhibited, but none of them more suggestive than that of the liberality of the church.

For several years they have paid into the treasury of the Board more than enough to support their pastor. Last year they paid upwards of $500 to sustain him, contributed $700 at the monthly concert, and nearly $200 for other objects. From the beginning of the present year to March 20th, less than three months, they have contributed $210 at the monthly concert, and have subscribed $1800 for the repair of their meeting-house, besides paying $100 for a son of their pastor, whom they have adopted as their beneficiary, and intend to educate in this country.

Nor is this all. Owing to the broken surface of the island, valleys lying here and there between precipitous hills, numerous houses of worship are needed for their convenience. In one of these valleys the inhabitants, not more, all told, than two hundred and fifty in number, are building a house, which, in addition to their own labor in getting stone, timber, lime, sand, etc., will cost them not far from $900, cash. And yet they have contributed more than $50 at the monthly concert the first three months of the year, have paid their proportion of their pastor's salary, and have also given for their poor. In another deep and secluded ravine, with but little more than a hundred inhabitants, they have put up a fine house, and introduced American chairs, and are now raising money for a bell. The house in the plain of Kalaupapa was not well built, and the inhabitants are raising funds for a new one, having resolved to appropriate the other for a school-house. Besides all this, the people are building houses of worship in small neighborhoods, that they may meet in them for conference and prayer, their dwelling-houses not being convenient for such purpose. The members of the church, entirely of their own accord, have already built seven of these within three miles of the station in either direction, and are now at work on the eighth.

Here is a church the foundations of which were laid only half a generation back, in the midst of heathenism, and in one of its darkest and most degraded domains. The darkness has fled apace before the light which the Gospel brings, the degradation will soon be only a matter of history. This church makes abundant provision for its spiritual wants, and with a full hand is extending the blessings to others, which it knows so well how to prize. It is an example to be considered. How many churches now without a pastor because they feel unable to support one, or without a house of worship because they think themselves too poor to build one, would continue unsupplied, if this same spirit prevailed in them! How soon the means would be furnished for giving the Gospel to all the world, if every church possessed the same spirit of liberality!

And yet who will pronounce that the course of this church is not such as will give them the liveliest pleasure in the world to come?

---

## NOTE B, p. 301.

The remarks of Sir George Simpson, Governor-in-chief of the Hudson's Bay Company's Territories, in his volume entitled "Overland Journey of a Voyage Round the World," are not less creditable to himself as a philanthropist and a close observer of mankind, than they are honorable to the American Missionaries at the Hawaiian Islands. While he perhaps awards to the natives a higher character than they have generally been deemed to deserve, he does full justice to the efforts of the missionaries to ameliorate the temporal condition of the lower orders. He remarks, that "perhaps the industry of the natives is the quality which promises to be most conducive to their civilization. A habit, if not a love of labor has been implanted and cherished in them by a combination of causes more or less peculiar to their condition, which chiefly, if not wholly, resolve themselves into the niggardliness of nature and the despotism of government. While many other Polynesian tribes almost realize the caricature of a copper-colored gentleman lying on his back under the branches of the bread-fruit, and doing nothing but keep his mouth open to catch the ripe rolls as they fall, the Hawaiians, as we have already had occasion to notice more than once, are compelled by the necessities of nature to earn their food by the sweat of their brow. Witness the construction of their fish-ponds, the preparation of their poi, and the cultivation of their kalo, with all its incidental toils of digging and embanking the beds, of erecting and maintaining the aqueducts, of fixing and regulating the sluices.

"So far as the kalo and poi are concerned, there are some localities, Lahaina, for instance, in Maui, in which the bread-fruit abounds, while, with a little care and attention, it might be made to grow in all parts of the group; but whether it be that this ready-made food be here of an inferior quality, or that the favorite dish of the natives has become indispensable to them, the bread-fruit is as little valued by the Sandwich Islanders as the kalo, which is indigenous in many parts of Polynesia, is valued by the indolent aborigines of the more southern groups. Nor is the despotism of government less influential in making the people work than the niggardliness of nature. Till very recently the commoners of this archipelago, like the peasants of France before the revolution, or of Canada before the conquest, were *taillables et corveables a misericorde*, or to invent English for the exotic abomination, *taxable and taskable at discretion*, while they were deterred alike from evasion or complaint by a mixture of feudal servility and superstitious terror.

"But, within the last year or two, certain laws, for their share in which the missionaries deserve great credit, have so far remedied this evil as to subject the amounts and times of tasking and taxing to fixed rules; and though the ascertained burdens are still too heavy and too numerous, comprising work for the immediate chief, work for the king, work for the public, rent for land and a poll-tax on both sexes, yet the restriction in question, if fairly carried into actual effect, will engender in the serf the idea of property, and inspire him at once with the hope and the desire of improving his physical condition by the application of his physical energies.

"Though in many quarters of the group an adequate motive for exertion may not at present be felt, yet in the neighborhood of Honolulu the sustenance of several thousands, who are exclusively consumers, constitutes at once the proof and the recompense of the industry of the adjacent cultivators. In fact, the demand of the town affords an ample market for the natives of the surrounding country, while there is certainly no reason for the buyers to murmur as to the amount or variety of the supply. In addition to the resources of a stationary market, which is usually well furnished with fish, meat, fruit, etc., the smaller dealers go from house to house to vend their wares, the whole scene, which is quite unique, savoring of any thing but indolence on the part of the rural population.

"Early in the morning a crowd of natives may be seen flocking into Honolulu, all carrying something to sell. Most of them have large calabashes suspended in a netting at each end of a pole, which they carry across one shoulder, the contents being all sorts of small articles, kalo and poi, and fruits and vegetables, and milk and eggs, and, what is the safest speculation of all, water fresh from the cold atmosphere of the mountains; some of them are loaded with bundles of grass for the town-fed horses; others carry a sucking pig in their arms, while the more substantial hog-merchants make the adult grunters, always there, as well as elsewhere, on the verge of insurrection, trudge along on their own petty toes; others again import ducks and fowls, and geese and turkeys, all alive, tied by the legs to long poles, which are carried like the poles with the calabashes; while last, though not least, a few individuals of more airy and delicate sentiments hawk about various kinds of curiosities, such as mats, shells, scorpions, etc., but above all, wreaths of bright flowers intertwined with their kindred leaves for the beaux and belles of the metropolis."

Evidence of the utility of the Sandwich Island mission, and of the vast benefit effected by it to the Hawaiian people, is constantly accruing from every quarter. A late number of the Journal of Missions presents the following: "A short time since, Mr. Coan's church at Hilo, by a contribution of $100, made his Excellency R. C. Wyllie, Minister of Foreign Relations at Honolulu, an honorary member of the American Board.

"In a note to Mr. Castle, acknowledging the reception of the certificate of membership, he says, 'Wishing as well as I do, and have ever done, to that benevolent Board, I ought to have become a member long ago.' As he was anticipated in this, he immediately, by the payment of $100, constituted Mrs. Lee, wife of the Chief-justice of the Islands, a member. In addition to this substantial testimony to the good effected by missions, he says, in a letter to the treasurer of the Board, whom he knew many years ago in Chili—'I consider that the diffusion of knowledge and Christianity throughout the Hawaiian Islands is at once the proudest achievement of any Foreign Missionary Society, and the greatest benefit that has been conferred on these Islands the last thirty-one years.'

"Few men are better qualified to give an opinion on this subject than Mr. Wyllie. He is a Scotchman by birth, has seen much of the world, is a man of close observation and of large intelligence, and has resided for a long time at the Islands, where, for several years, he has, with distinguished credit to himself, and great advantage to the nation, filled his present highly responsible office. While yet a private resident there, an extended series of articles from his pen, on the Sandwich Islands, their productions, capabilities, etc., gave proof of an intimate knowledge of all that pertained to this group, and a just appreciation of their future importance."

THE END.

www.ingramcontent.com/pod-product-compliance
Lightning Source LLC
LaVergne TN
LVHW021251110826
845151LV00002BA/385